Playing the Beethoven Piano Sonatas

Ludwig van Beethoven. Pencil drawing by Carl Friedrich August von Kloeber, ca. 1818.

PLAYING

The Beethoven Piano Sonatas

Robert Taub

Amadeus Press
Portland, Oregon

The author gratefully acknowledges permission to include material from:

Anderson, Emily, ed. and trans. *The Letters of Beethoven*. Copyright © 1961 St. Martin's Press; Macmillan. Reprinted by permission of Palgrave.

Beethoven, Ludwig van. *Klaviersonaten*. Edited by Heinrich Schenker. Revised by Erwin Ratz. Copyright © Universal Edition. Music examples reprinted with kind permission by Universal Edition A.G., Vienna.

Thayer, Alexander Wheelock. *Thayer's Life of Beethoven*. Copyright © 1964, 1967 by Princeton University Press. Reprinted by permission of Princeton University Press.

Whittall Collection, Music Division, Library of Congress. Portions of Sonata Op. 109 autograph score reproduced with permission.

While every effort has been made to trace copyright holders and obtain permission, this has not been possible in all cases; any omissions brought to our attention will be remedied in future editions.

Printed in Singapore

Published in 2002 by
Amadeus Press (an imprint of Timber Press, Inc.)
The Haseltine Building
133 S.W. Second Avenue, Suite 450
Portland, Oregon 97204 U.S.A.

Library of Congress Cataloging-in-Publication Data

Taub, Robert.
    Playing the Beethoven piano sonatas / Robert Taub.
        p.   cm.
    Includes bibliographical references (p.   ) and index.
    ISBN 1-57467-071-9
    1. Beethoven, Ludwig van, 1770–1827. Sonatas, piano. 2. Sonatas (Piano)—
Analysis, appreciation. I. Title.

    MT145.B42 T38 2002
    786.2′183′092—dc21

                                                        2001046126

For Tracy, Julia, Ben, and Daniel

Contents

Preface   *9*

PART ONE: PREPARATION

CHAPTER 1   The Basics   *15*

CHAPTER 2   Beethoven, His Hands, and His Feet   *23*

CHAPTER 3   Tempo   *44*

CHAPTER 4   Improvisation   *58*

CHAPTER 5   Trills, Pirouettes, and Good Humor   *66*

CHAPTER 6   Publishers and Editions   *79*

CHAPTER 7   The Myth of the Authentic Pianoforte   *89*

PART TWO: CONCERT PROGRAMS

Planning the Programs   *97*

PROGRAM 1   Sonata in F minor, Op. 2 no. 1 (1795)   *99*
             Sonata *quasi una fantasia* in E-flat major,
                 Op. 27 no. 1 (1800–01)
             Sonata in F-sharp major, Op. 78 (1809)
             Sonata in C major, Op. 53 ("Waldstein") (1803–04)

PROGRAM 2   Sonata in A major, Op. 2 no. 2 (1795)   *117*
              Sonata in E major, Op. 14 no. 1 (1798–99)
              Sonata in G major, Op. 14 no. 2 (1798–99)
              Sonata *quasi una fantasia* in C-sharp minor,
                  Op. 27 no. 2 ("Moonlight") (1801)

PROGRAM 3   Sonata in C minor, Op. 10 no. 1 (1796–98)   *129*
              Sonata in F major, Op. 10 no. 2 (1796–98)
              Sonata in D major, Op. 10 no. 3 (1796–98)
              Sonata in A major, Op. 101 (1816)

PROGRAM 4   Sonata in E-flat major, Op. 7 (1797)   *143*
              Sonata in G major, Op. 31 no. 1 (1802)
              Sonata in E minor, Op. 90 (1814)
              Sonata in C minor, Op. 13 ("Pathétique") (1798–99)

PROGRAM 5   Sonata in G minor, Op. 49 no. 1 (1798)   *162*
              Sonata in G major, Op. 49 no. 2 (1796)
              Sonata in E-flat major, Op. 31 no. 3 (1801–02)
              Sonata in F major, Op. 54 (1804)
              Sonata in F minor, Op. 57 ("Appassionata") (1804–05)

PROGRAM 6   Sonata in A-flat major, Op. 26 (1800–01)   *176*
              Sonata in C major, Op. 2 no. 3 (1795)
              Sonata in E major, Op. 109 (1820)

PROGRAM 7   Sonata in D minor, Op. 31 no. 2 ("Tempest")   *194*
                  (1801–02)
              Sonata in B-flat major, Op. 106 ("Hammerklavier")
                  (1817–18)

PROGRAM 8   Sonata in B-flat major, Op. 22 (1800)   *213*
              Sonata in G major, Op. 79 (1809)
              Sonata in A-flat major, Op. 110 (1821)

PROGRAM 9   Sonata in D major, Op. 28 ("Pastoral") (1801)   *229*
              Sonata in E-flat major, Op. 81a ("Das Lebewohl")
                  (1809)
              Sonata in C minor, Op. 111 (1822)

              Glossary   *249*

              Bibliography   *251*

              Index of Beethoven Piano Sonatas   *255*

Preface

*M*y earliest memory of the piano is of reaching up one day and pounding on the bass keys of the Steinway that my parents had just purchased. That these notes sounded like thunder pleased me no end. I was three years old, and this was the start. About 150 piano lessons and five years later, I ventured into my first Beethoven piano sonata: his Op. 10 no. 1.

From that moment on, the Beethoven sonatas were part of my life. No year was complete without working on a new one. There seemed to be a never-ending supply, each one with different moods, character, and pianistic challenges. When I was ten or eleven, it was hard to imagine playing them all, but occasionally I'd sneak glances at the really difficult ones, those that were many, many pages long with lots of black ink—the ones like Op. 106 and Op. 111. I never heard these pieces played when I went to concerts with my family, but I knew they were especially important, both because they took up so many pages of my two massive volumes of sonatas and because they each took up more than one side of a record in that large group that one of my heroes—Artur Schnabel—had made.

When I was about fifteen, I began studying with Jacob Lateiner, who had started teaching at Juilliard a few years earlier. My audition for him included the "Waldstein" Sonata. He was in the midst of playing a series of concerts at Hunter College, and it was there that I first heard the last Beethoven sonata, Op. 111. I then bought his recordings of the "Waldstein" and of Op. 109.

After three years of working with him and of learning several more Beethoven sonatas, I called one day and asked for permission to start working on Sonata Op. 110. It would be my first foray into the rarefied world of truly late Beethoven, and with hindsight, I suppose I wanted to feel that I was ready. Permission was granted.

But even as I was delving into territory that was new to me, I learned that the Beethoven piano sonatas could be appreciated on many different levels. The unending spectrum of expression can intoxicate a first-time listener as well as the most seasoned performer. For all of us the works repay repeated listening and deeper involvement; the more understanding I bring to the music, the more moving is my musical experience in performing or listening.

As I began to play more and more concerts, Beethoven sonatas naturally figured prominently in my repertoire. After performing several sonatas over the course of a concert season in programs that also included works of other composers, I would consider which one to learn next. This was always a difficult issue, for I didn't want to leave out any. Gradually I realized that I had worked on almost all of them.

I suppose that the idea of performing all the Beethoven sonatas as a cycle had been in the back of my mind since the time that I first encountered the Schnabel recordings. The opportunity came up unexpectedly, though, during a series of luncheon meetings at the Institute for Advanced Study in Princeton. The idea was proposed as a three-year project beginning in my first year as artist-in-residence. I felt keenly both the elation at finally being able to perform the cycle and the excitement and responsibility of the challenge. I first performed the Beethoven sonata cycle in Wolfensohn Hall at the Institute for Advanced Study during a three-year period from 1994 through 1997 and simultaneously recorded each program for VOX Classics. I have performed the cycle several times since, in New York and elsewhere, and will probably always continue to do so.

This book has evolved from these experiences and is intended for all music lovers, from the casual listener to the devoted performer.

MANY PEOPLE have inspired, helped, and cajoled me throughout this project. I gratefully thank:

The Institute for Advanced Study, which provided an invigorating and inspiring artistic home for my first Beethoven cycle and for the writing of this book;

Benny Goodman, who in the early 1980s advised me after a private performance of the "Waldstein" Sonata that if I wanted to really play a piece like this, I had to "make it my own," advice which I have taken to heart many times over;

Jacob Lateiner, whose high standards and expectations helped me establish a musical conscience;

Lewis Lockwood, who introduced me to the treasures of Beethoven autograph scores with a project in my third year as an undergraduate at Princeton that was devoted to examining the first movement of Beethoven's "Ghost" Trio;

William H. Scheide, who generously opened his extraordinary private collection that includes, among many treasures, a sketchbook used by Beethoven from March 1815 through May 1816 and a first edition of the "Hammerkla-vier" Sonata;

Bruce Brubaker, a friend and colleague, whose insights both at the keyboard and away from it have often provided fresh musical guidance;

Eve Goodman, whose editorial expertise and advice have been invaluable;

and my wife, Tracy, whose encouragement and support, always helpful and insightful, are evermore a source of inspiration.

I am also deeply appreciative of audiences the world over, for your continued enthusiasm and involvement contributes mightily to making worthwhile those many hours of practicing and traveling. All performances, whether live or recorded, are intended to connect with you, and this book is not only an extension of the types of connections I try to make, but also an acknowledgment of their importance.

PART ONE

Preparation

CHAPTER 1

The Basics

You must forgive a composer who would rather hear his work just as he had written it, however beautifully you played it otherwise.

—Beethoven to Czerny, 12 February 1816

The day before Beethoven wrote these words, pianist and composer Carl Czerny had performed the piano part in the Quintet for Piano and Winds, Op. 16. Having lost patience with Czerny's indiscriminate elaborations and aspirations of virtuosity, Beethoven addressed his letter: "For Herr von Zerni, celebrated virtuoso" (Anderson 1961, 560).

Why learn a particular piece of music? What draws us in? What makes us want to delve into the score, so that it becomes internalized, part of us? When we are so profoundly taken by a piece, we may ask further questions as well. Why did the composer create it? What is its *raison d'être*? What are the responsibilities of a performing artist toward a given work?

We perform because we have a burning desire to bring to life all the richness of emotion and artistry within a score, and to share this with as wide an audience as possible.

By doing so, I believe that we also enter into an implied moral contract with the composer—Beethoven in this case. The foundation of this belief is my underlying assumption that regardless of the degree of difficulty—whether considering Beethoven's own fingering in Sonata Op. 2 no. 2, or the pedaling in the "Tempest" and "Waldstein" Sonatas, or the specified tempos and the use of the left pedal in the "Hammerklavier"—Beethoven knew what he was doing. Everything in the score serves an intensely musical end. Beethoven's uncompromising compositional strivings—often impassioned—in the sketchbooks, the corrections in his autograph manuscripts of scores, the correspondence with publishers about corrections to proofs, the intense frustrations with imperfect editions—all reveal unwavering faith in his own creative processes.

He believed his works to be so organic and so thoroughly integrated that altering one aspect would change the nature of the musical vision. This is illustrated in his letter of 19 February 1813 to George Thomson in Edinburgh regarding the commissioned setting of Scottish airs for diverse instruments. Beethoven wrote that he

> learned with pleasure that you have at last received the 62 songs which I have set for you and that you are satisfied with all but 9 of them which you specify and in which you would like to have me change the ritournelles and accompaniments. I regret very much that I cannot accommodate you in this. I am not in the habit of rewriting my compositions. I have never done it, being convinced that any partial alteration changes the character of the composition. I regret that you will suffer the loss; but you can scarcely put the blame on me, since it ought to have been your affair to advise me more explicitly of the taste of your country and the small skill of your players (Thayer 1973, 554).

Beethoven went on to say that inasmuch as he refused to alter the nine songs in question, he simply "composed the songs wholly anew" but only after great reluctance.

The implied moral contract suggests that I question the very being of a particular work, and if convinced of its merit, immerse myself so fully in the style and essence of that work that it becomes its own world, with ties nonetheless to the musical universe of which it is part. I examine sketches and study autograph scores if available, read Beethoven's letters, try to understand his frustrations with the pianofortes of the time, delve into the reasons for his often unconventional fingering and pedaling indications, and internalize all this so that I can bring greater meaning to a performance, and move closer to the *Geist*—the spirit—of the music.

What can we expect when we begin to work on or listen to a Beethoven sonata? No two sonatas are identical in character. Consider the expressive variety and range of appeal, from the terse urgency of the first movement of the "Pathétique," to the languid introspection of the first movement of the "Moonlight," to the brilliant extroversion of the "Waldstein," to the gigantic challenges of the "Hammerklavier," to the transcendence of the final three sonatas. There is unabashed lyricism and fullness of sound in the slow movements of early sonatas, and there are works in all periods that converse not only in epic manner but in intimate tones as well. The expressive range is enormous.

Our appreciation and expectations may be refined by considering what is meant by a "sonata," what these works meant to Beethoven himself, and how he composed. The Italian term *sonata* had been used to denote a piece to be played as opposed to sung (cantata) as early as 1597 when Giovanni Gabrieli published a sonata for a group of strings and winds. Over the next century the term was applied to works of diverse types, although there was a tendency to limit it to extended compositions of contrasting movements. Bach used the term with greater precision when he differentiated between his suites (or partitas) which comprised dance forms and his sonatas which contained more serious allegros, adagios, and fugues.

By the time that Czerny claimed triumphantly in 1840 that he was the first to describe sonata form, the form was already ensconced in history, for C. P. E. Bach, Mozart, Haydn, and Beethoven had been forging ahead long before. Derived from drama inherent in the musical language of tonality, *sonata form* pertains to a movement that is of several parts: often two themes of contrasting key and musical character are introduced in the exposition; one or both of the themes are broken down into smaller motivic components and played in a greater variety of harmonic settings, usually with greater intensity, in the development; the themes recur, not necessarily in the same order, in the recapitulation, and as the original key of the work is attained there is a feeling of returning home; and the musical adventure can be summarized in an optional coda. Since Czerny, many others have written eloquently about sonata form. Among the most elegant and comprehensive descriptions is that by Charles Rosen in *The Classical Style*, a book that is now itself an invaluable classic. With sensitivity and eloquence, Rosen points out that "the concept of a style does not correspond to an historical fact but answer a need: it creates a mode of understanding" (Rosen 1997, 19).

With our perspective of hindsight, we can generalize and claim that during the classical era (Mozart, Haydn, Beethoven) a sonata was most often a multi-movement work (unlike the single-movement sonatas of Scarlatti) which frequently contained a lively sonata-form first movement, an expressive slow movement, and an extroverted rondo (ABACA) to conclude. Beethoven also included stylized minuets (a dance form borrowed from the baroque) in a number of sonatas through 1804. But to consider *sonata* or *sonata form* as a constricting structure is to disregard the creative energies of certain composers. To Beethoven the concept of a sonata as a totality was fluid, not a work to be cast from a preformed mold. His Sonata Op. 26, for example, starts with a theme-and-variation first movement, continues with a scherzo second movement, follows with a stylized funeral march for a third movement, and ends with a moto perpetuo–rondo, an idea he borrowed from Jean-Baptiste Cramer, a colleague whom he both rivaled and admired. There is no sonata-form movement in this sonata!

Beethoven designated each sonata of Op. 27 as Sonata *quasi una fantasia* (sonata in the form of a fantasy), implying close links between the movements; other sonatas he wrote are in four, three, or even only two discrete movements. Some begin with slow movements instead of allegro movements; some end with a slow movement. Some begin with introductions, some include theme-and-variation movements, some include fugues, a form decidedly associated with the baroque. The point is not that Beethoven wanted to try to write all different types of sonatas, but rather that the musical language of a particular piece—the expressive content itself—determined form. Form in his sonatas was molded from the inside out, not the converse.

Beethoven composed more piano sonatas than substantial works of any other single genre, and the piano sonatas span virtually his entire compositional career. His works are often divided into three periods (early, middle, late) to generalize about expressive and formal characteristics. Such groupings are too imprecise for the thirty-two piano sonatas, which I prefer to consider in five chronological periods, each defined by the dramatic and compositional content and the musical character of the works themselves:

1795–1800: Epitomizing classical styles
Thirteen sonatas: Op. 2 nos. 1, 2, 3; Op. 7; Op. 10 nos. 1, 2, 3; Op. 13; Op. 14 nos. 1, 2; Op. 22; Op. 49 nos. 1 and 2 (composed in 1798 and 1796, respectively, although not published until 1805)

1801–02: Experimentation
Seven sonatas: Op. 26; Op. 27 nos. 1, 2; Op. 28; Op. 31 nos. 1, 2, 3

1803–04: Post-Heiligenstadt, crossing the Rubicon
Three sonatas: Op. 53, Op. 54, Op. 57

1809: Compression, homogeneity
Three sonatas: Op. 78, Op. 79, Op. 81a

1814–22: Summation, transcendence
Six sonatas: Op. 90, Op. 101, Op. 106, Op. 109, Op. 110, Op. 111

Beethoven's relationship to his piano sonatas was fundamentally different from his relationship to his works of other genres. By the time of his debut of his Op. 2 sonatas at a soirée at the palace of Count Lichnowsky in 1795, Beethoven had already established himself as a leading pianist in Vienna. He composed his early piano sonatas (and piano concertos) not only on their own absolute musical terms, but also as vehicles for himself as pianist. Because of his fondness for and preeminence in improvising, and since quasi-improvisatory techniques are more possible in a solo work than in a work for many artists, Beethoven viewed his piano sonatas as more experimental and in many ways freer than his works for more than one instrument. Even later in Beethoven's life when he no longer performed in public, his piano sonatas still offered possibilities for immediate rehearsal—or even private performance—that works of larger forces simply could not.

Public concerts in those days were very different from concerts today. Although piano concertos were written for and performed in public concerts for general audiences, piano sonatas were the province of aristocratic salons. Beethoven made his reputation in both worlds: he performed and conducted in concerts for the general public (including several performances of Mozart piano concertos, as well as his own) and played his piano sonatas in private settings. He also taught piano to several patrons and dedicated some of his sonatas to them. It appears that only one of Beethoven's piano sonatas was performed in a public concert during his lifetime; an obscure amateur—Stainer von Felsburg—played what is believed to be Sonata Op. 90 in February 1816 (Stanley 1998, 2).

Regardless, the piano sonata was central to Beethoven in furthering his reputation as composer. Beginning in the 1790s, as the pianoforte began to evolve at a rapid rate throughout Europe, the market for published piano sonatas also grew. Despite (or possibly because of) uncompromising technical demands and hitherto unimagined musical complexity, Beethoven's published sonatas sold. This might also have been due in part to his exalted name. In any case, commercial success allowed the sonatas to transcend the boundaries of salons. Although not performed in front of the general public, the sonatas were nonetheless available to and consumed by them.

Beethoven was aware that his works would outlast him and his control over them. He cared deeply how they were performed. In a conversation with Johann Tomaschek (friend and confidant) in 1814, Beethoven remarked:

> It has always been known that the greatest pianoforte players were also the greatest composers; but how did they play? Not like the pianists of today, who prance up and down the keyboard with passages which they have practiced—putsch, putsch, putsch; —what does that mean? Nothing! When true pianoforte virtuosi played it was always something homogeneous, an entity; if written down it would appear as a well thought-out work. That is pianoforte playing; the other is nothing! (Thayer 1973, 599)

Although this quotation pertains to the art of improvising, it also reveals Beethoven's disdain for empty virtuosity and his ideal that playing should communicate the architecture and inner meaning of a work.

Beethoven was correspondingly concerned about the accuracy (or lack thereof) of printed editions. Today, in addition to published editions, we also have available to us published facsimiles of autograph scores of Sonatas Opp. 26, 27 no. 2, 53, 57, 78, 109, 110, and 111. While Beethoven certainly intended his autograph scores to be read by eyes in addition to his own—these are the scores that he sent to publishers for engraving—the idea that a Beethoven autograph score is a "final version" of a composition is not necessarily valid (Lockwood 1992, 4–17). Sometimes Beethoven's letters to publishers supplant information in an autograph, such as the addition—by post—of a "new" first measure of the Adagio of Sonata Op. 106. Beethoven may also have made changes during the processes of correcting proofs of first editions, such as the deletion of a flat sign before the bass F in Sonata Op. 53, first movement, m. 105. In this case, the first edition supercedes the autograph as the authoritative source. But at times publishers did not make corrections to their editions even though Beethoven mandated them. In such instances, the first edition (and possibly subsequent printings of it) is not authoritative. I take issues like these into account when I work on a piece, for they help shape musical gestures and contribute to my over-all interpretation.

Before he wrote out an autograph score, Beethoven experimented with and refined his ideas in his sketchbooks. He heard his music internally even before deafness became a major issue, and he began sketching as early as 1790, work-ing with musical ideas on paper at a point in the process when other composers might have worked at the piano. Beethoven needed to keep a record of his ideas and at first did so on individual sheets of music paper. In 1798 he began using bound books—sketchbooks—of music paper. Beethoven used his sketchbooks to experiment with, manipulate, develop, and refine all manner of musical ideas. He often worked on several compositions simultaneously, and therefore the record of Beethoven's compositional processes in the sketchbooks is uniquely rich and complex. For example, the sketchbook of March 1815–May 1816 (now in the Scheide collection) contains material for the second, third, and fourth movements of Sonata Op. 101, for the Cello Sonata Op. 102 no. 2, for an unfin-ished piano concerto in D major, and for several songs (including "An die ferne Geliebte"), as well as an isolated entry for what became the theme of the scherzo movement of the Ninth Symphony which was not completed until some eight years later. Beethoven also noted that this theme was specifically for the begin-ning of a symphony in which the instruments were to enter one by one; indeed, such is the beginning of the Ninth Symphony.

Beethoven's devotion to the process of sketching and to the sketchbooks themselves was unceasing. Even though he changed his place of residence twenty-four times after his initial move to Vienna (not counting the thirty-nine different summer residences he occupied), many of the original pages of sketches that he carried with him to Vienna in 1792 were within his reach when he died. While reading the sketches is challenging—they range, as Lockwood has said, "from the difficult to the undecipherable" (p. 11)—sketches can none-theless provide valuable clues to interpretation. For example, in the sketches for the "Appassionata" Sonata, the change of meter from 4/4 to 12/8 exerts a direct influence on our perception and interpretation of the first movement, as we shall see in Program 5.

Beethoven's autograph scores are usually easier to read than the sketches, although quite a few contain areas of rewriting with heavy crossings-out and multiple layers of revision. They are all imbued with life and emotion, and although they may not always represent the final word, they inevitably lead an interpreter closer to musical ideals in ways that printed scores simply cannot. The discussion of Sonata Op. 109 (Program 6) documents changes in musical terminology—not in notes—that Beethoven made in the autograph. Seeing the

Example 1: Autograph of Op. 111, first movement, mm. 131–138.

original terms that are crossed out and the subsequent changes clarifies notions of tempo which printed editions, lacking the original terms, can not possibly convey. Subtleties of calligraphy—ways in which notes are grouped, dynamics juxtaposed, even the spacing of phrases on the manuscript page—are direct indications of the composer's feelings about his own music as he was hearing it in his mind during the multifaceted processes of composing. One need only look first at the intense, propelled, forward-leaning writing of the first movement of Sonata Op. 111 to sense its character before even playing or hearing a single note. I am always inspired by playing from autograph scores as part of my own preparation (Example 1).

I learned the Beethoven piano sonatas initially from the Universal Edition score printed in Vienna, edited by Heinrich Schenker. But I also refer frequently to the Schnabel edition, both for his fingering and for his interesting footnotes that help reveal his artistry to those of us who know him only through his recordings. And there is a vast literature on these works. To name only a handful of valuable references, Sir Donald Francis Tovey's *Companion to the Beethoven Pianoforte Sonatas*, written in 1931, is absolutely wonderful in its descriptions of each work. Both of Kenneth Drake's books (*The Sonatas of Beethoven As He Played and Taught Them* and *The Beethoven Sonatas and the Creative Experience*) are sensitive and informative. Anything that Charles Rosen has to say is always of interest. From a purely literary point of view, Thomas Mann's descriptions of Sonata Op. 111 in *Doktor Faustus* are incomparable.

But this book differs from all these in that my perspective is that of a concert performer. My goal is to share my thoughts from living with these works for many years, getting them into my hands, committing them all to memory, performing them, thinking about them some more, hearing them in my sleep, and bringing them to life again and again—in front of audiences and microphones —with interpretations that evolve through time and experience.

In performance I try to tell the story as if it is being told for the first time, to play the Beethoven sonatas as if they are hot off the press. For that they once were, and many were strikingly revolutionary. I consider many more issues than simply "getting the notes." Concepts of tempo, fingering, pedaling, and phrasing, and ways that Beethoven's style evolved are all things that I think about, reconsider, internalize, and constantly challenge. I check on textual accuracy and delve into the myriad ways in which Beethoven imagined the sonic world of a piece. These elements are addressed in the first part of this book. Readers will then find a detailed consideration of each sonata in the second part of the book, indexed in the list of works as well.

Programs 1 though 9 explore the sonatas both individually and collectively in the order in which I have performed the cycle. This ordering balances aspects of Beethoven's creative evolution with contrasts among the works. I discuss the specific nature of each program and for each work look at the musical character and structure along with particular pianistic challenges, all of which influence our perceptions of what we hear and play. At times I mention external circumstances that may have affected composition, and I point out textual issues raised by subsequent publication. A glossary of terms appears at the end of the book, along with an index of the sonatas.

The idea is to foster a more meaningful appreciation in listening and an artistically valid interpretation. My perspective is that of a concert performer, playing on modern pianos, dealing with the exigencies of life as we know it, playing from the heart and the mind, for the heart and the mind.

CHAPTER 2

Beethoven, His Hands, and His Feet

From Beethoven's letter of circa 20 March 1819 to Ferdinand Ries in London, indicating more than one hundred corrections to be made to proofs of Sonata Op. 106 ("Hammerklavier"). The correction above—the addition of a pedal marking in the Adagio sostenuto (m. 72)—affects not the specific notes but the overall sonority and musical atmosphere.

Although Beethoven did not ordinarily specify fingering, he often included in his autograph scores—in passages where his musical vision set new stylistic precedents—fingering indications or pedal markings to more fully define the musical context. Such specific directions reveal how Beethoven used his own hands and feet, and can thereby help elucidate his musical reasoning on both local and global levels. Ultimately they can lead to a fuller interpretive understanding.

These markings are not secrets. When Beethoven indicated fingering and pedal markings, he intended them to be published for they are part of the fabric of the work. Yet amazingly, some of these markings are not taken seriously even today, if they are noticed at all. Instead they are dismissed as impractical, too difficult on the modern piano, or appropriate only on the older pianofortes with their smaller, more intimate sound. Such assumptions miss the point of these markings which are often of crucial musical significance, focusing upon specific musical and expressive goals. Many were intended as cautionary guides against presumably easier solutions. Certainly some of Beethoven's fingering is difficult not only on our modern pianos but on pianofortes as well: his fingering for mm. 84–89 in the first movement of Sonata Op. 2 no. 2 has caused consternation among many generations of pianists, but it helps influence texture and tempo. The same general ideas apply to some of Beethoven's long pedal markings in other works—the first movement of the "Tempest" Sonata Op. 31 no. 2, for instance. Even on a pianoforte, holding the right pedal down to the floor without regard to other musical dimensions (dynamics, touch, tempo) inevitably destroys the musical subtlety of such delicate passages. However, carefully regulating the degree to which the right pedal is depressed can create an aura of sound which stimulates the imagination and elevates this passage to a higher level of artistry.

THE CRAFT of playing is multifaceted. Perhaps the most obvious aspect is molding one's hands to the keyboard, being able to employ infinitely varying degrees of touch (motions with fingers, hands, and wrists)—and hence sound quality—which can seem onomatopoeic with the note and spirit of the score. Of paramount importance, also, is one's ear, both inner and outer. I think of the inner ear as guiding the artistic vision, leading to the exploration of new musical and interpretive realms. The outer ear allows me to adjust what I am projecting while playing and thereby helps me to realize my artistic goals.

To decide which fingers to use for specific passages, we might think on several different levels, beginning with the need simply to adapt the hand and fingers to the keyboard to reach the notes. Some classical principles apply: in single-note passages avoid the thumb on black keys, but in octaves use the thumb and fourth fingers on black key octaves (rather than thumb and fifth finger). Phrasing indications also determine qualities of touch and hence ways in which fingers are used. For example, from detached to semidetached to smooth, the staccato, portato, and legato markings require increasing amounts of weight in touch:

Staccato: detached   Portato: semidetached   Legato: smooth

Even within staccato playing, the degree of sharpness of detachment varies. Generally a softer dynamic level implies a more gentle staccato, whereas a louder dynamic level indicates a sharper staccato.

Portato touch is semidetached and weightier than staccato. It is not uncommon to use the same finger on several different notes in a portato passage for uniformity of sound. In Beethoven's Piano Concerto No. 3, first movement, mm. 160–164, the transition into the melodic second theme is also a transition of touch, from staccato to portato and finally to legato. In the portato measure, I prefer to use the same finger, the third, for each note (Example 2).

Example 2: Beethoven Piano Concerto No. 3, first movement, mm. 160–164.

Legato playing is accomplished with smoothness of fingering and help from the pedal. In the simplest of legato phrases—the two-note phrase—there is most often an implied decrescendo from the first to the second note, aided by a suitable fingering. For example, in the beginning of the "Tempest" Sonata, Op. 31 no. 2, I prefer to repeat the pattern of 3–2 for each slurred duplet in mm. 2–5. To achieve a smooth line in Sonata Op. 31 no. 1, second movement, m. 74, Beethoven himself suggested the fingering 1–3–1–3–1–3–1–3. While other fingerings are certainly possible, Beethoven's works very well, and I prefer to use it.

Another factor influencing fingering is the regulation of a piano's keyboard. I prefer a fair amount of aftertouch, the distance a key travels downward after the initial point of resistance at which the hammer-jack is tripped. Greater aftertouch—in which the point of resistance comes closer to the top of the keystroke—allows a pianist to control very soft, light, fast playing by ensuring that the keys are not depressed past the point of resistance. The hammers can seem to float gently up to the strings rather than being pushed up with full force. This type of setting for the aftertouch also allows for very rapid key repetition of the sort one might encounter in soft trills.

Of course, when a performer plays concerts on tour, the instruments are not always ideal. When I encounter a piano with less aftertouch than I would like, I might need to modify my fingering for trills. Ideally, and whenever possible, I prefer to trill with 1–3; I find the greatest speed and control of dynamics with this fingering. However, if aftertouch is so little that the trill speed is necessarily significantly reduced, I might change to 2–3 for a trill such as those at the beginning of the "Appassionata" Sonata, Op. 57. The fingering 2–3 will give me a slower trill, for the finger motion will be greater given the deeper point of resistance in the regulation of the keyboard.

Even with an ideal piano, one cannot always use the fingering of 1–3. At the end of the Arietta movement of Op. 111 there is a trill over a restatement of the main theme. Both are played by the right hand. The only fingerings possible for the trill are 4–5, 3–4, and 3–5 (I use all these possibilities), while 1 and 2 play the theme, all *pianissimo*.

Most often Beethoven did not specify fingering. When he did so, however, his fingering clarifies a manner of playing meant to achieve a specific desired musical purpose. Some fingerings may have been meant as a reminder to himself in the sonatas that he played, particularly those that predated his Heiligenstadt Testament (Beethoven's painful admission of the onset of deafness), after which he curtailed his public performances. However, even in these works and certainly in later ones, Beethoven also intended his fingering to help a hypothetical future performer realize specific musical ideals. His fingerings are not intended as merely challenging finger-wiggling exercises.

In the Allegro of Sonata Op. 2 no. 2, Beethoven indicated a fingering that is not immediately easy even on a pianoforte (Example 3). In fact, the most common way of playing this passage and the parallel figure in the recapitulation is to divide the notes between the hands. If one were to disregard Beethoven's fingering, the left hand could play the first note of each triplet with the third finger.

Example 3: Sonata Op. 2 no. 2, first movement, mm. 84–91. Fingering is Beethoven's.

A moderately skilled pianist could play this passage instantly in such a manner. However, the division between the hands makes it sound like unstylistic and simplified Liszt (he would have used interlocking octaves!), too pointillistic and probably too fast. Beethoven's fingering specifically guards against this result.

Following Beethoven's fingering here forces us to play much more smoothly and also allows for the tempo of the *espressivo* minor key second theme, which follows a long ritard (a slowing down), to be appropriately slower. We are dealing with musical elements, not merely "getting the notes." The difficult fingering ensures a certain level of awareness and care with these musical elements. And consider the striking visual element of playing this passage with only one hand: Beethoven was a virtuoso and was proud of it.

Another virtuosic passage for which Beethoven specified fingering is toward the end of the Prestissimo of the "Waldstein" Sonata (Example 4).

Example 4: Sonata Op. 53, third movement, mm. 463–474. Fingering is Beethoven's.

To reduce this passage to playing simple single-note scales in each hand (as is sometimes done, incredible though this may be) is to miss the point entirely. The fingering is there to ensure against such heresy, and following it by playing octave glissandos in each hand ensures that the Prestissimo will indeed be the ultimate in speed. The occasional argument that this type of playing is not possible on a modern piano (with heavier key-weight and deeper action) is specious—I have never encountered a well-regulated instrument on which these octave glissandos cannot be played. As a further indication that Beethoven meant exactly what he wrote, he provided an alternate (easier) way of playing the trill and melodic line that follows. No such *ossia* (literally "or" or "rather," an alternative, often easier, version of a passage) was composed for these octaves.

In these two cases in Op. 2 no. 2 and in Op. 53, Beethoven's fingering is concerned with qualitative musical dimensions: in the first instance, to ensure that a passage is played smoothly and not too fast (thereby allowing for a slightly slower second theme area); and in the second to ensure a revolutionary use of the keyboard for an astonishing musical effect and speed.

Fingering that Beethoven included in autograph scores can serve in other ways too. In the Adagio of Op. 106 and again in the recitatives of the Adagio movement of Op. 110, Beethoven wrote specific notes, tied to themselves (Examples 5a and b). The idea is not to double the length, as would normally be the case. Rather, the change of fingering indicates that the second note is to be rearticulated as an echo or rebound (the German term is *Bebung*) of the first. In Op. 110 I depress the key fully with the fourth finger for the first note of each group and then let it rise just beyond the point of aftertouch (but not fully up) before replaying the key, very softly, with 3. In Op. 106 I take the slurs connecting the octaves in m. 164 to mean the same idea, and rearticulate the second of each group.

Beethoven also provided fingering as a guide in certain passages that might otherwise seem difficult. The fingering for the chords in the Trio of Op. 2 no. 1, third movement, mm. 59–62, helps ensure a legato texture. And the fingering

Example 5a: Sonata Op. 106, third movement, m. 165.

Example 5b: Sonata Op. 110, third movement, m. 5.

for the left hand in Op. 111, first movement, mm. 26–27, although it might initially seem awkward, is actually brilliant when you learn and internalize it.

As we consider Beethoven's own fingering, another issue comes into play, that of redistributing passages for the hands, often defended as making them easier. I know of only one instance in which Beethoven clearly specified that the right hand is to help the left: Sonata Op. 2 no. 3, first movement, mm. 129–137. The stem of the tenor A indicates that it is to be played by the right hand. This I would do (Example 6).

Example 6: Sonata Op. 2 no. 3, first movement, mm. 128–130.

But I would not redistribute the hands in any other passage. For example, it might be tempting to rewrite the opening gestures of Op. 106 and Op. 111 in several different ways (Examples 7a and b). Yet the extraordinary drama inherent in these opening phrases derives, in part, from the way they are written and the way Beethoven meant for them to be played. If they are rewritten to redis-

Example 7a: Sonata Op. 106, first movement, mm. 1–4.

Example 7b: Sonata Op. 111, first movement, mm. 1–2.

tribute the hands with the idea of making them less treacherous, then tension will be reduced and the drama lessened. I relish these passages the way they are.

THE PIANO is a relative newcomer in the evolutionary time-scale of Western art music. Stradivarius had built some of the world's best violins some 130 years before the first Steinway of modern design was made in 1858. But pianofortes had been around since the time of Bach, and they evolved, particularly in the early nineteenth century, at an extraordinary rate. Various keyboard-shifting and damper-raising mechanisms were invented to alter qualities of sound; these were operated by raising levers with one's knees. Pedals replaced these knee-operated levers by 1810 or so. Gradually, high-quality steel strings and steel frames were employed in construction, allowing for greater string tension and greater sonority. Finally, the modern concert grand piano, essentially as we know it, was complete upon the invention and inclusion of the middle pedal. Certain subtle refinements are still ongoing, but the piano reached its general sophisticated evolutionary state—with copper-wound bass strings, steel overstrung frame, and the three pedals—at around the end of the nineteenth century.

By controlling the pedals, the feet do more than act as a conduit between the ears and the hands. The pedals, particularly the right (damper) pedal, are an integral part of the sound that we hear in the concert hall; the hands, ears, and feet are all inextricably linked.

The left pedal is referred to as the soft pedal (or the *una corda* pedal). When depressed, it shifts the keyboard slightly to the right, so that the hammers strike the strings with softer felt, thereby producing a softer sound. The degree of shift brought about by the left pedal should be adjusted only after the hammers have been spaced properly. If there is a large amount of travel, the keyboard will move far enough so that the hammers are hitting only two strings. If there is less travel, the hammers will still strike three strings when the left pedal is depressed, although on softer felt. There is a change in timbre (tone color) when the keyboard shifts, regardless of whether either two or three strings are struck when the left pedal is depressed. This change is caused by a different part of the hammers striking the strings than would strike them in normal playing. The change in timbre is more subtle when three strings, rather than two, are struck.

The keyboard of the early pianofortes was shifted so far that the hammers would indeed strike only one of the three strings of each note when the *una corda* pedal was depressed. However, construction evolved, changing the quality of the hammers and strings, the tension of the strings, and the overall geometry of the frame with the advent of overstringing. The degree of shift of the keyboard also lessened, rendering the term *una corda* anachronistic. However, even though the left pedal on the modern piano will not shift the hammers far enough to hit only one string, today's instrument nonetheless provides a much greater range of sound quality because of developments in materials and design.

I prefer that the hammers hit three strings at all times, even when the left pedal is depressed. I feel that I can play softly enough, and I certainly prefer the more subtle timbral change. Furthermore, when the keyboard shifts only very slightly, the response is much faster; the keybed takes less time to reach its final designated resting spot when the left pedal is depressed.

Once the keyboard-shifting mechanism and the hammers are adjusted well, I do not depress the left pedal with varying degrees; I depress it either fully or not at all. I know that depressing this pedal partially can bring about slight changes in qualities of sound, but I prefer to control these sorts of changes and subtle varieties of sound with my fingers. Thus, for me, the left pedal is either on or off. I generally use the left pedal whenever a passage is marked *pianissimo* or softer. Other indications to use the left pedal are the terms *una corda* (one string), *sotto voce* (in a low voice), and *mezza voce* (half voice).

Beethoven's use of the pedal was motivated by sensitivity to quality—not necessarily quantity—of sound. Although the vast majority of his pedal markings concern the use of the damper pedal, he was also precise about the use of the left pedal. In Op. 101 Beethoven indicates in the beginning of the Adagio *mit einer Saite* (with one string) as well as *sul una corda* (Example 8). The expressive intention is for a hushed, veiled sound.

Example 8: Sonata Op. 101, third movement, mm. 1–4.

The Adagio of the "Hammerklavier" Sonata includes many more directives for using the left pedal (*una corda* or soft pedal) than for the damper pedal, and many more than in any other work. The last such marking of this movement is fascinating, for the music moves from *una corda* (soft pedal depressed) to *tre corde* (soft pedal no longer depressed) even though the dynamics actually become softer, with the penultimate chord *pp* and the final one *ppp* (Example 9)!

To explain this seeming contradiction, some have suggested that the *tre corde* marking is misplaced and belongs at the *piano* start of the next movement. (Since the autograph score of Op. 106 is lost, this suggestion is at best only that.) However, if we look ahead to the fugue, Beethoven creates a similar false paradox in m. 269 of the Allegro risoluto; as we take leave of the choralelike abstrac-

Example 9: Op. 106, third movement, mm. 181–187. The *tre corde* in mm. 186–187 implies a subtle change of timbre for the last two chords.

tion of the fugue subject, another *tre corde* marking helps usher in the home key of B-flat major even as the dynamic level moves from *p* to *pp*.

Again, Beethoven's concern is with quality of sound. One does not absolutely need to have the left pedal depressed to play *pp* or even *ppp*. Lifting the left pedal in these instances, as Beethoven has indicated, makes the sound more immediate than that which would be produced with the left pedal depressed. Also, in each case, this new quality of sound, although still very soft, functions in an architectural dimension. In the Adagio, the two final chords—*pp* and *ppp* but *tre corde*, the only chords here which both hands play together—leave one suspended in F-sharp major after the movement-long immersion in F-sharp minor. This is a transformation of mode not unlike final cadences of many baroque fugues; stylistically it helps usher in the baroque counterpoint that motivates the movement that follows. In the fugue, the clarity of sound allowed by the *tre corde* at m. 269 helps define the beginning of the end—the return to the subject in B-flat major juxtaposed with the counterpoint from the chorale-like abstraction.

The *tre corde* indication can also influence the manner in which the last chord is rolled. Try playing this passage two ways: first, with the left pedal depressed from the *una corda* indication in m. 181 all the way to the end (ignoring the *tre corde*) and then once again, but this time incorporating the *tre corde*. The first way is easier; obviously, it is simpler to play *ppp* with the left pedal depressed. The second way, however, demands greater care and control with the fingers. I have found that in order to make the last rolled chord truly *ppp* and *tre corde*, I roll it a bit more slowly than I would if I were relying on the left pedal to help me make it softer. This slower roll leads in a more seamless fashion into the beginning of the Largo that follows.

Depressing the middle pedal (sostenuto pedal) immediately after a particular note or chord will cause the damper(s) for that note or chord to remain raised, thereby allowing only those strings to continue to vibrate for the duration that this pedal is employed. For example, one could play a C triad and then immediately depress the middle pedal; the dampers for C, G, and E will remain raised, allowing only those strings to continue to vibrate. Hence, only the sound of this triad will be sustained, even if other notes or chords are played (assuming the right pedal is not used); only the dampers for C, G, and E will remain raised by the middle pedal.

A pedal that sustained selective notes was patented by the Parisian piano maker Boisselot *et fils* as early as 1844, and although some interest was generated in the Paris exhibition the same year, his own interest in marketing the device was short-lived. Another French maker, Claude Montal, exhibited a similar device at the London exhibition in 1862, but he too made no further efforts, declining even to seek a patent. The modern version of this device and its position as the middle pedal was patented in 1875 by Albert Steinway (Rowland 1993, 24–25). Although in that year it became a popular option on American Steinway grand pianos, this pedal was absent from the Hamburg Steinways until well into the twentieth century, for European opinion about the value of this pedal was, at best, ambivalent.

The middle pedal is a simple mechanical switch; it is either on or off. While there are no gradations of use, the decision about when to use this pedal can involve musical and philosophical points of view.

As a matter of artistic principle, I do not use the middle pedal for music which predates its invention. This issue is different from that of playing—or pedaling—Beethoven, for example, on a modern grand piano rather than confining oneself exclusively to pianofortes of the types available to Beethoven throughout his lifetime. With the exception of the middle pedal, all aspects of the modern piano evolved in a linear fashion from the pianoforte. When Beethoven was presented with pianofortes of increased registral range, he immediately incorporated the "new" notes into new compositions: the range of the Érard piano of 1803 resulted in the higher compass of the "Waldstein" Sonata Op. 53 and the Fourth Piano Concerto Op. 58, and the increase in bass range of the Broadwood piano of 1818 was anticipated in Sonata Op. 101—the fugal climax specifically includes the new low E (contra E) in every chord. Although Beethoven composed additional cadenzas that used the larger registral span of his newest pianos several years after the initial publication of his First and Second Piano Concertos, he did not revise earlier compositions retroactively to incorporate expanded registral capabilities.

The middle pedal is a technological development completely separate and different from anything Beethoven encountered. While he certainly experienced increased sonorous capabilities of the pianos he knew, and undoubtedly wished and hoped for even more sound for the future, the advent of the middle pedal does not fit into this type of evolution; it is a development unto itself. Hence, I would never use the middle pedal for music of Beethoven.

The right pedal raises all the dampers, so that all strings are free to vibrate until the pedal is disengaged or the tones die away. Unlike the left and sostenuto pedals, the right pedal is used in varying degrees, thereby raising the dampers varying amounts and exerting different effects on the overall tone of the piano.

I prefer the pedal to be adjusted so that there is virtually no vertical free-play, and therefore the slightest motion of the right foot will cause the dampers to rise from their resting positions. (There should also be no vertical free-play in the middle and left pedals.) Damper regulation is important; all dampers should rise at the same time and the same rate when the pedal is depressed. They must also settle onto the strings at the same rate and time; otherwise some strings will remain undamped (vibrating) longer than others.

Research has shown (see accompanying chart) that when a hammer strikes a string, its maximum response—greatest vibration displacement and hence greatest decibel level—is reached not immediately but rather an instant later. But not all harmonic partials (overtones or sympathetic vibrations) die away at the same rate. In fact, several actually increase in intensity (decibel level) before beginning to decrease. In a well-tuned grand piano, depressing the pedal at the exact moment of greatest vibrational displacement can create the effect of a slight crescendo since the amount of sound is greater at that moment than when the strings were initially struck. This effect is quite subtle and is most noticeable within a context of *piano*, and with a concert grand, since the harmonic partials are more present with longer strings.

The damper pedal is also valuable in helping produce a legato sound. Although the manner in which sounds are actually produced on the piano is percussive (hammers striking the strings), sounds can be sculpted in an infinite variety of ways to lead and to blend into one another. To mold the sound in this manner is to play legato.

For example, a certain amount of weight on the C key followed by less weight on the D key will not only produce a decrescendo, but will help the note D grow smoothly out of the note C as long as the piano is well regulated and the C is held down until D has sounded. Pedaling between the two notes will help smooth the sound more. If the span between the two keys is such that it is impossible to connect them, then only with the pedal will legato be possible. Although in both these cases the hammers do indeed strike the strings in a more or less percussive manner, the pedal helps smooth together the sounds.

In producing a legato within a decrescendo, the pianist must use all resources to shape the sounds so that one sound molds into the next. I listen carefully, so

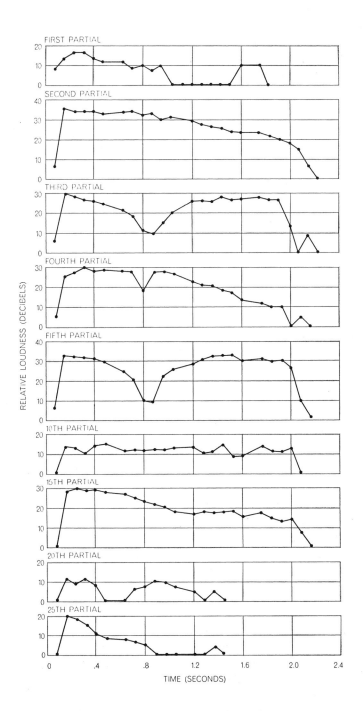

Decay curves for nine partial tones of the lowest C on the piano. In some cases the partial tones even increase in loudness before beginning to decay. For each curve, 30 measurements were made at 0.08 second each (Blackham 1965, 96).

that the initiation of a particular sound matches the decay of the previous one. Legato within a crescendo is more challenging to produce. Although I have mentioned the possibility of producing isolated subtle crescendos under special conditions, piano tones generally die away after being produced, unlike tones of string or wind instruments which can draw on more bow or more air to sustain or increase quantities of sound. Therefore, the legato crescendo on the piano is an issue of sonic illusion, albeit very convincing illusion if done well.

The role of the pedal in such a case is to smooth over the discrete initiation of each new sound, which, owing to the crescendo, is louder than the decay of the previous sound. Naturally, one tries as much as possible with one's fingers to produce a smooth series of tones. Use of the pedal in and of itself will not guarantee legato. In fact, it is certainly possible—and very easy—to play even the C–D example above nonlegato by accenting the note D. But with both hands and feet, the pianist can coax the piano into playing legato.

A good singing tone (like a good legato touch) is an element of the craft of playing that a performer always strives to improve. Nuances can be varied; for example, more pedal could be used at the beginning of the Arietta theme of Beethoven's Sonata Op. 111 than at the beginning of the Adagio of Sonata Op. 2 no. 1. Both chords are "singing," but the Arietta had a greater weightiness, even from the start, than the Adagio. The registral disposition is a factor, but also consider the total musical meaning—the ways in which the composer, the performer, and the audience have arrived at the beginning of each slow movement and where each is leading. Maintaining the top (or prominent) voice, often by sleight of foot, helps to make the piano sing. The degree to which the pedal is depressed in a particular passage affects the overall quality and quantity of sound. But pedal markings do not specify how far to depress the pedal and hence how high the dampers are raised off the strings, how free the strings are to vibrate, and the degree to which the overtone series is invoked.

Beethoven's pedal markings are integral to the totality of a composition. On one side of the sonic spectrum is Beethoven's use of the dampers to create as much sound as possible, as in the opening of the "Hammerklavier." Achieving this effect is rather straightforward: simply depress the damper pedal as far as it will go (Example 10).

Example 10: Sonata Op. 106, first movement, mm. 1–4.

Clearly, the pedaling here is essential to the enormousness of the opening. Changing the pedal at any point would significantly lessen the impact of these measures and alter the expectations they engender. On the other side of the spectrum are pedal markings of a nature far more subtle—those which help create a blurring of intermingled harmonies. Although use of the damper pedal in such cases is quite different, pedaling nonetheless is again integral to the organic nature of the composition.

Even within the rather improvisatory first movement of Sonata Op. 31 no. 2 ("Tempest"), the recitatives (mm. 143–148 and mm. 153–158) are wholly extraordinary (see Example 11). They are marked Largo, *pp*, and *con espressione e semplice.* Each is also marked to be played with the damper pedal depressed. This does not mean to depress the right pedal to the floor—it simply means to depress it just enough to lift the dampers slightly off the strings, allowing them to vibrate freely after being played, creating a hushed, suspended harmonic "mist." If Beethoven had not included the pedal mark, I would change the pedal

Example 11: Sonata Op. 31 no. 2, first movement, mm. 137–159.

in the normally accepted manner, with each new change of harmony. However, the inclusion of the pedal mark here guards against this and challenges the interpreter (and the listener) to more compelling sonic imagery.

While the initial pedal markings in this movement and at the beginning of the development each extend over a single rolled chord, each pedal marking beginning in m. 143 spans six measures, blending together different harmonies. However, to make sense of these markings, let's consider their local context as well as their role within the movement as a whole, and further, the place of this sonata within Beethoven's creative oeuvre.

After having composed the Sonatas Opp. 2, 7, 10, 13, and 14, Beethoven finally felt satisfied with his Sonata Op. 22. Not surprisingly, his next several sonatas were quite different from their predecessors: Sonata Op. 26 begins with a variation movement and includes a funeral march, and each sonata of Op. 27 is a Sonata *quasi una fantasia.*

Sonata Op. 31 no. 1 is a work full of good humor, but seriousness of mood returns with Sonata Op. 31 no. 2. The very opening is highly improvisatory: anything could happen; the arpeggiation could continue for at least two more octaves. Are we in A major? C major? There is no sense of harmonic stability until D minor is finally established in m. 21. After the dramatic and intense exposition and development, we are led back to the same harmony (A major chord, m. 137) as at the opening of the piece. Now, however, the chord is in root position, and the arpeggiation has become a grace note figure.

Even though this chord is now in root position, we hear it not as an A major chord but as the uneasy dominant of D minor. And indeed, m. 139 wrests us away (with the sforzando B-flat) with empty octaves—that very special sonority—to bring us down to the low C-sharp (leading tone of D minor) in m. 141, then back up and down again to C-sharp in m. 143, but this C-sharp is the bass of the rolled chord. At this moment, upon reaching the low C-sharp, Beethoven has written his pedal indication. The pedal marking lasts through the fermata in m. 148—a long time. Why?

A composer could have considered several alternatives at this point (m. 143). He could have written a literal repetition of the opening several measures of the work, aligning m. 144 with m. 148, leaving out the "new" music of mm. 144–148. He could also possibly have considered modulating from the harmony built on the A-six chord of m. 144 directly to the F-sharp minor harmony of m. 161, thereby leaving out this entire section (mm. 145–160).

These extraordinary recitatives are an improvisation upon a stylized improvisatory first theme. They help define not only this work but this particular stage of Beethoven's compositional maturity, and he has carefully indicated their meaning to him. The character marking is Largo—the slowest of the slow. The dynamic is *pp,* very soft. He also specified *con espressione e semplice* for touch and quality of sound. There is no crescendo; these five-and-three-quarters measures are all shaped within the dynamic of *pianissimo*. Depressing the pedal only slightly, thus barely raising the dampers from the strings, while observing the other indications (Largo, *pp*, *con espressione e semplice*) imbues this recitative with a very special quality, as if heard through a shimmering mist.

These pedal markings may seem quite unusual from today's perspective. But by the standard of the time, using the dampers in this way was not unique. C. P. E. Bach wrote in 1762 that "the undamped register of the pianoforte is the most pleasing and, once the performer learns to observe the necessary precautions in the face of its reverberations, the most delightful for improvisation" (Bach 1949, 431). Beethoven's contemporaries Jan Ladislav Dussek and Muzio Clementi specified use of the damper pedal in blurring together different harmonies even before Beethoven did, a technique that was not uncommon in the early years of the nineteenth century. (See particularly Dussek's Sonata Op. 39 and Clementi's Sonata Op. 40, fourth movement.)

I do not agree with the point of view that today's pianos are too sonorous for this kind of pedaling. One can certainly play this phrase badly and create harmonic sludge on any piano, even a pianoforte. However, while the sound of a pianoforte dies away more quickly, this phrase can be played well on a modern piano—in a manner true to the musical spirit—with careful attention to the pacing (Largo), the dynamic (*pp*), and the precise quality of touch needed to allow the notes to float. The pedal marking is not simply an add-on; it is essential to the music; its incorporation and internalization helps realize a musical whole much greater than the sum of its parts.

Beethoven also used the dampers to extraordinary musical effect in the second movement of the Piano Concerto in C minor, Op. 37. The markings in this score, however, are *senza sordino* and *con sordino*: without dampers (right pedal depressed) and with dampers (Example 12). Although this work was published in 1804 and thus assigned a higher opus number than the "Tempest" Sonata (which was composed in 1801–02 and published in 1803), it was actually composed during the summer of 1800.

The first movement of this concerto is so heavily grounded in C minor that one would normally expect the relative major (E-flat) as the key of the second movement. The key of E major, therefore, is a complete surprise; the music comes as if from another sphere. Thus, the Largo, *pianissimo*, the key, and the raised dampers (right pedal depressed) all combine to create a musical landscape wholly unexpected and very expressive. To dismiss any of these elements (including transposing the movement to the expected key of E-flat major) would be to destroy the musical ideal.

Once again, the pedal should not be depressed more than a small amount, just enough to allow the dampers to rise off the strings. Delicate voicing and touch are concomitant with careful pedaling to create a startling, and yet engaging and beautiful, musical texture.

Example 12: Piano Concerto No. 3, Op. 37, second movement, mm. 1–12.

Not all of Beethoven's contemporaries were as accepting of the damper pedal as he. Hummel was a leader among those who advocated a considerably more restrained approach to this pedal (Rowland 1993, 41). But another pianist who was also in Vienna at the same time—Leopold Kozeluch—wrote to his London publisher in 1799:

> On account of these three caprices [Op. 44], it is necessary to play from beginning to end with the open register. . . . One finds this mutation on every piano. The mutation is raised with the knee, which produces the effect of a [glass] harmonica, because the sound is not damped and continues sustained (in Flamm 1970, 75).

This letter predates Beethoven's use of the damper pedal throughout the first movement of his Sonata Op. 27 no. 2 ("Moonlight"), which was composed in 1801 and published the following year. Within the Adagio sostenuto Beethoven specified *Si deve suonare tutto questo pezzo delicatissimamente e senza sordini* (this whole piece ought to be played with the utmost delicacy and without dampers) and also *sempre pianissimo e senza sordini* (always very soft and without dampers). In this case, however, there is no *con sordini* indication to countermand the *senza sordini*. (Beethoven used both *sordini* and *sordino*.) In my opinion, the specification does not mean to keep the dampers uniformly raised from beginning to end of the movement; after all, although the indication is also for *sempre pianissimo*, there are in fact small crescendos and decrescendos throughout the movement. Thus, in an analogous fashion, one would change the pedal sparingly but judiciously. The *senza sordini* indication, in keeping with the *quasi una fantasia* character of this work, implies a generally "moist" sound, one which allows for some melding of harmonies, but not to the extent that the texture becomes opaque.

The Rondo movement of the "Waldstein" Sonata begins in a most awkward manner: the left hand crosses over the right hand to play the melody, and the right hand plays the arpeggiated accompaniment in the tenor range of the keyboard (Example 13). Why?

The entire musical context here is special. The pedal certainly plays a role: the long pedal marking allows the first bass note of each phrase to be heard throughout the phrase, analogous to the bass underpinning of the opening Allegro (and also the Adagio introduzione). In the Rondo, the bass notes are no longer only harmonic underpinning; they are also part of the main line. The pedaling also blends together the tonic and dominant harmonies—harmonies that have not been closely linked heretofore in this work in the usual classical sense—and cre-

Example 13: Sonata Op. 53 ("Waldstein"), third movement, mm. 1–12.

ates a delicate texture of suspended mist, in great contrast to the clarity of texture up to this point.

Once again, the dynamic is *pianissimo*, and although the character indication is Allegretto moderato, the harmonic rhythm (the rate of changes of chords) is slow. The pedaling and these other factors also help explain the unique disposition of the hands. Beethoven could easily have written the music to be played in the more traditional way, with the left hand playing the arpeggiated accompaniment and the right hand playing the melodic line. However, by writing the way he did, Beethoven forces the performer to play more carefully, for more care is required to play the main line softly with the left hand as it crosses over and to keep the accompaniment soft and transparent with the right hand as it plays in the tenor range. Careful pedaling links this all together; if the pedal is changed as the harmony changes, the extraordinary effect is rendered asunder.

In the early years of the nineteenth century, some European piano makers divided the damping mechanism to control the upper register of the keyboard with the right part of the pedal and the bass register with the left. However, there seems to be only one instance of a direction in Beethoven's music itself about the use of this mechanism, and it instructs the player *not* to use it. In the autograph score of his Sonata Op. 53 Beethoven wrote, "NB Where ped. is written, all the dampers from the bass to the treble should be raised. O means that they should be allowed to fall back again." (Although the first marking to use the pedal is not until the beginning of the Rondo, this directive was written at the very beginning of the sonata.)

In Sonata Op. 109 Beethoven used the damper pedal to help with another sort of musical connection—continuity between the first and second movements. The final E major chord of the first movement is held in pedal until the first E minor chord of the second movement is played. This pedaling helps create sonic continuity between the two movements. In the last movement, the last pedal marking for the final chord in this work is without an indication for the release of the pedal. The gentle sound lasts as long as the strings resonate.

In several instances Beethoven also specified pedal markings beneath rests. In these cases, such as the opening of Sonata Op. 111 and toward the end of the middle movement of Piano Concerto No. 4 in G major, Op. 58 (Example 14), the pedal indication works in conjunction with the note values of the chords to create a lighter, more hovering sound of specific duration. The quality of the sound is suggested by the note values and by their general context, and the duration of the sound is ensured by the pedal marking.

In these measures, Beethoven could easily have written each chord as a double-dotted quarter-note (♩··)—the full value that the pedal indication ensures—followed by a sixteenth-rest. However, because he wrote the chords as eighth-notes, we play them with a lighter, more floating touch, using the foot to

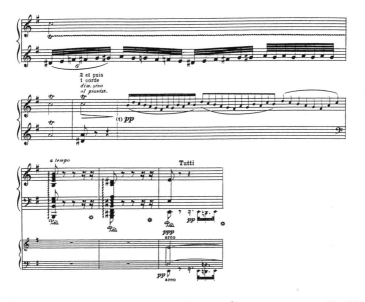

Example 14: Piano Concerto No. 4, Op. 58, second movement, mm. 59–64.

preserve the sound for the indicated duration. The same general idea applies to the opening measures of Sonata Op. 111.

With all his indications—fingering, pedaling, *una corda, tre corde*—Beethoven knew what he was doing and why. If, through careful attention to these markings, stylistic awareness of their meaning, and an understanding of the instrument, we can more fully hear with the master's inner ear, then we will be the richer for it.

CHAPTER 3

Tempo

Please tell me whether Andantino is to be understood as meaning faster or slower than Andante, for this term, like so many in music, is of so indefinite a significance that Andantino sometimes approaches Allegro and sometimes, on the other hand, is played like Adagio.

—Beethoven to George Thomson, Edinburgh, 19 February 1813, concerning progress on settings of Irish airs (Thayer 1973, 555)

*H*ow fast is allegro? How slowly should an Adagio be played? Tempo—our perception of the passing of time—is crucial to musical interpretation. Descriptive terms (allegro, adagio, andante, presto, for example) are more than simply directives of speed; they are implications of musical character. The stateliness of a Largo movement would be caricatured by playing it too fast; a Prestissimo would lose all urgency by playing it too slowly. These two terms are at the extremes of the tempo spectrum: largo, adagio, andante, allegretto, allegro, vivace, presto, and prestissimo, in order of increasing pace.

In his piano sonatas through Op. 81a (1809) Beethoven used these terms in ways generally consistent with classical style. However, when he returned to writing for the piano in 1814, his musical vision demanded more precise meanings on all levels, and he wanted to be ever more exact with movement headings. He tried German descriptions only (Op. 90) and German with Italian together (Op. 101). With Sonata Op. 106 onward, he returned to Italian terms (with the exception of the last movement of Sonata Op. 109, in which he used both Italian and German), but for Sonata Op. 106 he also ascribed metronome markings for each movement. In Sonatas Opp. 109, 110, and 111 he used headings for at least one movement in each work that pertain specifically to character as well as suggesting tempo implications: Gesangvoll, mit innigsten Empfindung (songful, with innermost feeling) in Op. 109; Arioso dolente (soulful, sad song) in Op. 110; and Allegro con brio ed appassionato and Adagio molto semplice e cantabile in Op. 111.

Of the total 111 piano sonata movements, forty-two are Allegro (and four are

44

Vivace), sixteen are Adagio, thirteen are Allegretto, eight are Andante, five are Presto. Only four are Largo and three Prestissimo. There are no Andantino movements. The other sixteen movements are headed by different sorts of character indications, such as the German ones of Op. 90. The two extremes—Largo and Prestissimo—are used sparingly and deliberately. The interpretive implication is that the subtle difference between each term and its nearest neighbor (Largo as opposed to Adagio, Prestissimo as opposed to Presto) should play an important role in determining tempo.

It is in the nature of tempo for several musical events to occur simultaneously. On the surface is the passing of the notes; underneath is the rate of harmonic change. Influencing the perception of both is the unit of metrical pulse. To which does a particular indication refer?

All, of course. The traditional Italian terms are descriptive and are relative to one another, with no absolute value. But the rate of harmonic change—not just the passing of notes on the surface—in an allegro movement is quicker than in an adagio. For example, the beginning of Sonata Op. 53 ("Waldstein") has many rapid notes, yet the harmonic rhythm is more expansive. However, the character of this first movement is Allegro con brio (lively, with brilliance). Thus, the tempo should ensure that the motion on the surface is rapid enough so that the progression from harmony to harmony, theme to theme, is perceived in the brilliant and often startling manner that is integral to this work.

In the Introduzione: Adagio molto that follows, the harmonic changes are more concentrated—there are more per phrase. A very slow tempo (Adagio molto) would ensure that not only would the notes on the surface be slower than in the first movement, but so would the actual rate (in real time) of harmonic change. The Allegretto moderato is back to a quicker pace, but initially the rate of harmonic change is made somewhat nebulous by the extraordinary pedal markings of the opening theme. By the time the Prestissimo coda is reached, the main theme is so familiar to a listener that the speed of the coda can really be as fast as possible.

Sonata Op. 7 also begins with repeated notes, but they resonate within a single harmony rather than moving in a linear course with the vectorlike quality of Sonata Op. 53. The tempo of Op. 7 is also quick (Allegro molto e con brio) but is limited by the clarity necessary for the sixteenth-note tremolando passages that conclude the exposition and recapitulation. The unit of pulse in this 6/8 movement is the eighth-note; in Op. 53, first movement (which is ¢ or 4/4), it is the quarter-note. Although the pulse in the first movement of Op. 7 is quicker than in the first movement of Op. 53 (Allegro molto compared to Allegro), the actual number of repeated eighth-notes per unit time is greater in Op. 53, and thus Op. 53 sounds faster. In other words, we should not assume that because Op. 7 is marked Allegro molto (as opposed to Allegro as in Op. 53), the surface motion of one should be faster than the other; the *molto* refers to the pulse of the repeated eighth-notes, which is faster than the pulse of a quarter-note in the first movement of Sonata Op. 53.

In the second movement (Largo, con gran espressione) of Op. 7, the surface motion, the harmonic motion, and the metrical pulse (3/4) are one and the same; all are very slow. The character indication *con gran espressione* implies that each chord is to be suffused with a sound of dignified weightiness.

The two polar extremes of speed are Largo (the slowest of the slow) and Prestissimo (fast to the extreme). The second movement of Sonata Op. 109 suggests the care with which Beethoven used both these terms. As was commonly his practice, he wrote out the autograph manuscript score in ink and then went back over it with a pencil to mark changes. The autograph of Op. 109 (Program 6, Example 61) clearly shows the second movement initially marked Presto (in ink) with the *issimo* added later in pencil (starting over the *o*). Beethoven explicitly differentiated between Presto and Prestissimo. He wanted this movement, with its relatively staid harmonic rhythm (one harmony per 6/8 measure), to have as dynamic a surface motion as possible, dramatic in and of itself, and in stark contrast to the movements surrounding it.

The meter of a work helps define the pulse and thus the perception of tempo. As Beethoven's conception of Sonata Op. 57 ("Appassionata") evolved, he changed the meter of the first movement (Allegro assai, very lively) from 4/4 to 12/8. An internal pulse of twelve eighth-notes per measure, rather than four quarter-notes per measure, heightens the dramatic excitement, brought to the fore in the *ff* syncopations of mm. 17 and 19. Thus, Allegro assai refers to the pulse of the eighth-note, not the pulse of the quarter-note. The subtle difference is that while an allegro quarter-note pulse in a 4/4 meter might, in fact, lead to a faster surface tempo than an allegro assai eighth-note pulse, one feels each eighth-note more in a 12/8 pulse, each musical event stands out more in relief, and thus the drama is heightened.

Similarly in Sonata Op. 109 Beethoven could have written the Prestissimo movement in 2/4, with quick eighth-note triplets, which would imply two main pulses per bar. But the 6/8 meter coupled with the Prestissimo indication implies a very quick pulse of six beats per bar.

In the scherzo movement of Sonata Op. 27 no. 1, the Allegro molto vivace refers to the pulse of a quarter-note, not a dotted half-note. The meter is 3/4, and the pulse is three beats per measure, not one longer beat per measure. This quarter-note pulse allows for the second-beat staccato notes (mm. 42–50) in the trio to be well-defined offbeat figures, with all their good-natured buoyancy; upon the return of the scherzo, the three-pulse allows the opening material to be clearly syncopated (with the top legato and the bass staccato) and thus more exciting and indeed molto vivace (with much life). With the less exact pulse of a dotted half-note (one per measure) and a correspondingly quicker surface speed, the movement would necessarily lose a lot of the detail and clarity.

The opening Grave of Sonata Op. 13 ("Pathétique") gives no indication of actual speed. The tempo, however, must be slow enough to allow the dotted thirty-second-notes, as well as the runs culminating in 128th-notes, to be clear. The tempo must also allow enough time for the *fp* chords to resonate, *piano*. This is not a question of the sound of the chord naturally decaying from *forte* to *piano*, which would have been notated differently: the first chord *f* and the next chord *p*, or a *p* placed at the tied end of the chord. However, a true, crisp *fp* can be affected—even, or rather especially, on the modern piano. On a well-regulated piano with dampers in good shape, the pianist depresses the keys rapidly in order to create the *forte*, then immediately allows them to rise so that the sound is damped almost instantaneously, and then depresses them immediately once again so that the dampers rise quickly, allowing the strings to vibrate further but presently with considerably less energy, *piano*. All this takes only a small fraction of a second. These chords then continue in a dramatic *piano* context, the harmonies unresolved, tension building, until the next *fp*. The slower the tempo (up to a point), the greater the tension, the longer the eventual resolution (the opening of the Allegro molto e con brio) is delayed, the more the musical line of continuity is stretched almost to the breaking point. The surface motion is slow but corresponds almost exactly to the harmonic rhythm.

By contrast, at the beginning of the exposition of the movement, the rate at which the harmony changes is considerably slower relative to the surface motion. Here, the surface motion can be fast, *piano*, and light, so that the tremolandos in the bass can be transparent (not overpedaled) in order to be realized as haunting and propulsive.

Another movement character indication that in itself is not explicit about speed in the usual manner is the In tempo d'un menuetto of Sonata Op. 54, first movement. Beethoven used this indication only here and in Sonata Op. 49 no. 2, second movement (Tempo di menuetto) and Sonata Op. 22 (simply Menuetto). Beethoven could well have assumed that his audience was musically literate enough that the tempo for a minuet was perfectly obvious.

But what is this tempo? The last sonata to include a minuet movement specifically designated as such is Sonata Op. 31 no. 3, and it is marked Menuetto: Moderato e grazioso. Minuet movements in earlier sonatas are divided between Allegretto designations (Op. 2 no. 1, Op. 10 no. 2, and Op. 14, the middle movements of which are minuets in everything but name) and Allegro (Op. 7 and Op. 10 no. 3, in which the Allegro movements contrast in mood and expression with the Largo movements that precede them). The minuet of Op. 22 has no such indication, but its gentle ♩. ♪ upbeat figure suggests allegretto.

With Op. 31 no. 3 firmly in the moderato mode, moderato rather than allegro also seems reasonable for the Tempo d'un Menuetto of Op. 54. The dotted upbeat figure further suggests this interpretation. The tempo of Op. 54, first movement, is determined by the counterpoint and sforzandos of the second (octave) theme as well.

The second movement of Op. 54 is only Allegretto. If it is played too fast, the startling and unstable harmonies and surprisingly quick harmonic rhythm will lose dramatic impact. Beethoven saves the più allegro for the coda, which is harmonically much more stable and can withstand a faster surface motion.

Sonata Op. 81a is the first sonata to include German headings in the movement indications. These headings are not directives of musical character *per se*; rather they indicate the musical program of each movement: "Das Lebewohl" (farewell, leave-taking); "Abwesenheit" (absence); "Wiedersehen" (return), referring to Archduke Rudolf.

The German included in the second and third movements, however, is intended to increase our understanding of the character suggested by the traditional Italian. Andante espressivo is clarified by In gehender Bewegung, doch mit Ausdruck (in forward motion but with expression), helping to ensure that this movement is imbued with a restless quality rather than a merely melancholy character. Vivacissimamente is clarified by Im lebhaftesten Zeitmaasse— in a tempo (spirit) most lively (not necessarily fastest).

Following the five-year hiatus from writing piano sonatas, Beethoven returned to the genre in 1814. Concerns with the inaccuracy of the traditional terms must have influenced his decision to abandon them altogether with his Sonata Op. 90, the very next one: Mit Lebhaftigkeit und durchaus mit Empfindung und Ausdruck (with liveliness and throughout with feeling and expression). In other words, the pace is quick but not fast. The pulse is strictly three quarter-notes per measure (not "in one," meaning one long beat per measure) and the rhetorical, declamatory opening, with its quick changes and contrasts of dynamics (*f* to *p*) and registers, guards against too rapid a tempo.

The heading for the second movement also guards against playing too fast: Nicht zu geschwind und sehr singbar vorzutragen (not too fast and to be performed in a very singing manner). The pulse of two quarter-notes per bar (as opposed to one half-note or four eighth-notes) along with the gentle harmonic rhythm suggest a tempo that allows the melodic line to be spun out in an unforced, unhurried, warm and loving manner.

For Sonata Op. 101 Beethoven also felt it was necessary to use German movement headings to help indicate the character of the music, but he added traditional Italian terms as well. The first movement, Etwas lebhaft und mit der innigsten Empfindung (somewhat lively and with innermost feeling), is in 6/8, not 2/4; a pulse of six eighth-notes, rather than two dotted quarters, per measure ensures a pacing for this movement that is expansive enough to allow for the elements of improvisatory fantasy with which Beethoven was concerned. (These elements are also manifest in its spiritual brethren Op. 102 no. 1 and the Sonatas *quasi una fantasia* Op. 27 nos. 1 and 2.) The Italian heading for this first movement is Allegretto ma non troppo; the *ma non troppo* keeps the gentle Allegretto feeling from becoming too lively.

The German and Italian terms—Lebhaft. Marschmässig (Vivace alla marcia)—used for the second movement are identical in meaning rather that clarifying each other. The march feeling dominates; the tempo should allow for a feeling of four beats per bar. For the third movement, the German (Langsam und sehnsuchtsvoll) is more concise than the Italian (Adagio, ma non troppo, con affetto). The slow and searching character of this movement contrasts completely with the marchlike character of the preceding movement. Even for the quasi-cadenza on the dominant chord at the end of this movement (m. 20) Beethoven has cautioned *non presto*.

When the affirming theme of the last movement is gathering momentum—crescendo within the trill on the dominant point (E); dominant seventh chords in the thematic rhythm of mm. 4–5 in the bass—the movement indication is Geschwind, doch nicht zu sehr, und mit Entschlossenheit (fast, but not too much, and with decisiveness). The Italian here is simply Allegro. A pulse of two beats per measure (2/4) rather than one would keep the tempo from becoming too fast and would keep the music rhythmically taut. Beethoven's use of both German and Italian in Op. 101 is complementary. He was not suggesting that one language or manner of description is primary over the other. Rather, he was searching for a new way of indicating to interpreters the tempo and character of each movement.

But he was not satisfied; there was still too much ambiguity. In November 1817, a year after completing Op. 101 and while in the midst of sketching Sonata Op. 106 (and the Ninth Symphony), he wrote to Ignaz Franz, Elder von Mosel, a Viennese composer, conductor, and writer about music:

> I am heartily delighted to know that you hold the same views as I do about our tempo indications which originated in the barbarous ages of music. For, to take one example, what can be more absurd than Allegro, which really signifies *merry*, and how very far removed we often are from the idea of that tempo. So much so that the piece itself means the *very opposite of the indication*—As for those four chief movements, which, however, are far from embodying the truth or the accuracy of the four chief winds, we would gladly *do without them*. But the words describing the character of the composition are a different matter. We cannot give these up. Indeed the tempo is more like the body, *but these certainly refer to the spirit of the composition*—As for me, I have long been thinking of abandoning those absurd descriptive terms, Allegro, Andante, Adagio, Presto; and Mälzel's metronome affords us the best opportunity of doing so. I now give you *my word* that I shall *never again* use them in any of my new compositions—But there is another question, and that is, whether by so doing we are aiming at bringing the metronome into *general use*, a thing which is so necessary? I hardly think so. Moreover I have no doubt whatever that we

shall be howled down as *tyrants*. If only the cause itself were thus served, it would still be better than to be accused of feudalism—Hence I fancy that the best solution would be, particularly for our countries where music has now become a national need and where every village schoolmaster will be expected to use the metronome, that Mälzel should try to sell a certain number of metronomes by subscription, and at a very high price. Then as soon as he has been covered financially by this number he will be able to dispose of the other necessary metronomes for the musical need of the nation so cheaply that we can certainly expect to see the greatest *universal use and distribution* of this commodity—It is clearly understood, of course, that some people must place themselves at the head of this movement in order to work up enthusiasm. You can certainly rely on me to do what lies in my power; and I look forward with pleasure to hearing what task you are going to allot to me—

> With kindest regards I remain, Sir, your most devoted
> Ludwig van Beethoven (Anderson 1961, 727)

Metronome markings measure and refer only to the speed of the surface motion. Character indications refer both to the rate of internal musical change with its inherent dynamic tension and to the surface speed. Beethoven believed that traditional terms, such as Allegro, no longer had a direct bearing on tempo, on the "body" of a work. He felt strongly that using the metronome could help clarify composers' intentions regarding tempo.

At the time of this letter (1817), Beethoven retroactively assigned metronome indications for each of his previous eight symphonies, as well as for the string quartets he had written up to this point (Op. 18, Op. 59, Op. 74, and Op. 95) and for his Septet Op. 20. Yet despite his spirited enthusiasm for the dissemination of metronomes and the accompanying forward-looking economic policy suggestion, Beethoven actually assigned metronome markings during the compositional processes only to Sonata Op. 106 ("Hammerklavier") and the Ninth Symphony, the major works he was sketching at this time. He did not go back and give metronome indications to any of his previous piano sonatas, nor did he give metronome indications to the three sonatas he composed following the "Hammerklavier"—Sonatas Op. 109, Op. 110, and Op. 111.

But his conviction about the necessity of metronome markings did not wane. In December 1826—some nine years after his letter to Ignaz Franz—Beethoven wrote to his publisher B. Schott's Sons, asking that they wait for his metronome markings for the Missa solemnis, which he had been sketching at the same time as the "Hammerklavier" and the Ninth Symphony, before publishing the work:

> The metronome markings will be sent to you very soon. Do wait for them. In our century such indications are certainly necessary. Moreover I have received letters form Berlin informing me that the first performance of the

[Ninth] Symphony was received with enthusiastic applause, which I ascribe largely to the metronome markings. We can scarcely have *tempi ordinari* any longer, since one must fall into line with the ideas of unfettered genius (Anderson 1961, 1325).

Beethoven was implying that his new works demanded a broader spectrum of tempo. Schott did wait, but the promised metronome marks never arrived. (The work was published—without metronome markings—in April 1827, one month after Beethoven died.)

At the end of March 1819, Beethoven sent a letter to his friend Ferdinand Ries, who was acting as his agent in London, detailing corrections to the proofs of Op. 106. (A composer and pianist, Ries studied with Beethoven from 1801 to 1805 and eventually became Beethoven's London publisher.) What has survived of this letter is incomplete; the first of the two surviving fragments begins with a correction to m. 31 in the Scherzo. In all, 113 corrections are entered to 102 areas in the proofs where Beethoven points out that the copyist misrepresented notes, ties, pedal indications, dots, and accidentals and also missed rests and articulation of trills. The portion of the letter referring to the massive first movement is lost. Many printed editions of this work mistakenly link the Largo and Allegro risoluto that follows into one last movement. Among the clearest points in this letter, however, is the separation Beethoven himself made between the Largo (as fourth movement) and the Allegro risoluto (as fifth movement). The letter has a separate heading for the corrections to each movement. In addition, Beethoven referred to corrections in the Allegro risoluto which reflect that he numbered the measures of the Allegro risoluto starting with m. 1, rather than continuing with m. 11 as if this were a continuation of the Largo.

Three weeks later (16 April 1819) Beethoven sent another letter to Ries with the tempos for Op. 106. In addition to specifying the metronome markings for the published edition of Op. 106, Beethoven also made further changes. One is the now famous insertion of the new first bar of the Adagio. Another subtle but important change is the deletion of *assai* from the heading of the first movement: "First movement Allegro, but only Allegro; you must remove the Assai: Mälzel's metronome $\rfloor = 138$."

So Beethoven initially conceived of this movement as even faster; when he assigned the metronome markings, he moderated his tempo to "only Allegro"! The metronome markings are not forgeries; Beethoven's metronome was accurate (an issue we shall revisit at the end of Program 7); the tempos span from allegro to largo (they are not confined to fast tempos only); and there is no musical justification for ignoring them.

Undue speed, however, has long been associated with the work, to sometimes amusing ends. In the astronomer Fred Hoyle's *The Black Cloud*, a sci-fi thriller of 1957, a pianist (Ann Halsey) performs the "Hammerklavier" at a soiree. She later comments: "The first movement of the B-flat major Sonata bears a metronome marking requiring a fantastic pace, far faster than any normal pianist can achieve." The Cloud, extraterrestrial matter whose intelligence supposedly exceeds that of humans, visits our solar system and requests information about the arts. Fortunately, Halsey's performance was informally recorded. The tape is transmitted to the Cloud, whereupon the response is "Very interesting. Please repeat the first part at a speed increased by thirty per cent." When this had been done, the next message was: "Better. Very good. I intend to think this over" (Hoyle, 152).

Beethoven abandoned German movement headings for Op. 106. The Italian character indications—together with the metronome markings—achieved the specificity for which he had longed.

I believe in the tempos Beethoven indicated for the "Hammerklavier" Sonata. But I don't stand in the wings backstage before a performance, metronome in hand, checking tempos before setting foot on the concert platform. Rather, I use the metronome in rehearsal as help toward internalizing the feelings of the tempos. I also confess that I worked on the "Hammerklavier" Sonata in private for eight years before performing it publicly; this is a longer period of internalization for me than for any other work with which I have been involved.

Is it musically valid to extrapolate the pacing of other works from the combination of Italian movement headings and metronome markings in Op. 106, to use the markings in Op. 106 as a guide? In other works did Beethoven consider the general pacing of an allegro movement to have a primary pulse of about 138? In Op. 106 the harmonic rhythm—in many instances—is two measures (four half-notes) per change. Although the surface velocity is fast, the designated speed of $\d = 138$ translates to a given harmony lasting approximately 1.75 seconds, not an unduly short time musically.

Even before becoming convinced of the metronomic of 138 for the Allegro of Op. 106, I found that I had gravitated toward 138 for the unit of pulse in several other Beethoven Allegro movements, such as Sonata Op. 27 no. 1, fourth movement (Allegro vivace); the C minor Piano Concerto Op. 37, first movement (Allegro con brio); Sonata Op. 111 (Allegro con brio ed appassionato). Some Allegro movements demand a faster pace—Sonata Op. 53 ("Waldstein"), first movement: Allegro con brio—and others demand a slower pace—Sonata Op. 78, first movement: Allegro ma non troppo. But as a general guide, I believe 138 to be a good starting point for Beethoven's allegro indications.

The second movement of Op. 106 is marked $\d\cdot = 80$. The unit of pulse (and in this case, of harmonic rhythm) is the dotted half-note which is slightly less than 1.5 seconds. What about other vivace movements? The first movement of Sonata Op. 109 works quite well with the unit of pulse (and harmony)—the quarter-note—at almost the same metronomic, $\d = 88$. The pulse per measure of Sonata Op. 79, third movement (also vivace), could be slightly slower (perhaps $\d = 76$), but the harmonic rhythm at the opening is twice as fast, since every beat brings a change of harmony. I play the second movement of Sonata Op. 101 Lebhaft. Marschmässig (Vivace alla marcia) at ♩ = 152–160, the equivalent of ♩ = 76–80. Since the harmonic rhythm of a good portion of this movement is by the half-note, there is a uniformity of tempo within the vivace character as well, since tempo is concerned with musical elements other than simply the notes on the surface.

The Adagio of Op. 106 is ♪ = 92. This pulse is not as slow as might initially be expected of an Adagio, but the harmonic rhythm is slow. The initial F-sharp minor harmony lasts eleven eighth-note beats. At ♪ = 92, this corresponds to about seven seconds, quite a long time in musical terms. Later in the work, there is frequently one harmony per measure, which translates to almost four seconds' duration.

An adagio designation is not always an invitation simply to play everything slowly; the harmonic and metrical pulse must be considered. The time signature of the Adagio sostenuto of Sonata Op. 27 no. 2 ("Moonlight") is marked ¢; the half-note rather than the quarter-note is the unit of metrical pulse. Beethoven thus intended the half-note as adagio; had he wanted the quarter-note to be adagio, he could have written the meter as 4/4, not alla breve. One must therefore guard against playing this movement too slowly; not only would it begin to sound like a dirge (which it is not), but the long, sustained singing top lines would be stretched beyond the breaking point. If a delicate, flowing undercurrent is established by the *pp* triplets and the dampers are raised judiciously throughout—just enough so that the music sounds as if from afar—then the adagio pulse of a half-note contributes to the lyrical and moving qualities of the music.

Within the thirty-two piano sonatas Beethoven wrote only four Largo movements (not including the Largo sections in Sonata Op. 31 no. 2, first movement), three of which are in works completed by 1798: Op. 2 no. 2, Op. 7, Op. 10 no. 3. The other is the fourth movement of Op. 106. It is marked ♪ = 76.

The three earlier Largo movements are the slow, intensely expressive centers of their respective sonatas. However, unlike Beethoven's use of the term *adagio*, in each case, the term *largo* is followed by an additional descriptive term of a particularly expressive nature: Largo appassionato (Op. 2 no. 2), Largo con gran espressione (Op. 7), Largo e mesto (Op. 10 no. 3).

The Largo of Op. 106 is the only such designation that does not include an additional term. The expressive function of this movement, however, is fundamentally different from that of previous largo movements. As discussed earlier, this Largo is improvisatory, suggesting (and rejecting) themes that lead to the contrapuntal texture of the fugue that follows. Additionally, this Largo follows a long adagio movement which is, instead, the more intensely expressive.

While nothing is slower in Beethoven than a largo movement, the main difference between adagio and largo is the manner in which the music is slow. Adagio movements are built with long, singing lines; largo movements tend to be more monolithic in harmonic motion. (Among the most powerful characteristics of the Largo e mesto of Op. 10 no. 3 is that it combines both these musical features.) The pacing of harmonic change in an adagio movement may be the same as—or even slower than—that of a largo movement. For example, I play the Adagio of Op. 2 no. 1 at $\flat$ = 72–76 and the Largo of Op. 7 at $\flat$ = 76–80. However, most largo movements have less surface motion, and thus they give the impression of being more stately and slower.

The pacing of the unit of pulse in the last movement of Op. 106 (Allegro risoluto) is actually faster than the pacing of the unit of pulse in the opening Allegro: $\downarrow$ = 144 as opposed to $\downarrow$ = 138. However, the unit of harmony (the measure, in each case) proceeds more slowly in the Allegro risoluto than in the Allegro; three beats of $\downarrow$ = 144 take about 1.2 seconds, while two half-notes at $\downarrow$ = 138 take about 0.875 seconds.

Both certainly are very fast, and at face value, the metronomic of $\downarrow$ = 144 is at the upper end of the allegro scale. However, both are consistent with Beethoven's concept of allegro movements and with the implications of the terms (allegro as compared to allegro risoluto), for regardless of the higher number in the metronome indication of the final movement of Op. 106, the rate of harmonic change is not as fast here as in the opening Allegro.

The metronome markings for the Ninth Symphony (the only other work to which Beethoven assigned such markings at the time of composition) appear to be reasonably consistent with those for the "Hammerklavier," as the accompanying table suggests. The slowest movement of the symphony—the Adagio—feels expansive at $\downarrow$ = 60. At this tempo, the pace of harmonic change (the $\downarrow$) is extremely close to the pace of harmonic change (the $\downarrow\cdot$) of the Adagio of the "Hammerklavier." One half-note at $\downarrow$ = 60 is within 0.05 seconds of three eighth-notes at $\flat$ = 92.

The fast movements of the symphony are undoubtedly very fast on the surface, but even in the Scherzo (Molto vivace, $\downarrow\cdot$ = 116) the rate of harmonic change is the four-bar phrase, which, at this tempo, takes about two seconds. This is actually slower than the rate of change in the Scherzo of the "Hammerklavier" which is about 1.5 seconds.

The fact that sound production on the piano can be faster than that of some orchestral instruments (the strings of a piano can be set into vibration faster than can the initial column of air in a wind instrument) is not really relevant to the question of tempos throughout a movement. A good orchestra can play these tempos. Although some are fast, the challenge is in living with the score and internalizing the music, and when necessary, thinking at the suggested pace.

With Sonata Op. 109 Beethoven discarded the metronome markings. Did he feel they too were now superfluous because those which he ascribed to Op. 106 represented his thoughts on tempo? He reverted to Italian headings for the

Metronome Markings for Symphony No. 9, Op. 125

Movement	Metronome marking
1. Allegro ma non troppo	♩ = 88
2. Molto vivace	♩. = 116
Presto	♩ = 116
3. Adagio (Tempo I)	♩ = 60
Andante moderato	♩ = 63
4. Finale presto	♩. = 96
Allegro ma non troppo	♩ = 88
Allegro assai	♩ = 80
Alla marcia	♩. = 84
Andante maestoso	♩ = 72
Adagio ma non troppo, ma divoto	♩ = 60
Allegro energico, sempre ben marcato	♩ = 84
Allegro ma non tanto	♩ = 120
Prestissimo	♩ = 132
Maestoso	♩ = 60

first two movements of Op. 109 but chose to use German as well to describe the character of the last, the one that is both the expressive center of the work and the most revolutionary. In addition to the Italian heading, Andante molto cantabile ed espressivo, Beethoven wrote Gesangvoll, mit innigsten Empfindung (full of song, with innermost feeling). When, for Variation III, the meter changes from a triple meter to a duple meter (3/4 to 2/4), the pacing is Allegro vivace; a reasonable tempo would be ♩ = 144, which is consistent with our discussion of allegro pacing. Following Variation IV, which reverts to a triple meter (9/8) and is somewhat slower than the theme, the fugato variation that follows is back to a duple meter (c) and is Allegro ma non troppo. The tempo would be slightly slower than a pure allegro, perhaps approximately ♩ = 96.

Of the character indications that imply moderate tempos, Beethoven used allegretto in the piano sonatas more than andante or any others. (He used the term *moderato* only once—in Op. 110, first movement: Moderato cantabile molto espressivo (moderate [in pacing], singing, and very expressive). Beethoven designated a range of styles of movements as allegretto, from the minuet or scherzo movements of early sonatas to the rondo last movements of Opp. 7, 22, 31 no. 2, 53, and 54, to the first movement of Op. 101 (where the term *allegretto* complements the German Etwas lebhaft und mit der innigsten Empfindung). The character of Allegretto movements is lively in a way often more gentle and playful (less boisterous and less extroverted) than allegro; the pacing is not as rapid.

Beethoven used andante (walking pace) for the themes of both the Op. 26 variations and those of Op. 109, as well as for the theme and variations of the middle movement of Op. 57 ("Appassionata"). Andante is also the pace of the ambling first section of Op. 27 no. 1, first movement. In a middle movement, the andante pace depends on context; it can be slower than an allegretto (Op. 14 no. 2, second movement; Op. 79, second movement) or not as slow as an adagio (second movements of Op. 28 and Op. 81a). Perhaps Beethoven never actually used andantino in the piano sonatas because he was too aware of the further confusion it would cause.

Beethoven also at times suggested a lessening of the pace by means other than the conventional terms *ritard* or *ritenuto*. In Sonata Op. 109, second movement, he specified *un poco espressivo* in m. 28, the point at which the second theme is harmonized (and starts leading to the dominant of the dominant). Four measures later, he wrote *a tempo*. The direct implication is that the *espressivo* measures are slightly under tempo.

One can interpret the term *espressivo* at the unfolding of the second theme in Op. 2 no. 2, first movement (mm. 58–59) to mean the same idea—expressive and slightly slower paced. In this case, there is no *a tempo* marking later. However, the slightly slower tempo could continue through m. 91—Beethoven's own fingering at the octave arpeggios is an integral part of this pacing—and tempo primo could be regained at m. 92 onward. This pacing would allow for a smooth transition back to the exposition and ahead to the development.

Beethoven also manipulates time internally in another instance in the sonata literature, in the last movement of Op. 110, where he thereby creates feelings of musical reaffirmation and exuberance. Following the intensely moving second arioso, the theme of the fugue is transformed both musically and metrically: the theme is inverted and set simultaneously in double augmentation (twice as slow) in counterpoint against triple diminution (three times as fast).

The autograph manuscript score of Op. 110 states—in pencil—"tempo I-mo" (tempo primo) in m. 174, the point at which the theme recurs in its original metrical and melodic shape, now in *forte* bass octaves. (This *tempo primo* is missing in some printed editions; see Chapter 6.) To me, Beethoven's penciled notation implies that the directives *poi a poi più moto* and *nach und nach wieder geschwinder* (gradually faster) of mm. 172–173 lead back to the *tempo primo* indicated in m. 174 but not beyond. Once the original tempo is reached and the beginning of the musical affirmation attained, the tempo and pulse remain constant until the end of the piece.

In the Arietta movement of Op. 111 Beethoven does the converse: he guards against an internal change of tempo by specifying *L'istesso tempo* (same tempo) at the metrical changes as the second and third variations unfold. Initially, this seems simple enough, but as usual—and not surprisingly—there are musical decisions to be made. The initial meter of the movement is 9/16, with the character indication Adagio molto semplice e cantabile. The pulse could either be nine sixteenth-notes to the bar or three dotted eighth-notes. Since the directive is adagio (and not molto adagio) and considering the calligraphy of the autograph manuscript, the intention seems to be a pulse of three. So when Beethoven changes the meter to 6/16 in m. 32*b* and writes *L'istesso tempo*, the pulse of three remains constant and not the pulse of the sixteenth-note. This change of meter means that the new sixteenth-notes are actually fifty percent longer than those of the 9/16 meter. However, the music sounds faster because the actual smallest rhythmic unit is now ♩ as opposed to ♩ and the pulse is six sixteenth-notes per measure rather than three eighth-notes.

The 12/32 meter of the following variation again halves the basic rhythmic cell, and the pulse is a rapid twelve thirty-second notes per measure, divided into three groups of four. The transition back to 9/16 (m. 64) is seamless. The three groups of four ♪s of the previous music are now three groups of ♪ triplets or ♪·, as in the opening of the movement. The *L'istesso tempo* directives ensure that the basic three-pulse has remained unchanged.

In his article "Tempo and Character in Beethoven's Music," Rudolf Kolisch asserted that difficulties in playing one's instrument were not the only reason for disregarding Beethoven's tempos. Rather, "Beethoven's musical language, because of its newness, was not understood by his contemporaries, and . . . therefore the new tempi for his unprecedented expressive characters simply could not be conceived" (Kolisch 1993).

Perhaps a greater understanding can be reached by hearing works afresh at Beethoven's suggested tempos. In piano performance, decisions about the most minute details of tempo are influenced physically by two major factors: the acoustics of the concert hall and the responsiveness of the piano at hand. I prefer a somewhat resonant hall, for dry acoustics are sonically unrewarding, and overly live acoustics create too much of a sonic blur. I also prefer a very precise level of regulation of a piano's action—quick, responsive repetition springs and careful settings of the backchecks (parts of the piano action that stop the hammers after they strike the strings), slightly on the high side so that the hammers do not slip down too low after striking the strings.

Interpretive parameters that influence decisions about tempos are informed by an understanding of both the composer's particular use of descriptive terms and the meanings of the musical contexts to which they are ascribed. By considering the ways in which Beethoven designated tempo and character indications throughout the sonata cycle, we can understand more fully the meaning of any one specific designation.

CHAPTER 4

Improvisation

No man in these days has heard extemporare playing unless he has heard
Beethoven.

—Johann Baptist Cramer to Samuel Appleby, ca. 1799–1800

*J*ust as Bach repeatedly demonstrated his extraordinary skills in weaving complex counterpoint spontaneously on a given musical theme, so did Beethoven's vivid musical imagination and command of the language and keyboard
allow him to conjure up intense and complete musical offerings when he was
called upon to improvise.

Joseph Gelinek, one of Vienna's finest piano virtuosos of the 1790s, reported
when he first heard the young Beethoven upon his arrival: "Ah, he is no man;
he's a devil. He will play me and all of us to death. And how he improvises!"
The noted pianist Johann Baptist Cramer (b. Mannheim 1771, raised in England), was well-regarded by Beethoven; his comments to his musical friend
Samuel Appleby of Brighton echoed the same sentiment (Thayer 1973, 139,
209). And in 1812, in the midst of his longest hiatus from composing piano
sonatas, Beethoven sat down at the keyboard, observed by the young Franz
Glöggl, later a music publisher in Vienna, then a youth in Linz:

> Among the cavaliers who were in Linz was Count von Dönhoff, a great
> admirer of Beethoven, who gave several soirees in his honor during the
> composer's sojourn. I was present at one of these. Pieces were played and
> some of Beethoven's songs were sung, and he was requested to improvise
> on the pianoforte, which he did not wish to do. A table had been spread
> with food in an adjoining room and finally the company gathered about it.
> I was a young lad and Beethoven interested me so greatly that I remained
> always near him. Search was made for him in vain and finally the company
> sat down without him. He was in the next room and now began to impro-
> vise; all grew quiet and listened to him. I remained standing beside him at
> the pianoforte. He played for about an hour and one by one all gathered
> around him. Then it occurred to him that he had been called to the table

long before—he hurried from his chair to the dining-room. At the door stood a table holding porcelain dishes. He stumbled against it and the dishes fell to the floor. Count Dönhoff, a wealthy cavalier, laughed at the mishap and the company again sat down to the table with Beethoven. There was no more thought of playing music, for after Beethoven's fantasia half of the pianoforte strings were broken. I recall this fantasia with pleasure because I was so fortunate as to have heard it so near him (Thayer 1973, 541).

Not surprisingly, Beethoven incorporated qualities of improvisation into his piano sonatas, even those that required extensive work in the sketchbooks. One such element is the fermata—the long, dramatic pause on a rest or particular note or harmony which leaves a listener suspended while the performer seems to be gathering musical thoughts before continuing. The first phrase of the first Sonata (Op. 2 no. 1) ends with a fermata over a quarter-rest. Silence is thus prolonged and drama heightened as the performer waits before taking up the opening theme again, but hereafter in the bass. In the parallel place in the recapitulation (m. 108), the pause indicated by the fermata is dramatic in a different way, for at this point, the *ff* dynamic carries on, straight through the rest, until the main theme reenters *piano*, and in the tonic harmony. These fermatas help create the drama of this movement.

So are the fermatas which pervade the first two movements of Sonata Op. 31 no. 3. In this work, they prolong specified chords rather than silences. In the first movement, the fermatas play a teasing role by prolonging E-flat six-four chords as Beethoven deliberately (but playfully) delays truly defining the tonic harmony until the recapitulation of the second theme. This structuring of the movement lends a stylized improvisatory quality, further heightened locally by the fermatas.

In the Scherzo that follows, the fermatas are over sforzando E-flat notes, which are now dominant pitches in A-flat major. Here the pauses heighten the tension and yearning for the return of the tonic, which always occurs in these instances in the following measure.

The opening of the tightly organized "Waldstein" Sonata also uses fermatas for dramatic effect. The opening phrase comes to a halt in m. 13, having reached a G embedded in a local C minor harmony, over which there is a fermata. The parallel place in the recapitulation also has a fermata, before continuing in a contrasting harmonic context, and the seventh chords in the coda of the first movement are all held by fermatas. In all cases, the pauses engendered by the fermatas vastly increase harmonic and motivic tension.

Delaying definition of the tonic harmony of a work is an element of improvisation that helps shape Sonata Op. 31 no. 2 ("Tempest"). The opening twenty measures—with five successive tempos (largo, allegro, adagio, largo, allegro), three fermatas, extremes of dynamics, and abrupt harmonic changes—eventually settle down to a tonic of D minor, but all are part of a stylized improvisation that unfolds from the first note of the opening rolled chord.

The Introduzione movement of the "Waldstein" Sonata Op. 53 is also quasi-improvisatory insofar as it lacks firm harmonic grounding until the tonic (F major) is finally reached in m. 9. In this first phrase, the bass makes a chromatic descent analogous to that of the first phrase of the opening movement, albeit at a slower pace.

The most improvisatory movement of all is the brief (nine measures, two minutes and thirty-six seconds) Largo movement of the "Hammerklavier" Sonata Op. 106. These measures lead from the profound introspection of the Adagio to the brilliant enthusiasm of the fugal Allegro risoluto, and no functional tonality is ever established. As the harmonies spiral downward by thirds, three different contrapuntal themes are tried and rejected internally, amidst fermatas and vast changes of tempos and dynamics. (An analogous situation is created in the last movement of the Ninth Symphony, with internal trials of various themes.) In the Largo of Op. 106 the themes are tried and ultimately rejected, their contrapuntal nature paving the way for the fugal theme of the Allegro risoluto to eventually emerge as the "right" theme.

In the first movement of Sonata Op. 101, the tonic—A major—is carefully avoided until the end of the movement. Sophisticated notation implies a different type of touch for each note and therefore four different qualities of sound,

which, along with the judicious use of rests and the continual postponement of the tonic, engenders feelings of suspenseful fantasy.

Another type of musical delay is that of a theme emerging gradually. In Sonata Op. 57 ("Appassionata"), the end of the second movement leaves one suspended on the dramatic *ff* dominant seventh chord within a fermata. The context changes as the key signature shifts from D-flat major to F minor, and the same harmony is repeated in a lower register to start the Allegro. Sixteenth-notes fill in the outline of the chords, initially *piano*, starting in the register of the last chord of the second movement. Momentum builds as the registers descend and the crescendo leads to *forte*. Gradually the main theme of the movement is attained (Example 15).

Piano concertos of the classical era include long cadenzas toward the end of the first movement (and frequently also, the last movement) which prolong the unstable six-four chord to heighten tension before the true final cadence. The cadenzas provide occasions during which the soloist could improvise without the orchestra, weaving together themes of the work in different keys in a com-

Example 15: Sonata Op. 57, second movement, leading into the third movement.

positionally and instrumentally virtuosic manner. Classical concertos also frequently included shorter cadenzas, usually in the last movement, during which the soloist might briefly extend a local dominant harmony—either a series of arpeggios, chromatic scales, or trills, or a succinct combination of these. The last movements of Beethoven piano concertos contain several such passages (Example 16).

Since sonatas are solo works, we would not expect them to include cadenzas. But even in the first group of published sonatas, Beethoven transcended expectations and included a brilliant cadenza toward the end of the first movement of Sonata Op. 2 no. 3 (Example 17). This flourish, improvisatory in nature, is built entirely from musical material of the opening motive. It has the effect of expanding the motive's already considerable scope—both formal and virtuosic—and of helping to conclude, in a whirlwind fashion, a sonata movement of unprecedented dimension. (Mozart also included a cadenza in the first movement of his Piano Sonata in B-flat major, K. 333, but this was hardly the norm.)

The dramatic role of improvisation in Sonata Op. 101 is entirely different. One aspect of the spiritual kinship that Sonata Op. 101 shares with the Op. 27 sonatas is that the slow movements of Op. 101 and of Op. 27 no. 1 are not truly independent movements, but rather continue without a break of silence into the concluding movement of each work. In Op. 27 no. 1, the Adagio leads, via a

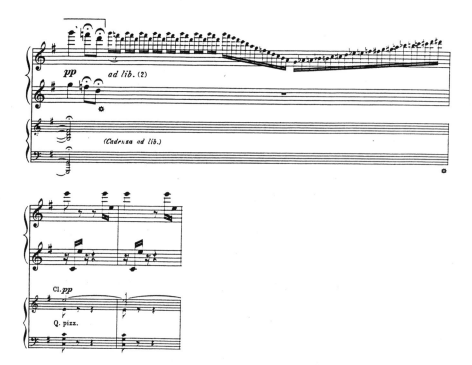

Example 16: Piano Concerto No. 4, Op. 58, third movement, mm. 415–417.

spun-out prolongation of the dominant, into the final movement. And indeed, when the slow music returns before the Presto coda, an analogous improvisatory passage leads from the slow music to the fast. In Op. 101 Beethoven specified *non presto* for the area of stylized improvisation. Although it is anchored in the dominant harmony, it leads from the probing music of the Adagio to a recurrence of the opening theme of the first movement, initially within an *una corda* context (Example 18).

This is not the stuff of flamboyant virtuosity, but rather searching music of great intimacy, demanding of the performer subtle control of touch, dynamics, and tempo. The feeling of improvisation continues as the music of the opening of the sonata returns, fragmented, and leads through a series of harmonic changes and trills of gathering intensity to the luminescent theme of the last movement.

Even within the frequently improvisatory Sonata Op. 31 no. 2 ("Tempest"), the recitatives within the recapitulation are a surprise. Sustained within a single light pedal marking (see Example 11), each of these recitative sections creates the illusion of further improvising upon the improvisatory nature of the rolled chords (A major and C major, respectively). Again, every careful marking

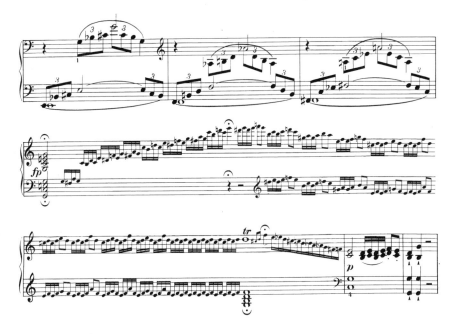

Example 17: Sonata Op. 2 no. 3, first movement, mm. 229–234.

(Largo, *pp*, pedal) contributes to the feeling of improvisation—of one long sustained aura and mood; change the pedal and the magic is gone.

Beethoven was also daring and dramatic with an "improvisation" in the middle of Sonata Op. 110. In the third movement (Adagio ma non troppo), the recitative starts by arpeggiating and prolonging the E-flat minor chord on which we are left suspended in m. 3. At this point (m. 4) a listener might wonder if a dominant harmony is being established, a cadenza being performed. The ensuing music is highly improvisatory and even creates the illusion of establishing the dominant, for the first harmony of the arioso theme is in A-flat minor. But the key signature at this point indicates E-flat minor, so the entire Arioso dolente is as a dominant to the A-flat major fugue that follows.

In m. 4 Beethoven actually writes *Recitativo* and specifies seven tempo changes within this intense but relatively short improvisation (Example 19). There are also two long pedal markings to sustain specific sonorities, an enharmonic change from C-flat major to B major under the *Bebung* A (m. 5) as the dominant within E major, and finally the reestablishment of the minor mode as the music changes from a recitative to a profoundly moving song.

Every aspect of these measures indicates what we can consider as a composed improvisation; even strict meter is abandoned. Beethoven's writing in the autograph score is sprawling, especially the terms (sempre tenuto, andante, *una*

Example 18: Sonata Op. 101, third movement, m. 19, through fourth movement, m. 7.

corda) that he later added in pencil. It is as if he heard the music in his mind's ear while making a second pass through the autograph with pencil, and his spacious handwriting reflects the feelings of freedom from a generally more regular metrical backbone which embody this recitative.

Yet another kind of feeling is engendered by sudden, unexpected harmonies. A dramatic impression that anything can happen, that no ground is safe, is made manifest by the cataclysmic climax of the first movement of Sonata Op. 106 "Hammerklavier." In m. 267 the theme that we have heard so many times in the key of B-flat major is suddenly hammered out in B minor. This chromatic clash leaves one hanging, as if wondering what could possibly happen next. It is ironic —but perhaps not surprising—that in this, one of the most carefully planned sonata movements, such feelings of improvisation come to the fore at the most dramatic moment, when we least expect them.

Example 19: Sonata Op. 110, third movement, mm. 4–10.

In the sketchbooks, in the autograph scores, and even in letters to his publishers, Beethoven may have considered every nuance of his piano sonatas. So do dedicated performers. Our responsibility includes internalizing the life and spirit of the music so completely that in performances the music seems to be created spontaneously, even to the point that the performer convinces himself—and therefore feels as though—he is improvising during these special moments. Daring to allow feelings of spontaneity of stylized improvisation to enter the spiritual world of these works infuses them with freshness and new life.

CHAPTER 5

Trills, Pirouettes, and Good Humor

Who makes the rules!

—Beethoven to Ferdinand Ries when the latter questioned the parallel fifths in the String Quartet in C minor, Op. 18 no. 4 (Newman 1988, 192)

Trills

*T*here is no prescribed single way to play trills. Some are blindingly fast, some less so; some are loud, others are soft; some direct musical energy forward within a crescendo, while others serve to dissipate energy, vanishing into ethereal shimmers. The musical context of a trill determines its expressive function. In the Beethoven piano sonatas, not surprisingly, trills occur in manifold variety, ranging from the charmingly ornamental to those that are fully woven into the music.

Beethoven wrote extended trills in the last movements of Sonatas Op. 53 ("Waldstein"), Op. 109, and Op. 111. In each case the trills are on dominant pitches and thus preserve and even heighten the underlying harmonic tension that dominant cadential harmonies engender. The trills of Op. 53 and Op. 109 are the embodiment of speed; that of Op. 111 is concerned more with a reflective quality of sound rather than with sheer speed.

The long trill of Op. 53 is in the Prestissimo coda and follows the extraordinary glissando octaves in mm. 465–474. The trill begins on the dominant G (m. 477) and, along with the figuration of the left hand beginning in m. 485, forms a new, reconsidered, faster "accompaniment" for the thematic melodic line. With the introduction of the A-flat in m. 493, the harmonies move away from the stability of C major through a short but expressive progression to C minor, A-flat major, F minor, and then via a chromatic expansion of the F minor chord (F becomes F-sharp) to G major, once again to the dominant of the home key of C major. With the return of G major in m. 511, a crescendo and a double trill lead to the reaffirmation of the C major in m. 515, now *ff.* The trill was the underpinning of the changes of harmony, then became the foreground and led back to home territory.

Beethoven wrote an alternate version of this trill, one which preserves the evenness of motion but is less intense than a pure trill. The alternation between pitches in the *ossia* is measured and at a slower rate than would be the case in a pure trill. Beethoven seems to have been most concerned here with the general undulating effect of the alternation of pitches and the clarity of the theme, for in the manuscript he wrote:

> Those for whom the trill, in combination with the theme, appears too difficult, may simplify it in the following way:

> or may double it in accordance with their ability:

> Two notes of each sextola [group of six] are played to one quarter-note in the bass. It is not of crucial importance if the trill loses some of its normal speed (Beethoven 1947, 2: 400n).

That Beethoven is not overly concerned with the overall speed of the trill suggests that the Prestissimo indication at the beginning of the coda is sufficient for the speed of the theme, and the trill speed is secondary. Here we have the only alternate version of a trill that Beethoven ever offered. Even in the cadenza that he composed for the first movement of his C minor piano concerto, although the texture and difficulty of the double trill in both hands is similar, there is no alternate version. In contrast, the speed of the coda in this movement in Sonata Op. 53 is so fast that the easier trill was indeed acceptable to Beethoven. Wherever the tempo is not as fast, however, alternate versions would not be acceptable. Similarly Beethoven did not compose an alternate version of the glissando octaves that precede these trills in Op. 53; the fingering Beethoven specifies is enough to ensure a rapid glissando in the Prestissimo. I prefer the trill as Beethoven initially intended it. Even at the Prestissimo tempo I try to trill as softly, lightly, and quickly as possible to produce a delicate underpinning for the main theme which floats above.

The final movements of Sonatas Op. 109 and Op. 111 are theme-and-variation movements. In each case, successive variations are of increasingly smaller note values and therefore greater surface speed. This progression is particularly overt within the last variation of Sonata Op. 109; the thematic line is restated in quarter-notes, then with eighth-note accompaniment which moves to triplet eighths, then triplet sixteenths and thirty-second notes before finally becoming trills in both hands in m. 12. These trills are at top speed; once it is reached, the diminution is complete. The trills start on the main note, taking the cue from the thirty-second notes that lead into them, and as they are part of the crescendo begun in m. 8, they help propel the music forward.

Once the dominant bass pedal-tone trill is reached in m. 16, the theme is made more abstract in the right hand. The trill here intensifies the harmonic and melodic tension. This tension is increased even more when the trill moves to the B in the treble (m. 25), with the thirty-second note thematic abstractions now in the left hand and syncopated thematic melodic notes above the trill in the right hand. The tension starts to lessen ever so slightly when the pedal begins to sustain the bass tonic E in m. 22 which has been yearned for throughout the trill measures. As the trill continues within this dominant-tonic pedaled misty context, the pace of the trill can slow so that the afterbeat A-sharp–B in m. 35 can lead smoothly into the restatement of the theme that follows.

In the second movement of Sonata Op. 111, diminution of note values (increased surface speed) and increased abstraction of the "theme" lead to the trill that begins in m. 106. ("Theme" is in quotation marks because Beethoven himself did not designate this movement as a theme-and-variation movement. Although its first part consists of four variations on the Arietta theme, the entire movement is ultimately a synthesis of variation and sonata form.) This trill, *forte*, is the apogee of speed (diminution), and the signature motive of the theme (C–G–G, in its original pulse) is played below it. The grace note C-sharp that precedes this trill is placed well before the main trill note, D, in the autograph score, implying that the grace note is played before the first beat of the measure rather than on it. The trill gradually softens, so that the change to minor in m. 108 occurs within a longer diminuendo. For the first time in this movement, the music moves away from the C major–A minor–G major of the theme as the trill leads into different harmonies.

The trill here plays a pivotal expressive and structural role. There is no trill passage in any other music like this one. As it expands to a triple trill (mm. 112–113) and then ascends chromatically (mm. 114–117), the musical tension increases dramatically. Structurally the trill acts in a manner to both dissolve the "variation" form of the first part of this movement and to lead into the "development" area (mm. 120–130) in which new harmonies are explored before the arietta theme recurs in m. 131 ("recapitulation").

The string of trills that recurs at the end of this movement is analogous in musical function to the trills toward the end of the variation movement of Op. 109. But rather than the *forte* dynamic of the bass and treble dominant trills in Op. 109, the trills at the end of Op. 111 are light and *pianissimo*. They are on the dominant G, with the exception of the very first trill—m. 160, on D—itself the dominant of G and therefore leading to it. For the high G trill with the theme underneath, I use any fingering possible to achieve a gossamer and even trill. The fingering can change somewhat depending on the action and voicing characteristics of the piano, but generally I use 4–5 and 3–5, even occasionally 3–4. The afterbeat grace notes C-sharp–D fit in at the end of the third sixteenth-note beat of m. 160, and once again, the autograph score indicates that the D-sharp grace note comes in before the fourth sixteenth-note beat.

The rate at which to trill is determined by hints and suggestions within the music itself. In Sonata Op. 27 no. 1, leading from the Adagio con espressivo third movement to the Allegro vivace fourth movement, Beethoven wrote out a measured alternation of G and A-flat as thirty-second notes, followed by a trill on A-flat. The trill is played faster than the alternation that precedes it. In addition to speed, two other issues bear consideration. Should we trill from the A-flat to the upper neighbor (B-flat) or to the lower neighbor (G), and does the trill begin on the main note or on the neighbor note?

I would suggest beginning the trill on the main note and including the upper neighbor (B-flat). The previous alternation begins with a G, repeating the final note of the flourish in m. 24 which leads to it. The crescendo throughout the measure of alternating G and A-flat leads to the *sfp* of the trill (m. 26), which accentuates the A-flat, the last note of the tremolando. The pirouette in m. 26 that leads away from the trill begins with G–A-flat–B-flat, uniting the three pitches that have played so prominent a role in this cadential area. In a parallel figure, the trill in m. 263 begins with the B-flat and includes the C, its upper neighbor.

In the third movement of Sonata Op. 81a ("Das Lebewohl"), Beethoven wrote another alternation of pitches as alto accompaniment to the counterpoint of the soprano and tenor lines (Example 20a). Unlike the *ossia* of Sonata Op. 53 ("Waldstein"), the tempo—although fast—is not prestissimo. Hence this alternation of pitches maintains a smooth speed, slightly slower than a very fast trill. Such a fast trill is reserved for the cadential m. 68 (Example 20b).

A gentle alternation of pitches occurs even more slowly in Sonata Op. 90. Beginning in m. 40 of the second movement, the tenor F-sharp–G-sharp colors the F-sharp tonality as it is established as the dominant of B major. The alternation of F-sharp and G-sharp is considerably slower than any trill, yet it creates an expressive area of gentle harmonic destabilization within the slow tempo. Far from being ornamental, the alternation creates the music.

In the second movement of the good-humored Sonata Op. 31 no. 1, Beethoven took the highly unusual step of beginning with a trill. Considering the playful character of both this sonata and this movement, and the *piano* dynamic, the trill could begin on the main note at a medium speed and then increase in rapidity, reaching the maximum speed by the third eighth-note of the left hand. The texture should remain light, with a slight shaping upward through the trill

Example 20a: Sonata Op. 81a, third movement, mm. 53–56.

Example 20b: Sonata Op. 81a, third movement, mm. 67–69.

suffix to the long E. This helps give a sense of forward direction to the trill while the left hand remains virtually static in its accompaniment, thus heightening the drama of virtuoso singer versus accompanist that this movement parodies. The trills that follow can be played in the same character (Example 21).

In the Presto coda of the last movement of this sonata, the long left-hand trill (mm. 241–247) makes possible the crescendo to *forte* and keeps the dominant pedal pulsating under the rapid right-hand trill cadence figures (E–D–C-sharp–D). I prefer the tempo fast enough so that the right-hand figures are at

Example 21: Sonata Op. 31 no. 1, second movement, mm. 1–6.

trill speed, not only harking back to the beginning of the third movement but also suggesting a recollection of the trills of the second movement.

The four trills in the opening first phrase of Sonata Op. 57 ("Appassionata") are more than mere ornaments. They help maintain—and can even increase—the extraordinary tension of this phrase. The dynamic context for the first two trills is *pp*, but the trills can still be very fast. I start the trill with the lower auxiliary note on the beat, creating a greater dissonance (and thus more tension) when played together with the left-hand chord. The third trill has a slight crescendo-decrescendo, which adds to the drama. The last trill of this phrase adds even more: the higher pitches increase tension, and the expected pretrill auxiliary note is not there. I make the crescendo-decrescendo slightly more intense than in I do with the previous trill. Although the trills are all of the same rhythmic pattern, maximizing the minute details that differentiate them makes each one contribute more to the overall shape of the phrase.

The two right-hand trills at the end of the Adagio movement of Sonata Op. 31 no. 2 ("Tempest") are both short trills, and yet both help establish the direction of the musical momentum. The first of these trills (m. 100) directs the line forward, since it arrives near the apex of the crescendo. The trill continues the crescendo through the main note (D) to the downbeat F of m. 111. The second trill helps dissipate the intensity of the musical line by smoothly continuing the diminuendo to the B-flat of m. 112. In both cases, playing a *Nachschlag* (or trill suffix) makes for a smoother transition to the note after the trill, a smoothness which is desirable here.

Although Beethoven frequently specified a *Nachschlag* for given trills, in many instances he did not. So should the pianist add a *Nachschlag* if there isn't one printed? I believe that the answer depends upon musical circumstances. In the second movement of Sonata Op. 31 no. 2 ("Tempest"), as we have seen, addition of a *Nachschlag* for each trill enhances the smoothness of a musical line that is slow, legato.

In the first movement of Sonata Op. 31 no. 3, the trills in m. 65 and m. 67 do not have *Nachschläge*, but my tendency would be to add them. Each of the following six trills (mm. 68–71) does have a *Nachschlag*, but that is because two of these *Nachschläge* include nonharmonic notes (B-natural and E-natural) that Beethoven may have felt necessary to specify. Beethoven may not have indicated them for the trills in m. 65 and m. 67 because the music at this point is harmonically more stable than that of the following chain of trills, and the *Nachschläge* would not include any nonharmonic notes. The parallel passage in the recapitulation (mm. 191–201) also includes *Nachschläge* for the second chain of trills (mm. 194–201), and although the first trill in m. 191 has no *Nachschlag*, the second trill (m. 193) does, even though there is no nonharmonic pitch. Beethoven thus seems to have assumed *Nachschläge* for this passage and for the parallel passage in the exposition but did not include them, feeling they were obvious.

For the three trills later in the development of this work I would not add *Nachschläge*. In mm. 123–127 (Example 22) the three trills on the F-seventh, B-flat–seventh, and E-flat–seventh harmonies do not have *Nachschläge*, but the trills on the following Cs (within A-flat, A-flat augmented, and inverted F minor harmonies in mm. 128–130) do. The first three trills are *forte* in a rapidly changing harmonic and registral landscape. The latter three trills, all on the same pitch, are the static ceiling under which the left-hand harmonies evolve with the chromatic ascent of one pitch (E-flat to E to F). Also, these trills can be phrased to the following note; the *Nachschlag* helps the forward direction in each instance. By contrast, the trills in mm. 123–127 come away from the highest note (sforzando) of each group; there is an implied subtle decrescendo or shaping down of the musical gesture. Addition of a *Nachschlag* to these trills would obviate this sense of direction and lessen the contrast with the trills of opposite direction that follow.

Example 22: Sonata Op. 31 no. 3, first movement, mm. 123–131. I do not play the editor's *Nachschläge* in parentheses.

At the end of the third movement of Sonata Op. 101, a chain of three treble trills ascends chromatically, leading gradually and with increasing intensity to the theme of the last movement, Geschwind, doch nicht zu sehr (fast, but not too much so). Adding *Nachschläge* would make the musical landscape more florid, which would compromise the vectorlike qualities of the chromatic line. Beethoven's addition of the D-sharp grace-note before the trill on E helps set off this final trill, as the crescendo begins here as well.

Beethoven invokes another chain of three trills, also without *Nachschläge*, to herald the theme of the last movement of the very next sonata, the "Hammerklavier," Op. 106. The trill of the theme, however, does include a *Nachschlag* whenever musically and pianistically possible. Certainly the initial statements of the theme all include them; as the trill builds in intensity and forward direction, the *Nachschlag* helps direct the musical energy forward. Even so complicated an area as the augmentation and strettos in mm. 101–103 includes them. (The measure numbers in Example 23 assume the start of the Allegro risoluto as m. 1. If the Largo and Allegro risoluto are numbered consecutively, add ten to these measure numbers.)

Example 23: Sonata Op. 106, last movement, mm. 101–104.

But beginning only four measures later, the musical direction of the trills is reversed—initially the intensity diminishes from the first note of the trill, rather than building through the trill to the note following the trill, as the contour is inverted. Accordingly, Beethoven writes no *Nachschlag*. In m. 114 when the note following the trill is higher than the trill note, the trill again leans forward, and *Nachschläge* reappear.

Just before the choralelike abstraction of the theme (m. 240), Beethoven compresses to a rhythmic extreme the thematic leap of a tenth to the trill. These trills, by definition and necessity, are short. No *Nachschläge* are specified, for they would be irrelevant.

Pirouettes

In addition to the many types of trills and the extraordinarily rich and diverse music of which they are part, Beethoven also used musical pirouettes for expressive purposes—often free from local metrical pulse and incorporating feelings of improvisation—before moving on to vigorous musical material.

The transition from the third to the fourth movements of Sonata *quasi una fantasia* Op. 27 no. 1 involves a scale flourish to a tremolo to a trill, which dissolves into a figure that pirouettes downward, ending on the A-flat with a fermata (completing the dominant seventh harmony), before resolving to the Allegro vivace that breaks in, *piano*. This gentle figure adds to the feeling of spontaneity while prolonging the unstable dominant harmony; it can be played in a quasi-improvisatory manner consistent with other qualities of this sonata.

In the first movement of Sonata Op. 2 no. 3, a cadential flourish (m. 232) built from the opening motive heralds the return of the main theme in the coda.

One might expect a cadenza of this sort in a piano concerto but not in a piano sonata. Even though the massive scale of this movement warrants a coda to balance the development and the general overt virtuosity, the cadenza adds an element of quasi-improvisation free from the confines of the strict tempo which is otherwise so propulsive throughout this work.

The first time that a listener feels any sense of stable harmonic grounding in the first movement of Sonata Op. 31 no. 3 is in the second theme, for the first is harmonically unstable. But at the end of the first phrase of the second theme, Beethoven offers a cadenzalike pirouette (mm. 53–56) which gradually winds its way up to a higher register. Feelings of improvisation return as the first of these measures proceeds from four sixteenths in a beat to five, and then to twelve thirty-second notes. Even in mm. 54 and 55 where there are twelve sixteenths in each measure, the barring of these sixteenths is not by the standard groups of four but rather for the entire group of twelve, implying a dissolution of metrical pulse.

In the midst of the coda toward the end of the first movement of the "Appassionata" Sonata Op. 57, Beethoven writes a series of virtuosic arpeggios (mm. 227–234) just before the tempo increases to più allegro. While these are played in tempo and are written in the same size notes as the rest of the score (unlike the "cadenza" of the first movement of Sonata Op. 2 no. 3 and unlike many of the pirouettes discussed earlier here), they nonetheless feel somewhat improvisatory, suggesting a brilliant and dynamic cadenza.

The *non presto* pirouette in the third movement of Sonata Op. 101 leads to a restatement of the opening theme of the work. But brilliant pianistic virtuosity does not motivate this cadenza. There is no feeling of inevitability about the eventual arrival of the main theme. Rather, the whole musical point of this slow movement is to create the feeling of quasi-improvisation to which the slow flourish adds, so that the recurrence of the opening theme is in fact a complete surprise. Coupled with the *non presto* tempo (unusual, for the pirouettes are generally faster tempos), this feeling implies that the character of this pirouette is searching and introspective.

Twice in the slow movement of Sonata Op. 31 no. 1 Beethoven composed pirouettes, the second being even longer than the first. In each instance these flourishes further the parodic nature of this movement by extending the stylized soprano "diva" character of the right hand ever upward into the coloratura stratosphere. Each pirouette evolves from the trill that precedes it. The speed and intensity increase as the figures ascend. The dynamic changes in the second flourish (crescendo–piano–crescendo–diminuendo) serve only to increase the feelings of improvisation (Example 24).

In some early sonata slow movements, Beethoven incorporated pirouettes into the score in a noncadential fashion. The Adagio of Op. 2 no. 1 is florid in this manner; the playing requires flexible and subtle dynamic control that

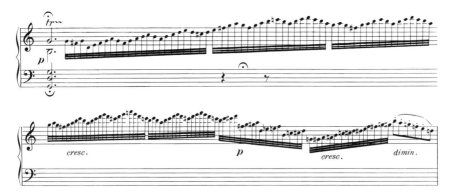

Example 24: Sonata Op. 31 no. 1, second movement, m. 90.

reflects the contour of the ornate musical line (Example 25a). Similarly in the Adagio of Sonata Op. 10 no. 1 ascending flourishes of sixty-fourth notes are always played in a graceful and lyrical fashion, *pianissimo* (Example 25b).

And again in Sonata Op. 22, which Beethoven himself felt epitomized his early classical style, long lines of rapid notes are woven into the gentle and singing musical current that turns around itself as it descends or ascends (Example 26).

Good Humor

Profundity, passion, exuberance, and introspection abound in the cycle of Beethoven sonatas. But there are also times of great good humor. Every movement of Sonata Op. 31 no. 1 is musically funny. The first pokes fun at an issue every pianist faces—that of playing with the hands exactly together. In this work, the pianist seems to lack the control to stop the right hand from being slightly ahead of the left—until the final two chords. The second movement parodies singers who go off on long excursions displaying their vocal ingenuity, leaving their accompanist to wonder when, and musically where, they will return. While the last movement is ostensibly a graceful rondo, both these elements—particularly that of the "poorly" played chords of the first movement—return to draw the work to a humorous conclusion.

If it is funny that a pianist can't play with his or her hands properly together, then it is probably even funnier if he plays an obviously "wrong" note. Beethoven must have enjoyed the joke he played on his audience, when—in the first movement of Sonata Op. 2 no. 3—he wrote the fortissimo octave D-sharp in the bass in m. 74. This chord is not only "wrong"—one might expect an E at this point in the cadential C harmony, but certainly not a D-sharp—but it is played

Example 25a: Sonata Op. 2 no. 1, second movement, mm. 48–51.

Example 25b: Sonata Op. 10 no. 1, second movement, mm. 26–32.

forcefully, with great conviction. The right hand must then incorporate this "mistake" in order to get back on the "right" track, hence the augmented arpeggio that follows (Example 27).

An analogous "mistake" is made in the recapitulation (m. 208). After the initial "wrong" note, which I play in tempo, I like to take a little time in the right-hand arpeggio, as if spontaneously figuring out a smooth way to get back on course.

Humor of the unexpected also fueled Beethoven's imagination in the recapitulation of Sonata Op. 10 no. 2, first movement. Rather than a simple wrong note, however, he brought in an entire statement of the theme, but in the "wrong" key. In mm. 117–118, the opening theme returns, but it is in D major (the submediant). This sounds funny but unsatisfying, since the tonic is the key that is expected. By quickly reasserting the tonic (mm. 136–137), Beethoven lets us know that it was all a musical joke.

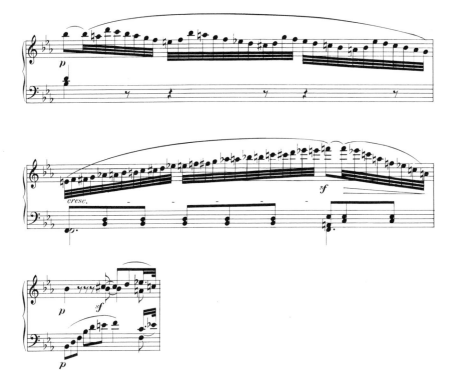

Example 26: Sonata Op. 22, second movement, mm. 25–27.

Example 27: Sonata Op. 2 no. 3, first movement, mm. 71–75.

Sonata Op. 31 no. 3 is also a good-humored piece. Although there is no element of parody, the constant slowing down, stopping, and starting again of the first theme of the Allegro is musically humorous. The Scherzo second movement is of remarkable jocundity. The energy in the staccato arpeggiated left hand, along with the offbeat sforzandos, contributes to the astonishingly vibrant musical character.

Jumping ahead seven years to Sonata Op. 78 (1809), we also find good musical humor in the second of its two movements. The contour and abrupt dy-

Example 28: Sonata Op. 78, second movement, mm. 21–31.

namic changes in the passages of groups of two sixteenth-notes alternating be-tween the hands helps make these passages amusing within the overall bright sound of this movement (Example 28).

Op. 78 thus offers the last instance of musical amusement in the piano so-natas. Even though feelings of exuberance recur (last movement of Op. 81a, second movement of Op. 110, and carried almost to extremes in the first and last movements of Op. 106), the sonatas that follow Op. 78 focus upon more serious expression.

CHAPTER 6

Publishers and Editions

It is unpleasant for me if my works come out so full of mistakes. The proof copy will be corrected here immediately and returned to you; whereupon you may then circulate the work throughout the world. I must insist that this be done, for, if not, it will be your own fault if your edition is pirated.

—Beethoven to Moritz Schlesinger in Paris, 31 August 1822,
regarding publication by the Schlesinger firm
of Sonata Op. 111 (Anderson 1961, 965)

*B*eethoven was intensely frustrated by errors in printed editions of his work. Not surprisingly, his bouts of exasperation led to relationships with publishers that often were convoluted. In 1822 four different firms published his Sonata Op. 111 more or less simultaneously, and owing to their lack of care, Beethoven eventually settled on making sure that a pirated reprint from a fifth firm was, in fact, the most accurate. Efforts toward securing a publisher for the Missa solemnis (beginning in 1822 as well) were also convoluted and even more protracted. On 22 August 1822 Beethoven wrote to Artaria:

Being just now overwhelmed with work, I can only say briefly that I have always returned your favors whenever possible. As regards the Mass I have been offered 1000 florins C.M. for it. The state of my affairs does not permit me to take a smaller honorarium from you. All that I can do is to *give* you the *preference*. Rest assured that I do not *take a heller more* from you than has been *offered me by others*. I could prove this to you in writing. You may think this over but I beg of you to send me an answer by tomorrow noon as tomorrow is post-day and my decision is expected in other places—I will make a proposition to you concerning the 150 florins C.M. which I owe you, but the sum must not be deducted *now*, as I am in urgent need of the 1000 florins—In addition I beg of you to keep everything secret about the Mass. As always

your grateful friend Beethoven (Thayer 1973, 794)

The other offers to which Beethoven refers include negotiations with Simrock and then with C. F. Peters. He had also indicated intent with Schlesinger and later with Schott, who eventually (18 January 1825) received the manuscripts of both the Mass and the Ninth Symphony (Thayer 1973, 927). Thus, he involved a total of five publishing firms regarding the Missa solemnis, and he asked Artaria not to deduct the 150 florins that he already owed them from the requested fee of 1000 florins.

To understand such a position, we need to consider Beethoven's personality and the manner in which he lived. Beethoven had undertaken to care for his nephew Karl in 1815, and in addition to the psychological strain this engendered, Beethoven was forced into an even more precarious financial situation. He no longer considered his bank shares as exclusively his own, but rather as an inheritance for his nephew. Also, his income diminished noticeably, owing both to the smaller payments he received from his various patrons (who themselves faced financial insecurity) and to his decreased productivity (measured in discrete works, which is how publishers paid him) from about 1814 on.

In addition, Beethoven's health was, at best, fragile. On 19 May 1822 he wrote to Franz Brentano (a friend, occasional patron, and agent) that "during the last four months I have again been constantly suffering from gout on my chest and have been able to do only very little work" (Anderson 1961, 944). To his brother Johann van Beethoven, he wrote (also May 1822): "Just have a look at my rooms here. You will then see the results, you will realize what happens, simply because when I am seriously indisposed I have to be *at the mercy of strangers.*" The next month he seemed no better; to C. F. Peters he explained on 5 June 1822 that he has "been ailing for the last five months" (947).

It is not surprising that Beethoven negotiated with several different publishers simultaneously. With hindsight however, it does seem surprising that he did not try to establish more competitive bidding among them.

In stark contrast to the sublime spirituality, optimism, and elegiac qualities of his late works, Beethoven could not help but be disillusioned with publishers. Not only was he continually angered by rampant inaccuracies, but he also remained frustrated by his attempts to formulate a complete edition of his works. In the letter to C. F. Peters dated 5 June 1822, in which he referred to his ailments and also proposed the Mass for publication, Beethoven expressed that

> what I wish for more than all these is an *edition of my complete works* which I could superintend myself. . . . I myself would superintend and edit the whole edition in two, even possibly one or one-and-a-half years with the necessary help, and supply for each composition category a new work. For example, for the variations a new set of variations, for sonatas a new example of a sonata and so on; for each type in which I have, I would supply a new work (Thayer 1973, 789).

Again, to the publisher Schott (on 22 January 1825): "You might reflect upon my suggestion that it would be better to have the edition done now *by* me rather than after my death. . . . I am inclined to have more confidence in you . . . for each type of work, such as, for example, sonatas variations and so forth, I would compose a new work of the same type" (Anderson 1961, 1168). On three other occasions after age forty, Beethoven approached four different publishers with the desire for a correct and complete edition of his works (Breitkopf und Härtel in 1810, Simrock in 1817 and 1820). Sadly, this project remained rejected during Beethoven's lifetime.

Among Beethoven's posthumous papers is a document (ca. 1822) that addresses this issue. It reveals much about his bitterness toward publishers who issued his works in imperfect editions over which he had little control. Yet almost triumphantly he asserts his sovereignty over the creative process:

> The law-books begin without more ado with a discussion of human rights which nevertheless the executors trample underfoot; and in like manner the author commences his statement.
>
> An author has the right to arrange for a revised edition of his works. But since there are so many greedy brainpickers and lovers of that noble dish, since all kinds of preserves, ragouts, and fricassées are made from it, which go to fill the pockets of the pastrycooks, and since the author would be glad to have as many groschen as are sometimes disbursed for his work, the author is determined to show that the *human brain* cannot be sold either like coffee beans or like any form of cheese which, as everyone knows, must first be produced from milk, urine, and so forth. . . .
>
> The human brain in itself is not a saleable commodity (Anderson 1961, 1450).

Believing unequivocally that music ennobles the human spirit, Beethoven created a world of expanding musical expression. He had a musical vision for each composition, a vision in which his particular use of musical notation, and form, harmonic language, rhythm, dynamics, and phrasing are all inextricably bound. Attentiveness to Beethoven's continual struggle for an accurate portrayal of his vision and a greater sense of interpretive responsibility can lead ultimately to a more meaningful musical statement.

Hence my belief in an implied moral and aesthetic contract between performer and composer: not only must I consider why I would perform a particular work, I also concern myself with why the composer wrote it and what its creation means both in itself and in relation to his more general oeuvre. I would want to offer the most complete artistic journey through the music, entwining the emotional with the intellectual.

For performances of the Beethoven sonatas or the works of any other composer of genius, developing a highly refined craft of playing is not sufficient. Neither is studying simply the printed page. The musician must delve into the creative spirit of the composer; we must first immerse ourselves thoroughly in his expressive world and then in the conception and genesis of a specific work—why that work was created, what about it was new and revolutionary. In performance the music is then free to soar, fresh and spontaneously.

On a practical level, the text from which a performer works should represent the most finalized ideal of the composer. This means having a good edition and more than occasionally working from a number of editions and sources simultaneously.

Some fifteen different publishers were involved in the first printings of the piano sonatas. Furthermore, beginning with Sonata Op. 106, several publishers brought out each work simultaneously in different countries. However, Beethoven was far from being happy with the situation. His frustration and anguish with inaccurate editions grew from this point forward, bringing forth the statement of 1822 about his rights as a composer being trampled.

Given the inaccuracies of the first editions and the loss of so many autograph manuscripts, what is a performer to do? Many editions of the Beethoven sonatas are available today, but I know of no editor more responsible than the respected theoretician Heinrich Schenker who supervised an edition for Universal Edition. In his preface Schenker reveals his understanding of Beethoven's idiosyncratic notational calligraphy:

> Beethoven's powerful and direct thinking produces, physically as it were, a style which is also convincingly perceptible to the eye of the reader:—the ascending and descending of the lines: here they ascend from the lower to the upper stave, there they descend from the upper to the lower; the deep significance of the cross beams: they convey to the eye the desire of belonging together or of being separated; the subtle, intelligent language of the slurs: sometimes they unite what belongs together or emphasize their parts, at other times they purposely contradict a continuity in order to increase the desire for it, often counteracting each other simultaneously in different parts; the up or downward stroke of the stems: they make us perceive the notes like contrasting actors, sharply marked in co- or counter-action, which is best observed where, for example, a downward stroke of the stem foretells, a long time ahead, the counterplay of a sequence of notes with their stems upwards or vice versa; the notation of the rests: they are omitted now and then, thus enabling the parts in their entirety to be presented more spaciously and not more than necessarily emphasizing the coming and going of a part, etc. (Beethoven 1947, Preface)

Whenever possible, I rehearse privately from autograph scores (or facsimiles thereof) and first editions, and read Beethoven's letters to publishers, which record his corrections and occasional changes. I also try to make sense of sketch material in order to form a more thorough understanding of the genesis and nature of a specific work. Generally I rely on Schenker's edition as a basic guide and also consult his wonderful "Erläuterungen zu den Sonaten Op. 101, 109, 110, 111" (in Schenker 1970) for further detailed commentary about the autographs of these works. (Op. 106 is not in the series because the autograph is lost.) The Schenker edition is not only generally textually accurate but also accurately represents Beethoven's own fingering and pedaling. I also find the Schnabel edition interesting, not for its textual authority, which is occasionally lacking, but rather for Schnabel's commentary, which is fascinating. He also suggests frequently marvelous fingerings in passages for which Beethoven did not include any.

I always consider several issues in selecting an edition from which to play. Who is the editor? What are his interests in editing? What sources have been consulted? Are the composer's own indications clear (phrasing slurs, dynamics, fingering, pedaling), and distinguishable from any editorial suggestions? When textual questions arise, are they clearly indicated as such?

In the nineteenth century, music publishing firms frequently engaged famous performers to prepare "performing" editions. They included their own preferred fingering and pedaling, and also phrasing, dynamics, and often tempo markings. These suggestions inevitably obscured the composer's original intentions, particularly since most often no effort was made to differentiate between the editor's suggestions and the composer's own notation.

As a counter-reaction the Royal Academy of Arts in Berlin began printing editions in the 1890s that were free of such obfuscation. These were the first Urtext editions (original text; Ur considered as the first true city in the Fertile Crescent). The original intention of these editions was to present the composer's ideas and notation so that they could speak for themselves. But noble as this goal may be, it is not easily attained.

Consider the remarks of Günter Henle, of G. Henle Verlag, Munich, the firm that during the period after World War II capitalized greatly on the use of the term *Urtext*. Henle noted correctly that occasionally a composer's autograph score and the first edition differ, creating a situation in which the editor (not the composer) must decide what to print (Grier 1996, 11). Henle does not point out that such an edition is no longer Urtext, nor does he elucidate how such decisions are made. As a performer, I would prefer to know these points, for I may draw conclusions different from those of the editor.

Such a non-Urtext edition should more correctly be called a critical edition. A performer should expect documentation of editorial decisions and could possibly even revise some of these decisions based on his or her own research and interpretation of a composer's musical ideals.

A responsible edition will point out areas of textual controversy, such as the A versus A-sharp issue in the development of the first movement of the "Hammerklavier" Sonata (see Program 7) and the question of whether there are valid repeat signs for the first part of the trio in the second movement of Sonata Op. 101 (see Program 3).

A good edition will also be careful about the placement of dynamic indications. At the end of the first movement of the "Moonlight" Sonata, a two-measure phrase is repeated, with the only difference in the repetition being the placement of the crescendo-decrescendo marking (Example 29). The result is a subtle but clear difference in performance of the two phrases. The exact placement of the dynamic marking should be accurate in all editions.

Example 29: Sonata Op. 27 no. 2, first movement, mm. 60–69.

The ideal version of a work would be the autograph that Beethoven (or any composer) sent to the publisher. But even with Beethoven autograph scores the situation is far from unambiguous. Some markings that are in an autograph score have not survived into all currently available editions. An example is the *tempo primo* at m. 174 in the last movement of the autograph of Sonata Op. 110, the point at which the fugue theme returns in bass octaves. The autograph in Beethoven's hand, with this directive, was sent to the publisher Adolf M. Schlesinger (Schlesinger *père*) in Berlin. However, a fair copy (not made by Beethoven but corrected by him), which does not include this *tempo primo*, was sent to Moritz Schlesinger (Schlesinger *fils*) for publication in Paris. (This copy was bought by Brahms and remained in his estate.) Of the leading editions available today, the Schenker edition inexplicably does not include this marking, but the Henle edition does. Although Beethoven seems to have left no correspondence about this point, I believe that the *tempo primo* at m. 174 makes good musical sense, and I follow the *tempo primo* of the autograph score. Thus I do not continue the previous *nach und nach wieder geschwinder* past this point.

Another instance in which a performer has to make a textual judgment is in the first movement of the "Waldstein" Sonata Op. 53 (Example 30). Although all printed editions have an F as the first left-hand note in m. 105, the autograph has an F-flat at this point. So did the initial engraving plates, for a space for the flat sign is still visible in the earliest first editions as is a very light impression of the flat sign left over from when the engraver imperfectly effaced the flat. (The lack of a flat preceding the F changes the character of this passage, weakening the temporary establishment of C-flat major in the second half of the measure.) Again, there is no documentary evidence about this change, but it seems likely to have been made at Beethoven's request. In this case, an early first edition takes precedence over the autograph.

Example 30: Sonata Op. 53, first movement, mm. 103–111. The autograph score has an F-flat in the bass (instead of F-natural) in m. 105.

As we have seen, Beethoven's letters to publishers can include vital aspects absent from the autograph score, such as the first movement of the Adagio of the "Hammerklavier" Sonata Op. 106 and the metronome markings for this work. Autograph facsimiles, first editions, letters, even sketches—all can be used in collaboration with a responsible published edition to gain greater insight into a work.

Beethoven's ideal of a complete edition of his works was undertaken by Breitkopf und Härtel in 1864. The last of the forty volumes was published in 1890. However, this *Gesamtausgabe* (complete edition) is considered today to be both incomplete and not totally reliable. With the uncovering of more source

The Beethoven Piano Sonatas: Autographs and First Editions

Sonata	Date of composition	Autograph	First edition
Op. 2 nos. 1–3	1795	lost	Artaria, Vienna, 1796
Op. 7	1796–97	lost	Artaria, Vienna, 1797
Op. 10 nos. 1–3	1796–98	lost	Joseph Eder, Vienna, 1798
Op. 13	1798–99	lost	Joseph Eder, Vienna, 1799
Op. 14 nos. 1–2	1798–99	lost	Mollo, Vienna, 1799
Op. 22	1800–01	lost	Hoffmeister und Kühnel, Leipzig, 1802
Op. 26	1800–01	Deutsche Staatsbibliothek, Berlin	Cappi, Vienna, 1802
Op. 27 no. 1	1800–01	lost	Cappi, Vienna, 1802
Op. 27 no. 2	1801	Beethoven-Haus, Bonn	Cappi, Vienna, 1802
Op. 28	1801	Beethoven-Haus, Bonn	Kunst und Industrie-Comptoir, Vienna, 1802
Op. 31 nos. 1–2	1801–02	lost	Nägeli, (*Répertoire des Clavecinistes*, Vol. 5), Zurich, 1803
Op. 31 no. 3	1801–02	lost	Nägeli, (*Répertoire des Clavecinistes*, Vol. 11), Zurich, 1803
Op. 49 nos. 1 and 2	1798 and 1796, respectively	lost	Kunst und Industrie-Comptoir, Vienna, 1805
Op. 53	1803–04	H. C. Bodmer, Zurich	Kunst und Industrie-Comptoir, Vienna, 1805

Op. 54	1804	lost	Kunst und Industrie-Comptoir, Vienna, 1806
Op. 57	1804	Conservatoire de Musique, Paris	Kunst und Industrie-Comptoir, Vienna, 1807
Op. 78	1809	H. C. Bodmer, Zurich	Breitkopf und Härtel, Leipzig, 1810
Op. 79	1809	H. C. Bodmer, Zurich	Breitkopf und Härtel, Leipzig, 1810
Op. 81a	1809	First movement: Gesellschaft der Musikfreunde, Vienna; second and third movements: lost	Breitkopf und Härtel, Leipzig, 1811
Op. 90	1814	T. Odling, London	Steiner, Vienna, 1815
Op. 101	1816	Louis Koch, Wildegg, Switzerland	Steiner, Vienna, 1817
Op. 106	1817–18	lost	Artaria, Vienna, 1819 (two editions, one with French and the other with German titles)
Op. 109	1820	Library of Congress, Washington, DC	A. Schlesinger, Berlin, 1821
Op. 110	1821	Deutsche Staatsbibliothek, Berlin, and H. C. Bodmer, Zurich	A. Schlesinger, Berlin, 1822; M. Schlesinger, Paris, 1822
Op. 111	1821–22	First movement: Beethoven-Haus, Bonn; second movement: Deutsch Staatsbibliothek, Berlin	Clementi, London, 1823; M. Schlesinger, Paris, 1823; A. Schlesinger, Berlin, 1823; Cappi & Diabelli, Vienna, 1823

materials (autograph scores, sketchbooks, letters) since that publication, the Beethovenhaus in Bonn started, in 1961, an ambitious project entitled simply *Beethovens Werke*. As of mid 2001 twenty-six volumes are available.

In preparing a Beethoven sonata for performance, I use the Schenker edition as my primary printed source. I consult the Schnabel edition for his annotations and also check the Peters and Henle editions. Of course I study autograph scores in facsimile reproductions whenever they are available; the table at the end of this chapter is a guide to surviving autograph scores and to the first publishers of the sonatas. I also study whatever sketches might be extant. Beethoven's sketches might seem a surprising choice on a practical level, for he ultimately rejected most of what they contain. But examination of sketches can have exert a profound impression. For example, the fact that Beethoven altered the original meter in his sketches of the first movement of Sonata Op. 57 ("Appassionata") from c to 12/8 exerts a strong impact on my interpretation. This change is not mentioned in any edition; the only way one could know about it is through examination of sketch material. Perhaps one day a critical edition could be prepared which incorporates not only the final product but also significant stages of creative evolution, such as this metrical change or the changes (Presto to Prestissimo; deletion of ritard) in the second and third movements of the Sonata Op. 109 autograph. A more complete perspective could greatly enhance the bond of understanding between performer and composer.

CHAPTER 7

The Myth of the
Authentic Pianoforte

Clavicembalo miserabile

—Beethoven's comment on a leaf of sketches of 1824

It is and remains an inadequate instrument.

—Beethoven to his friend and confidant
Karl Holz in 1826 (Thayer 1973, 984)

*T*here was nothing holy to Beethoven about the many pianofortes he had throughout his life. He did not allow himself to be restricted compositionally by their limited sonorous capabilities, and by all accounts of his playing, he preferred to break instruments rather than to compromise his range of expression. Yet although continually frustrated, he composed some of his most daring and expressive works for the piano. He knew that as pianofortes continued to evolve, his works would be played on better and better instruments. In 1819 Beethoven advised the publisher Artaria that upon receipt of his Sonata Op. 106 ("Hammerklavier"), they now had "a Sonata that will keep the pianists busy when it is played fifty years hence" (Marston 1991, 448).

What does "authenticity" mean in terms of the sound of Beethoven's piano works? What type of piano should be used to perform these works? Should we perform the sonatas on the period instruments that were prevalent at the times of their composition? Are the pianos against which Beethoven railed to be considered as holy? Beethoven's own powerful and direct manner of playing is the stuff of legend. The description of him improvising in 1812 (see Chapter 4) depicts the weakness of pianoforte sound and construction that fueled his frustrations with them. To what extent should we consider what the audience heard? If Beethoven were playing, many strings would quickly be broken and many more out of tune. Should the concept of authenticity be applied to what Beethoven himself heard? Beethoven was largely deaf for a significant portion of his mature life (deafness was bothersome from 1802 onward). Beethoven's inner ear was the important and uncompromised guide, unaffected by his hearing loss or the sonorous limitations of the pianoforte.

Let us consider the limitations that were imposed upon Beethoven by external factors and how he dealt with them. A typical Viennese pianoforte in 1795—the year of composition of the Op. 2 sonatas—had a range of five octaves (FF–f³). Some pianofortes retained hand stops (vestiges of harpsichords), but many had two knee levers: one to raise the dampers, another to shift the keyboard to *una corda*. Pedals crept in gradually during the first decade of the nineteenth century, as we have seen, and Beethoven changed from *senza sordino* indications (knee levers used to raise the dampers) to pedal markings with the Op. 31 sonatas, composed in 1801–02. His involvement with piano technology was in the vanguard. The demands that Beethoven's piano sonatas placed upon the instruments of the time pushed the pianoforte manufacturers to keep up. In 1802 Beethoven wrote, "The whole tribe of pianoforte manufacturers have been swarming around me in their anxiety to serve me—and all for nothing. Each of them wants to make me a pianoforte exactly as I should like it" (Anderson 1961, 82).

In 1803 the Érard firm in Paris made a gift of one of their pianofortes to Beethoven. He was delighted with its expanded registral range: five-and-a-half octaves (FF to c⁴). This pianoforte had two pedals: a damper pedal and a keyboard shift (*una corda* pedal). Beethoven immediately took advantage of the expanded upper register. The "Waldstein" and "Appassionata" Sonatas (Opp. 53 and 57 of 1803–04) make full use of these "new" notes, as does the Fourth Piano Concerto Op. 58 (1805–06). There were no uniform standards for pianofortes; not all instruments had this expanded range. But obviously Beethoven intended these works to be played on only the newest of instruments, for the older ones (even those less than eight years old) and others less technologically advanced could not accommodate them.

In 1818 he was once again honored with the gift of a pianoforte, this time from the London firm of Broadwood. This instrument had a compass of six octaves (CC–c⁴) and again two pedals—damper and shift (*una corda*). Two years previously Beethoven had incorporated the new bass notes in the climax of the fugue of Sonata Op. 101 (1816). Just to ensure against any misunderstandings about these "new" notes being played and against the work's being played on an instrument with a smaller range, Beethoven specified in a letter to the publisher "contra E" for each of the six consecutive times this new low E is used. (The publisher printed only one contra E.) In addition to the six-octave range, Beethoven was also initially pleased with the relatively larger sonority of the Broadwood.

During his lifetime Beethoven owned or borrowed at least fourteen pianofortes. Eleven of these came from Viennese piano makers, four of which were from the Streicher or Stein companies, to which Beethoven felt a great allegiance. Only the two pianos honoring Beethoven (the Érard and the Broadwood) as well as a piano from a Hungarian maker (Vogel) were from non-Viennese makers (Newman 1988, 53).

It is perhaps ironic that none of Beethoven's favored Viennese pianos are among the three instruments of his that have survived. The Érard that he received as a gift in 1803, with which he was dissatisfied because of its heavy action, is in the Kunsthistorisches Museum in Vienna. About the Broadwood, which is in the National Museum, Budapest, Beethoven reported to his friend Johann Stumpff that the instrument had not fulfilled his expectations. A Graf piano made in 1825 and loaned to Beethoven is in the Beethoven-Haus, Bonn. It has quadruple-unison stringing (four strings for each note rather than the customary two or three) and a special resonator, the purpose of which was to make the instrument audible to Beethoven. But by then his hearing was too far gone, and Beethoven never felt close to this instrument.

Beethoven composed the "Hammerklavier" Sonata Op. 106 some seven years before the loan of the Graf piano. At that time no piano known to have been at Beethoven's disposal was able to accommodate both the extreme bass and the extreme treble registers he required—the six-and-one-half-octave range (CC to f^4).

We might question, then, how to interpret passages that Beethoven seemed compelled to write in ways that were directly affected by restricted registral ranges. For example, might one be tempted to add octaves to the bass in several measures of Sonata Op. 10 no. 3, first movement (Example 31)?

Example 31: Sonata Op. 10 no. 3, first movement, mm. 268–274.

The analogous scale in the exposition of this movement (mm. 87–92) continues in octaves throughout. Perhaps among the reasons that later in life Beethoven wanted a new edition of his works was to compose again such passages that may have been compromised by registral limitations. Of course Beethoven never realized the new edition. I would argue against such recomposition at this date for several reasons, even for playing on a modern instrument. I believe that it is possible to obtain a stylistic consistency with the five-octave range of

Beethoven's early pianos and to maintain this style in performance today on our modern instruments. Furthermore, Beethoven demonstrated several times —for example, in his letters of 13 July 1802 about his transcription of Op. 14 no. 1 and of 19 February 1813 about his setting of Scottish airs—that if rewriting were to be done, only the composer was qualified to do it (see Program 2 and Chapter 2).

The two main innovations in piano technology of the nineteenth century were Érard's double escapement action of 1821 which allowed for a faster repetition and lighter touch; and Alpheus Babock's cast iron, one-piece frame of 1825 in Boston (Harding 1978, 158, 204) which made possible far greater string tension and therefore considerably fuller sonority. Beethoven never saw or tried either of these innovations, but there is every reason to suspect that he would have welcomed them.

The German (and Viennese) piano action was distinguished by a fast, light, responsive touch which produced a clear, singing, very controllable tone. By contrast, the English action was deeper and less responsive; the tone was fuller but more muffled and of a broader dynamic range. Beethoven maintained his friendship with and allegiance to the Viennese piano maker Andreas Streicher and even influenced Streicher to imbue his pianos with some of the better characteristics of the English pianos:

> Streicher has left the soft, the excessively pliant, as well as the bouncing rolling of the older Viennese instruments, and—upon Beethoven's advice and request—has given his instruments more resistance and elasticity so that the virtuoso who performs with strength and significance has power over the instrument for sustaining and supporting the tone and more sensitive pressure and release of the key. Through this change he has given his instruments a greater and more diverse character so that more than any other instruments they will satisfy the virtuoso who seeks more than easy glitter in performance (Newman 1988, 64).

Many pianofortes have survived from Beethoven's time and even earlier. Others have been restored, and still more reproduction pianofortes have been built. We can play Beethoven's works of a particular era on a contemporaneous instrument to understand how they may push that instrument to its limits not only in speed and volume, both loud and soft, but also in delicacy of pedaling and phrasing. We can then take the same work to the modern piano and, viewing the music afresh, as though newly composed, push the instrument to its limits in certain pivotal passages, such as the opening of the Rondo in the "Waldstein." Once again, these are not necessarily limits of speed or volume but rather of subtlety in playing. Studying the pianofortes available to Beethoven and trying them in rehearsal is important to the way I shape a fully considered interpretation and maintain stylistic integrity. I begin to understand Beethoven's frustrations with his pianofortes and bear these in mind as I work with the fuller capabilities of today's instruments.

Any discussion about music from an earlier time should consider general aural environment. For better or for worse, our sphere of hearing has been irrevocably enlarged. Beethoven's audience never heard lawn mowers, airplane engines, or public address systems. We are bombarded constantly with aural phenomena (mostly noise) that in sheer volume is far beyond that of earlier times. In Beethoven's era a big thunderstorm, with its accompanying aural drama, was viewed as a major event; to us, it's at most a minor inconvenience.

I believe that Beethoven's works should be performed on the best possible instruments currently available, in a most sympathetic artistic manner. Again, this conviction implies stylistic awareness as well as consideration of the *very essence* of each particular work, consulting responsible editions, understanding pedaling concepts, honoring the moral contract. If a concept of authenticity demands slavish adherence to period instruments exclusively, it becomes invalid.

Even though performances of musical works—including recorded ones—are for the moment, each is nonetheless unique. We have all had special experiences in listening and can imagine conditions in concerts that are associated with particularly inspired performances, ones that stand out in our memories. For me, inspired performance involves having a piano to play that is capable of a wide range of sound and tone color and having good "natural" acoustics that do not interfere with the qualities of sound. In my experience an inspiring performance may be inseparable from the general conditions and the specific concert hall. Or considering another artistic domain, individual paintings are also unique, but their locations are not. Moving a work of visual art from one lighting situation to another is certainly feasible. An analogous concept of authenticity for paintings, therefore, might suggest viewing Rembrandts only under natural light or by aid of candles. But I do not know of a single museum that does not offer modern lighting conditions for viewing and appreciating its treasures.

Beethoven wrote the deprecating comments that head this chapter after he had completed his last piano composition, the Bagatelles Op. 126. He had never been content to pour his compositional ideas into a preformed mold but rather was always pushing musical perception forward, linking expression with formal experimentation. Similarly, he was never content for very long with the limitations of contemporaneous pianofortes. He had already allowed the sonata cycle to come to an end, feeling there was nothing more he needed to accomplish in this domain. One could speculate about his writing more bagatelles of extremely concentrated form, such as the intermezzos that Brahms was to espouse. But Beethoven's declining health, his desire for new musical challenges, and his lifetime of frustrations with the pianoforte led him to forego that instrument and concentrate instead on other genres—choral and orchestral (Missa solemnis,

Ninth Symphony) and string quartets. Continuing his comments in 1826 to Holz, Beethoven claimed that "in the future I shall write in the manner of my grand-master Händel annually only an oratorio or a concerto for some string or wind instrument, provided I have completed my tenth symphony (C minor) and my Requiem" (Thayer 1973, 984). Nothing more for the inadequate pianoforte.

Beethoven was right: the "Hammerklavier" and his other works have indeed kept musicians busy many years hence. The pianoforte has grown up. The demands placed upon the piano makers by the music of Beethoven and others forced the use of stronger, more durable materials. Design changes in the action, concomitant with the incorporation of the cast iron frame, have produced an instrument capable of tremendous power and of the most searching intimacy. Why not use the full palette of sound to bring fresh life to these works of time-less value?

PART TWO

Concert Programs

Planning the Programs

*T*he thirty-two sonatas span twenty-seven years (1795–1822) and range in duration from about seven to almost forty minutes. Each creates its own universe of expression, and each is pianistically challenging in different ways. Preparing for a performance of the cycle involves ordering them into concert programs, and of course many different combinations are possible. When I set out to plan my sonata programs for the first time, I had some tough but exciting decisions to make.

I began by sitting myself down in front of a large piece of blank paper to ponder the alternatives. I will never forget the sense of challenge, trepidation, exuberance, and awe that I felt at that moment. Such is the beginning of an exultant journey unlike any other—rich in drama, brilliance, and intimacy; daring in its ambition to forge new qualities of musical perception and pianism; humbling in its prospect of embracing these works. But the beginning—determining concert programs—happens quietly behind the scenes.

If programs proceeded chronologically, many would share a large degree of stylistic uniformity. Chronological order might be effective if the concerts were played over a short time span, but it might otherwise imply a false sense of linear evolution in Beethoven's creative development. Every time I have performed the cycle, the concerts have been spread over the course of at least a season, and in any case, I prefer a different type of ordering—one that highlights on a global level the enormous range of contrast and diversity of musical character among the works and on a more local level particular threads of commonality.

So, with these general ideas in mind, I wrote "Sonata Op. 2 no. 1" in the upper left corner of the paper and "Sonata Op. 111" in the lower right corner. I would start with the first sonata and end with the last. I then decided that I preferred to plan enough concerts to allow for a reasonable appreciation of each work on a given program; I did not want to cram too many works into any one program and thereby lessen the amount of concentration that both the audience

97

and I could devote to each sonata. I planned to let the programs themselves determine the total number of concerts rather than superimposing an arbitrary number from the outset.

I also wanted to end each program with a work that would allow the audience to leave the hall feeling exultant, with a sonata that is rousing or transcendent or both. For instance, although Op. 90 is one of my favorite works, its best placement is not at the end of a program. But Op. 57 ("Appassionata") is a different story.

Another consideration is Beethoven's sensitivity to key. Two of the sonatas in E-flat major (Opp. 31 no. 3 and 81a) are both ebullient and generally fast-paced; the three in C minor (Opp. 10 no. 1, 13, and 111) are all terse and dramatic occasionally to the extreme. The two sonatas in B-flat major (Opp. 22 and 106) are large works of boundless enthusiasm, and the two in C major (Opp. 2 no. 3 and 53) display brilliant virtuosity. To maximize contrast I would try to avoid consecutive works in the same key.

Some of the sonatas (Op. 27 no. 1, Op. 54, Op. 78, and Op. 90) are heard less frequently; I would try to intersperse these with sonatas that are generally better known, such as the "Pathétique," "Moonlight," "Waldstein," and "Appassionata." Although the order would not be strictly chronological, I did want to weight the first several programs in favor of earlier works and include at least one late sonata on each of the later programs.

Keeping all this in mind, I listed works with which to end programs—Opp. 53, 57, 106, 109, 110, and 111. Other possibilities included Op. 13 ("Pathétique"), Op. 27 no. 2 ("Moonlight"), and Op. 101. I then decided that it would be nice to try to include Op. 26—the only sonata that begins with a theme-and-variation movement—on the same program as Op. 109, which ends with one. (The last movement of Op. 111 also involves a theme with variations, but after the third "variation" the music assumes a more abstracted form.)

Among the strikingly expressive features of the epic Op. 106 ("Hammerklavier") is the quasi-improvisatory Largo in which Beethoven seems to search for just the right theme for the enormous fugue that follows. The "Tempest" Sonata Op. 31 no. 2 is also quasi-improvisatory but in different ways, including two recitatives that appear to embellish earlier themes spontaneously. I decided that these two works would make an effective concert pairing, and since Op. 106 is the longest of the sonatas, this program would thereby be complete.

I decided that I would separate the three sonatas of Op. 2 and also the three of Op. 31. Each is a long opus and would constitute a major part (if not all) of a concert program, and I preferred to construct programs of greater stylistic diversity. However, I decided to keep together the two works of Op. 14 and also the three Sonatas Op. 10. The former are shorter works and make a good pairing, and the latter display wholly different dramatic styles, even within the same opus.

Balancing these considerations, I came up with nine programs encompassing the thirty-two piano sonatas. These are discussed in the chapters that follow.

Sonata in F minor, Op. 2 no. 1 (1795)

Sonata *quasi una fantasia* in E-flat major, Op. 27 no. 1 (1800–01)

Sonata in F-sharp major, Op. 78 (1809)

Sonata in C major, Op. 53 ("Waldstein") (1803–04)

The first program displays the wide range of expression, form, style of composition, and imaginative pianism that these sonatas embody. It seems reasonable to start with the first piano sonata that Beethoven published—Sonata Op. 2 no. 1. By contrast, this is followed by the first of the two sonatas that Beethoven labeled *quasi una fantasia*—Op. 27 no. 1. The "brother" sonata to the "Moonlight," Op. 27 no. 1 is played much less frequently, perhaps because it is more experimental in form.

The second half begins with Sonata Op. 78, a work also rarely played. Its two movements are both in F-sharp major, an unusual key choice for Beethoven (but not for Scriabin!), which helps imbue this short work with both forward-looking and evanescent qualities. This first program ends with the mighty "Waldstein" Sonata Op. 53, a work of both compositional and pianistic virtuosity.

In autumn 1795 the twenty-five-year-old Beethoven played the three Sonatas Op. 2 for his former composition teacher Haydn, to whom they are dedicated, at a Friday morning concert at Prince Lichnowsky's (a friend of Mozart and a great supporter of music in Vienna). Beethoven considered these works illustrative of his ideals as a composer and pianist and worthy of publication, and they furthered his introduction into Viennese musical society. Unlike the enthusiastic testimony spontaneously offered by Haydn to Leopold Mozart about the genius of his son, there is no record about what Haydn thought of Beethoven's Op. 2 sonatas. But neither are Beethoven's words of dedication of Op. 2 particularly affectionate; the simple and direct "Dedicated to Joseph Haydn" is merely a sign of respect.

These sonatas are not Beethoven's first attempt at this genre. He dedicated a set of three sonatas without opus numbers (WoO 47: E-flat major, F minor, D major) to Maximilian Friedrich, Elector of Cologne, in 1782–83. There is also an unfinished sonata in C major WoO 51 from 1790–92. Beethoven's withholding these works from publication implies that he did not feel that they represented him in the ways he wished to be perceived by the public at that time. (Works which Beethoven withheld from publication were designated as Werk ohne Opuszahl or WoO—work without opus number—by Kinsky-Halm in their thematic catalog of Beethoven's complete works.)

Of the nineteen Mozart sonatas, only two are in minor keys: No. 9 in A minor, K. 330, and No. 14 in C minor, K. 457, often played paired with the Fantasy in C minor, K. 475. Haydn chose minor keys for only five of the sixty-two sonatas that he completed: No. 19, E minor, Hob. XVI:47; No. 25, E minor, Hob. XVI:2e (lost); No. 47, B minor, Hob. XVI:32; No. 49, C-sharp minor, Hob. XVI:36; and No. 53, E minor, Hob. XVI:34. In the late eighteenth century minor keys were less frequently used, but none of these sonatas is an "early" work, and both Mozart and Haydn were revered beyond compare in Vienna. It was a sign of great self-confidence that Beethoven chose the F minor sonata as the first in his Op. 2, his first group of sonatas to be published. Perhaps he felt particularly comfortable with this key; he may have recalled his earlier sonata also in F minor (WoO 47 no. 2). In any case, Beethoven's Op. 2 no. 1 helped establish his compositional voice from the outset.

The challenges of playing this piece begin with the first note. It has no phrase marking; it is not staccato, but neither is it legato, for it is not slurred to the following staccato notes. I play the opening C with more weight than the following staccato notes, but I make sure not to connect it in phrasing by separating it with a slight air space from the following F (Example 32).

The opening figure (a) increases in intensity and corresponding sharpness of touch as it rises, and each time the turn at the end (b) is played, it is also at a

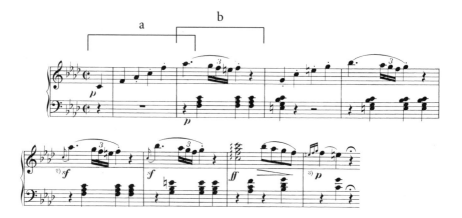

Example 32: Sonata Op. 2 no. 1, first movement, mm. 1–8.

higher dynamic level. The use of dynamics is immediately striking—the first six measures build from *p* to *ff*, then fall away back to *p* by m. 8. There is no slowing down as the first phrase stops abruptly in m. 8. Rather, the fermata over the rest, along with the phrase ending on the dominant, leaves one hanging until the theme recurs in the bass, starting in the dominant. A ritard to round off the phrase would lessen this intentionally startling effect.

Although the second theme is simply an inversion of the first, the entire musical feeling is different. The top line is now as legato as possible while the undulating left hand playing only E-flats (dominant of A-flat major, the key of the second theme area and relative major of the home key of F minor) now gives a feeling instability. The F-flat (flat-sixth degree of A-flat major) lends a minor-key feeling to this area by implying an A-flat minor harmonic context; it can be played with a special weighting of the hand, both at the beginning of each descending figure and at the sforzando downbeats (mm. 22 and 24).

The *con espressione* marking that begins the ending of the exposition implies a slight lessening of the tempo (as in the Prestissimo of Sonata Op. 109). The C-flats here give a hint of E-flat minor; a weighty touch can help emphasize this subtlety.

Initially the dynamic in the development is *piano*. The crescendos, *fp*, and *sf* markings, and the increased pace of harmonic change and increased registral range of the second theme (played in the bass beginning in m. 67) all generate greater intensity in this area of the piece. A clear sound, gradual increase of tension in the touch, and spare pedaling will allow the tensile strength of the counterpoint to prevail. An abstraction of the second theme (mm. 73–79) with incisive sforzando markings leads to the loudest measure of the development—m. 80—as the seventh chords prepare to resolve into C major, which itself begins a trajectory of resolution as the dominant of the home key of F minor.

This path leads to the single, *pianissimo* pulsating C of mm. 93–94 upon which the drama and forward momentum are concentrated. The phrase marking is portato. I would suggest a weighty touch, using light pedal for each note but changing the pedal to allow for a bit of air space between the notes. In the remaining six measures of this phrase leading to the recapitulation, it is nice to subtly weight the left-hand chords in favor of the new pitches introduced in each measure.

The importance of silence in music is often overlooked. Rests—silence—contribute to drama by leaving a listener hanging or by allowing a listener to breathe before a new passage. It is therefore crucial for a performer not to rush ahead during rests; although there are no notes, the silence is still an important part of the music.

The rests in m. 147 of the coda leave the listener suspended on an unstable harmony. But the length of the phrase up to this point (mm. 140–147) is the same as that of the parallel passage in the exposition. The extension of the phrase of this final coda makes the music more intense, as does careful observance of the rests and of the offbeat sforzando markings in mm. 150–151, which demand an incisive touch along with light pedaling. In observing the repeat sign for the second part of this movement, I maintain the tempo, saving the fermata over the last rest for the conclusion of the movement. I keep my hands poised above the keyboard for the duration of this fermata (about an extra three or four quarter-rests). This is a visually dramatic effect that maintains the intensity of the movement beyond the final sound.

The first sixteen measures of the Adagio of Op. 2 no. 1 are a transcription of the second movement of a piano quartet (WoO 36) Beethoven had composed (but had not published) some ten years earlier. Even though the music beginning in m. 17—with the excursion into D minor and the crossing of the hands—is rhetorical and dramatic rather than lyrical, a four-part texture is preserved. Clarity of lines is important; textures are spare, and the general quality of sound is *dolce* (rather than the more syrupy *espressivo*). I would, for example, play the top F in m. 52 with a clear *pianissimo* tone that would last for its entire duration, and play the alto and tenor lines softer so that they do not interfere with the sustained F. This preserves the lyrical quality of the top line, and also allows for the gently shifting harmonies to influence the ways in which we hear the top F.

Italian opera was in vogue in the last years of the eighteenth century in Vienna, and Beethoven was enthralled. Although he never wrote an *opera buffa*, this early interest influenced the lyrical style of many of his slow movements. In the coda of this Adagio the repeated postponements of the final cadence lend poignancy, like the prolonged leave-takings in Italian opera. The emotion is further heightened by the long appoggiatura D-flat first heard as a sforzando dissonance against the dominant arpeggiated chord three measures from the end. The chord that follows in the penultimate measure can be voiced with a slight extra pressure on the repeated D-flat—even though it is *pianissimo*—to heighten this feeling.

The graceful Menuetto and the Trio remain in F (minor and major respectively). Both break with the pattern of eight-bar phrases, again postponing local cadences and thereby creating feelings of suspension. I believe that the dynamic contrasts in the second part of the Menuetto are sudden contrasts, not to be anticipated by crescendos or decrescendos. Thus, I play both the *pp* in m. 21 and the *ff* three bars later as *subito* contrasts. In repeating each section of the Trio, I vary the dynamic prominence of the voices, as if altering instrumental timbres in an orchestral trio. This is not merely a question of making one hand more prominent than the other but has more to do with qualities of voicing and sound, achieved by subtleties of touch and pedaling.

Beethoven used the term Prestissimo sparingly (see Chapter 3). When he wrote it, he meant it. Hence, the last movement of this sonata is played very fast indeed. The ubiquitous triplets at the beginning of this movement and the concentrated juxtaposition of dynamic extremes create an underpinning of urgency. I take just a millisecond before the *piano subito* markings to allow the *forte* sounds to disperse and the *piano* areas to be really quiet. When the melodic second theme begins (m. 34 on), I try to maximize the legato contrast with the staccato opening theme, connecting the right-hand octaves by changing the top fingers on the second and third octave of each group from 4 to 5. This fingering allows for a smooth connection from one octave to the next (Example 33).

Example 33: Sonata Op. 2 no. 1, fourth movement, mm. 34–36. Suggested fingering for legato octaves.

The middle section of this movement, marked *sempre piano e dolce*, provides an extraordinary contrast to the intensity of the first section. But the music at the beginning of this area is structurally a transmutation of the music at the beginning of the sonata: the repeated left-hand chords and the rising right-hand arpeggio that begins the now arialike theme hark back—perhaps subliminally for a listener but certainly consciously for the composer—to the material of the first movement. Of course the context is wholly different, and so the music is played very differently and the feeling is completely different.

In contrast to the first part of the Prestissimo, the middle section is played with consummate grace and lyricism. As we will hear in Sonata Op. 2 no. 2—the next one in the initial series that Beethoven offered for publication—the drama of the last movement is reversed. Whereas the dramatic scheme of the Prestissimo under discussion is intense–lyrical–intense, that of the graceful Rondo of Op. 2 no. 2 is lyrical–intense–lyrical. In performance, even though the two sonatas are in different programs, I try to maximize these characterizations and contrasts.

Beethoven included repeat signs for both parts of the last movement, which allows the opportunity to play (and hear) the repetition of the music slightly differently from the way we hear it the first time through. Inevitably we hear the repeated music in a different way if only because of familiarity. The entire dramatic line, however, can be enhanced. Consider, for example, the feelings engendered by returning to the *sempre piano e dolce* area immediately following what initially seemed like the conclusion of the movement. Calm is in stark contrast to agitation, and we wonder, perhaps, what can happen next: the movement was supposed to end, and here we are back again, fully ensconced in the lyrical part. When playing the end of the piece for the final time, from m. 173 onward when the second theme is in the home key of F minor and we are preparing for the end, I take just a little more time for the last group of descending octaves, voicing them a little bit more to the top, making the drama just a bit more intense, for this is truly the last time we will hear this music. There are no more repeats. The final *fortissimo* is a little stronger than the others; the final cascade is strong to the last note.

WHEN I PLAY Sonata Op. 2 no. 1 I highlight the contrasts in mood among the four movements both by imbuing each movement with its own character and by pausing between the movements, framing each in silence. But Beethoven designated each of the two Op. 27 sonatas as *quasi una fantasia*, implying departures from expected structures and indicating a sense of temporal continuity throughout each work. Thus in playing Sonata Op. 27 no. 1 I would be sensitive to the links between movements and to the transplantation of musical material (and the subsequent feelings of recollection this engenders) from one movement into another.

Indeed, after each of the first three movements of Op. 27 no. 1 there are no heavy double bars to indicate a cessation of musical momentum and a period of silence. Rather Beethoven wrote, between the first and second movements, *Attacca subito l'Allegro* (begin the Allegro at once), adding parallel *attacca* indications following the second and third movements as well. The only heavy double bar comes at the very end of the piece.

Composed in 1800–01, Op. 27 comes in the second of five periods of Beethoven sonatas. Having completed his Sonata Op. 22, about which he was particularly pleased, Beethoven moved on to further experiments in form beginning with the next sonata, his Op. 26 (more about this in Program 6). The Op. 27 sonatas continue to expand musical perceptions and the notions of what a sonata can be.

The pacing of Op. 27 no. 1 was unusual by contemporaneous musical expectations. Rather than beginning with a lively Allegro first movement, the opening is Andante. The harmonic rhythm is leisurely: only two harmonies—the tonic and the dominant—are heard for the first minute or so. Because of this relaxed pacing, subtleties of voicing and dynamics are particularly important.

When finally in m. 13 a surprise C major harmony is heard, the *pianissimo* dynamic draws in the listener. A slight leaning of the right hand to the top E of these chords can help impart a sense of quiet wonder in keeping with the fantasy element of the work.

When C major recurs as the allegro interruption beginning in m. 36, clean articulation—only slight pedaling—of the arpeggios along with the considerable contrast engendered by the *forte* and *piano* dynamics can help maximize the visceral excitement. On the surface, this mood is completely contrary to the gentle opening, but the music is still harmonically confined to the local tonic and dominant (C and G) with a brief foray into C minor in m. 57. I prefer to start this C minor phrase with a more gentle touch that both sets it apart somewhat from the phrases of a similar nature that precede it and gives it a longer trajectory, since after two measures it develops a crescendo that leads to *forte*. The fermata of the dominant seventh harmony in m. 62 can be held sufficiently long to allow the sonority to diminish to a soft enough level so that the recurrence of the music of the opening Andante can begin without a break in sound but at a *pianissimo* level. The crescendo and decrescendo in mm. 82–83 can be delicately sculpted to convey first the sense of leading toward the tonic harmony and then the sense of coming away from it. The final chord, *pianissimo, senza sordino*, is a hollow sound, which is filled in by the sudden and unbroken start of the next movement. In this fantasy nothing is wasted, for just as the surprise of C major in m. 13 led to the entire C major Allegro middle section beginning in m. 36, the C minor of m. 57 is more fully developed in the Allegro molto vivace second movement that follows.

A characteristic of the second movement is the rapid pulse of three, which leads first to playful syncopations within each measure in the trio and next, when the opening music of the scherzo recurs, to syncopations at a more intense level within the beat. A tempo that is too fast and that leads to a feeling of one beat per measure—rather than three beats per measure—will not allow the full impact of the syncopations to be felt (Examples 34a and b).

Careful phrasing in the opening of this movement can help heighten the dif-

Example 34a: Sonata Op. 27 no. 1, second movement, mm. 42–49. Syncopations in the trio.

Example 34b: Sonata Op. 27 no. 1, second movement, mm. 94–98. Syncopations within the recurrence of the scherzo. If the tempo is too fast, the feeling of syncopation will be lessened.

ference between the *piano* measures, which are legato within the bar, and the *forte* measures, which are staccato. When the music of the scherzo recurs, syncopated, the eighth-rests in the right hand are important, for they help impart a breathless feeling which adds to the excitement, whether the dynamic is *piano* or *forte*.

Once again, there is no break in sound as the scherzo movement leads to the Adagio. But finally, in contrast to everything that has come before, there is a distinct singing line throughout this movement. Voicing, therefore, is important, as are subtleties in the left-hand touch. For example, in mm. 13–16, when the right hand plays a line of syncopated octaves, the left hand is staccato for the only time in the movement. This contrast allows the top line to sing through more but also provides an accompaniment that is sharper-sounding than elsewhere. The cadential flourish that leads to the ensuing Allegro vivace covers a large registral range and is distinctly pianistic. I like to differentiate between the sixty-fourth notes of mm. 24–25 and the actual trill in m. 26: the trill is faster. The entire Adagio is closely aligned to the key of A-flat major (the subdominant of the home key of E-flat major), so the establishment of the dominant harmony in the last three measures (the pirouette measures) is crucial to the arrival back in the home key of E-flat major at the beginning of the Allegro vivace. In m. 24, the first of the last three measures, it is nice to bring out the bass descent as well as the flourish upward in the right hand. In m. 26 with its trill and two fermatas, the figure that meanders down one octave from the high A-flat can be shaped with slight dynamic fluctuations according to registral contour, arriving at the final A-flat, *pianissimo*.

At the beginning of the Allegro vivace, which again enters without a break in sound, the left hand should be well articulated in order for the right to be heard distinctly, and the right pedal used only sparingly. When the main theme is played in chords (without the sixteenth-note accompaniment) in mm. 25–35, enough time should be taken before the *piano* echos so that the contrasts between the dynamic levels are maintained and the *piano* chords—even the first of each group—stand out. This is part of the vitality of the movement.

Aside from this section and the corresponding section in which the musical material recurs (mm. 191–203), the sixteenth-note accompaniment is incessant—with one exception: the most improvisatory area of this movement, mm. 139–166. It follows the more intense development area in which the main theme is played in different registers and harmonies (mm. 106–138). It can be played as though searching spontaneously for just the right harmony, as the music descends by thirds from the dominant B-flat octave of m. 139, gradually and incrementally leading back to the home key of E-flat when the opening theme is heard once again. The sequence of dynamics—*pp*, crescendo, crescendo, *p*—in mm. 160–167 gives the idea of starting in a direction, leading somewhere, then starting over again, contributing to the overall idea of fantasy and stylized improvisation. I keep the *pianissimo* until the crescendo marking in m. 163, build up the sound, then drop back to *pianissimo* again in m. 165, and again build up the sound with the ensuing crescendo until the *piano subito* in m. 167 when the theme recurs.

At the end of the movement we are left suspended on the dominant harmony, where the music of the Adagio recurs, no longer in A-flat major, but rather in the home key of E-flat major. A fantasy involves the recurrence of musical elements, but even though this recurrence surprises a listener, the home key lends feelings of reminiscence and, in a sense, of the beginning of the end. Only the first phrase of the Adagio is played, and as the cadence at the end of this phrase is first repeated and then postponed, the feeling of improvisation—of spinning out the line—deepens.

Beethoven, and the pianist, have one little trick left—a Presto coda. Of course it enters *attacca* (at once, without a break), drawing its musical impetus from the interval of a descending third, first heard at the very beginning of this work and then again at the start of the last movement. But the syncopated left hand harks back to the syncopations of the second movement, and once again, the tempo should allow for clarity of these syncopations and for the offbeat sforzandos. The final flourish is brilliant and virtuosic, and the last two chords impart a special air of finality, for not only are they *fortissimo*, they are also the only V–I cadence at the end of a movement in this work.

THE CHALLENGES of playing Sonata Op. 78 are different from those of the previous two sonatas on this program. Although Op. 78 is a much shorter work, its themes are more concentrated and it is more intense in manner, but it is also more intimate and evanescent. This sonata, one of Beethoven's favorites, offers subtle glimpses into the future: the concentration on small thematic motives is characteristic of the organic, meticulously composed works of the last period, works in which every nuance is an integral part of the whole. Distinctions between melody and accompaniment begin to dissolve in Op. 78 as thematic motives of equal importance are frequently juxtaposed as counterpoint. The very nature of its closely interrelated themes demands that each be as fully characterized and realized as possible, played so as to distinguish each theme individually but nonetheless to weave them all into a carefully constructed luminescent musical fabric.

Sonata in F-sharp major Op. 78 was composed in 1809. Its immediate predecessor, Sonata Op. 57 ("Appassionata"), was completed five years earlier; extroversion gave place to intimacy. A precedent for the two-movement scheme of Op. 78 is Sonata Op. 54, both movements of which are also in the same mode (F major). But both two-movement sonatas that followed Op. 78—namely Op. 90 and Op. 111—are of a different dramatic scheme; the first movement is more turbulent and in a minor mode (E minor and C minor respectively), and the second movement is lyrical and introspective, in a major mode (E major and C major, respectively).

Sonata Op. 78 is in the fourth of the five groups of Beethoven sonatas; three of this group (which also includes Sonatas Opp. 79 and 81a) are heterogeneous in character, and although they do not include weighty slow movements, they foreshadow in their concentrated thematic focus the late sonatas, which were to follow with Sonata Op. 90, composed some five years later.

The themes of Sonata Op. 78 are closely related, and I try to be precise in interpreting the musical markings in order to give each theme its own character, thereby setting each into relief against the others and simultaneously creating a sense of musical unity that encompasses the entire work. For example, the opening figure of the Allegro ma non troppo is abstracted throughout the exposition, both melodically and rhythmically (Example 35).

In the development, as the same rhythmic figure forms a counterpoint to the right-hand sixteenth-notes, I shape the subtle dynamics of the right hand to mirror the contour of the phrase. The dynamic level falls slightly as the line does; the left-hand dynamics reflect local harmonic changes, particularly the series of dominant-tonic resolutions (Example 36).

Among the most expressive markings of the first movement is Beethoven's *te-nu-te* (holding back) which he specified in m. 24 (and again in m. 83) for

Example 35: Sonata Op. 78, first movement.

Example 36: Sonata Op. 78, first movement, mm. 47–51. I shape the dynamics to reflect the contours within the phrase.

three left-hand chords. At this point he also added an articulation marking for the right-hand sixteenth-notes:

I play these three beats at an immediately slower tempo, with a sonorous left hand and articulated right hand so that the first and fourth sixteenth-notes of each beat receive a little extra weight. This pattern, of course, is another manifestation of the opening rhythmic cell , setting up the top C-sharps as a steady line under which harmonies evolve to the cadence in mm. 27–28 (and mm. 86–87).

This same dotted rhythm ( ) forms the basis for the first of the two themes of the second movement. However, the rhythmic values are doubled ( ) and the metrical position is changed so that the figure begins on the downbeat (Example 37). The feeling is thus completely different, much more akin to the half-cadence figure first played in mm. 31–32 in the first movement.

The incorporation of the dotted rhythm in the second movement changes the character of this figure; the second chord is played with a sharper sound, as is the eighth-note downbeat of m. 2. The entire figure, although *forte* both in mm. 31–32 of the first movement and at the beginning of the second movement, is more incisive in the latter.

Another musical motive in this movement is the grouping of sixteenth-notes by twos. (This motive foreshadows linear aspects of the first theme of Sonata Op. 109.) The barring of these groups by twos rather than by the more conven-

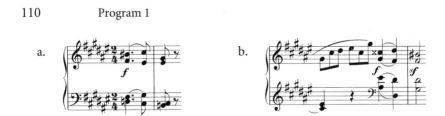

Example 37: Sonata Op. 78, second movement, opening figure (a), which is closely related to the figure from mm. 31–32 of the first movement (b) and to the dotted rhythmic figure of m. 1 of the first movement.

tional four sixteenth-notes—and this is very clear in the autograph score—is a direct indication that Beethoven had in mind detached two-note groups (even though playing four notes in a group is sometimes easier) and that he intended the feelings of breathlessness that this treatment engenders as the second note of each group is detached from the first of the following. The left-hand line therefore should really be as legato as possible, contrasting vividly with the right-hand groups above it and creating a situation of further contrast when the two-note groups alternate between the hands (mm. 22 on). Because of the *forte* dynamic and the very nature of the two-note groups, I play this area with a lot of energy. This vigor is further intensified in mm. 57 on, when the pedal is employed (and the left hand is staccato), now *fortissimo*. Because of the long pedal marking, I use a sharp staccato touch in the left hand and detach the right-hand groups sharply as well, creating a very bright sound.

In keeping with the jocundity of this movement, I like to hold the fermatas in mm. 175, 176, and 177 a long time, allowing the surprise to build with each harmony. I then play the final six measures back in tempo, with the left hand as the main line. The rambunctious character of this coda comes in complete contrast to the quiet dignity of the opening Adagio cantabile of the sonata; even though this piece lasts less than eleven minutes, it creates a fully expressive universe.

Sonatas Opp. 53 ("Waldstein"), 54, and 57 ("Appassionata") form the third of Beethoven's five groups of sonatas. Op. 53 is the first of the post-Heiligenstadt sonatas, and, along with his Symphony No. 3, Op. 55 ("Eroica"), immediately and palpably demonstrates his extraordinary resolve to continue to develop his artistry.

Expressive qualities of Sonata Op. 53 push to new heights the limits of what could be demanded from the piano. Virtuosity is not demonstrated exclusively through loud playing but rather by exquisite control: each movement of the "Waldstein" Sonata begins *pianissimo*, and among the most frequently used dynamic markings is *sempre pianissimo* (always very soft).

Count Waldstein was a connoisseur of music, but he was also the first to recognize—in 1787—the extraordinary gifts of the young Beethoven and to bestow assistance upon the young genius in such ways as not to offend his sensibilities. Therefore, Beethoven's dedication of this sonata to the count years later was the gesture of a mature man and the proof of gratitude; hence the nickname of this sonata. Sketches for this work appear in the "Eroica" sketchbook which Beethoven used from approximately June 1803 to April 1804.

Referred to as Landsberg 6, the sixth volume in the formerly private collection of Ludwig Landsberg (1805–1858), the "Eroica" sketchbook had been in the Preussische Staatsbibliothek in Berlin but was missing after World War II. In the mid-1970s it was located in the Biblioteka Jagiellonska in Krakow. This sketchbook also contains entries of early ideas for the Fifth Symphony Op. 65 and the Sixth Symphony ("Pastoral") Op. 68, as well as entries for the Triple Concerto Op. 56. But the two major works sketched extensively are, in fact, the Third Symphony ("Eroica") Op. 55 and the "Waldstein" Sonata.

On 6 August 1803 the French piano firm of Érard made a present of a piano to Beethoven. (It is unknown whether this is the date that the piano was sent from Paris or the date on which Beethoven actually received it.) This instrument still survives; its highest note is c^4—higher than the f^3, the previously accepted upper limit of the piano. Sketches for the coda of the first movement and the finale Op. 53 include notes higher than f^3; Beethoven used the expanded registral compass of the Érard piano in this work.

Both the "Eroica" Symphony and the "Waldstein" Sonata are strikingly original—even revolutionary. (Tovey declared in *A Companion to Beethoven's Pianoforte Sonatas* that with the "Waldstein" Sonata Beethoven crossed the Rubicon, referring, of course, to Julius Caesar's famous crossing of the River Rubicon that forever enlarged the scope of the Roman Empire.) In both, the sonata form is expanded well beyond its previous conceptions. Initially the "Waldstein" was to be a full three-movement sonata until Beethoven reluctantly decided that including a full Andante before the unusually spacious Rondo would be too vast a scheme even for him. The Andante was removed (and published separately in 1805—the same year as the sonata—as the independent Andante favori (WoO 57). In its place Beethoven composed a shorter and more profound Adagio introduzione to the Finale.

The importance of the roles of the first note—the bass C—cannot be over-emphasized. Locally the ear can hear it in two ways: as beginning the bass chromatic descent to the dominant (C–B–B-flat–A–A-flat–G) in m. 13 and as skipping up a tenth to the right-hand chords that immediately follow (Example 38).

The latter, of course, is wrong, for the right-hand eighth-rest on the downbeat of the first measure is there to guard against this role. Therefore, I weight the left-hand chords slightly to the bottom, preserving the low Cs all the way throughout mm. 1–2 and continuing the vectorlike chromatic descent to the G octave in m. 11. This descent helps infuse the work with its unique tension and

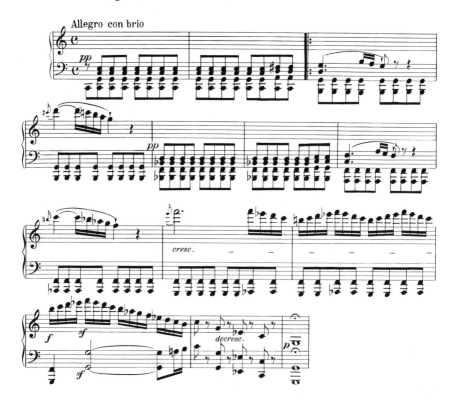

Example 38: Sonata Op. 53 ("Waldstein"), first movement, mm. 1–13. Note the chromatic descent of the bass from the initial C to the dominant G, first heard in m. 9 and then held under the fermata of m. 13.

urgency. The first right-hand chord comes in very softly, almost secondary to the low C. (But in the Rondo the long, arching melody does in fact start from the same low C, which is still played by the left hand.) Although the harmonic motion is striking, it actually proceeds quite slowly; therefore, I like a fast tempo —Allegro con brio, *pianissimo*—creating the feeling that the opening chords are pulsating restlessly.

The bass underpinning continues to be of crucial importance, for when the music resumes after the fermata on the dominant (m. 13), the left-hand line moves upward, expanding rapidly toward B major, a surprising harmonic move. I make sure the crescendo in mm. 21–22 continues all the way through to the *piano subito* in m. 23, setting up the arrival of B major dramatically. The B major harmony here must have a palpable presence; it cannot be too soft—it is marked only *p*, not *pp* as in the opening of the piece. Heard retrospectively as the dominant to E major, it helps establish the smooth transition to the second theme which is in the mediant key (E major), an unusual key relationship. (This key relationship is first explored in Sonata Op. 31 no. 1, but everything in Op. 53 is on a grander scale.) In no previous sonata had Beethoven characterized the themes so strongly; the unexpected choice of key for the choralelike second theme enhances the overall contrast.

The marking for the second theme, *dolce e molto legato*, implies voicing the chords to the top (as initially indicated by the upper-voice stems). Both hands are legato, and changing fingering on several keys after playing them is frequently the only way to achieve a smooth, connected sound. When this theme becomes somewhat abstracted by triplets in the right hand, I let the left-hand chords become the melodic anchor.

In the development, the left hand again leads the changes in the chromatic harmonies while the right hand plays fragments of the first theme in different harmonic settings. Sensitivity to the roles of the harmonies and to the dynamic indications is crucial to the propulsion here. I lead with the left hand beginning in m. 112 when harmonies amass as notes are sustained.

So far the music has progressed through many harmonies but has not been particularly centered around the home key of the piece—C major. However, the low *pianissimo* G in m. 142 brings an incipient feeling of expectation, which can be heightened by clearly articulating all the sixteenth-notes (particularly those in the low bass) and by keeping the dynamic level very soft until the crescendo in m. 151. This crescendo leads to the first F-natural in this passage, *forte*, in m. 152, establishing the local G harmony as a massive dominant preparation for the return to C major. The key of C is finally established in dramatic fashion in m. 156, as the hands come together in contrary motion, *fortissimo*, dropping immediately to *pianissimo* at the return of the opening theme.

The next surprise is the A-flat in m. 168. In the exposition, and indeed what we would expect here, the corresponding note was G. The A-flat leads not only to a brief local excursion away from literal restatement of the opening music, but ultimately and chromatically to the recurrence of the second theme in A major. To help emphasize the importance of this A-flat, and to add as much drama as possible to the initial surprise of hearing it, I take a small amount of time before playing it.

At the beginning of the coda, when the repeated chords of the main theme are played by the left hand (m. 261), the tension of prolonging the final cadence to C major can be increased by giving each right-hand syncopated octave a slight accentuation. This adds a new dimension—rhythmic strength—to the theme that has already been heard repeatedly. Both chords under the fermatas in mm. 282 and 283 can be held a long time, for the music is about to lead to the second theme finally in C major—the home key; the end is near. Once again, for the final statement of the main theme beginning in mm. 295, I weight the left-hand chords subtly to the bass, allowing the chromatic line to lead to the low G. The final chords are sharp staccato, pedal used for each one to enhance sonority. Hands are held over the keyboard for the rests in the last measure, ensuring the piece is framed in silence.

I consider this sonata to be in two movements, with the Introduzione: Adagio molto as a true introduction to the Rondo: Allegretto moderato. Unlike the Andante that Beethoven had originally intended as a second movement for this sonata, the Introduzione does not stand on its own musically; rather it is meant to prepare us expressively and emotionally for the Rondo that follows. The choice of key—F major—is the same as that of the original Andante, but in the Introduzione the feeling is more concentrated, more focused. In several other instances during this general period Beethoven composed slow movements that are linked directly to the finale: in the Sonata Op. 57 ("Appassionata"), the Fourth and Fifth Piano Concertos Opp. 58 and 73, in the last of the String Quartets Op. 59, and in the Violin Concerto Op. 61. However, in each case, the musical context is different. For example, the last movement of the "Appassionata" Sonata breaks in dramatically, *fortissimo*, whereas the Rondo of the "Waldstein" slips in gently, *pianissimo*.

Although very different in character and function from the first movement, the Adagio molto begins with an analogous descending bass chromatic line. As in the first movement, this line generates tension and a feeling that anything can happen. Following a tenor melody, based on the opening dotted figure, the chromatic descending bass line returns, this time continuing to G, the dominant of C, the eventual goal. The enharmonic change of A-flat to G-sharp allows the music to proceed to the point of the cadence, which, prolonged by a fermata and spanning the bass, middle, and upper registers of the piano, increases the anticipation of the resolution into the beginning of the Rondo.

The tenuto markings in the right hand and the portato articulation insure a feeling of hesitancy. Ascending intervals, initially hollow, are filled in with counterpoint beginning in m. 10 but return gaping even wider in m. 23 as octave Fs in huge, tension-fraught, dominant ninth chords. The sforzando markings here are placed carefully on the left-hand A-flats and the right-hand Fs that follow, not on the G–F pairings, thus giving these A-flat–F combinations even more dynamism. The dynamic markings and different types of phrasing indications are far more concentrated in this Introduzione than in the first movement. The sound—the playing—is intense, not relaxed; the expressive function of the movement is to create tension that is diminished only with the texture and melodic line of the Rondo.

I hold the last note of the Introduzione long enough so that the sound diminishes of its own accord nearly to the *pianissimo* with which the Rondo begins. The texture is shimmering, the melodic line beginning with the low C floats both above and below the mist of the accompaniment. Tempo is indeed moderate, and judicious use of the pedal—raising the dampers just barely off the strings—for the durations indicated by Beethoven is an invaluable and integral part in this music.

So is the unusual disposition of the hands. The hands are crossed: Beethoven indicated for the left hand to play the melodic line in the part of the keyboard most often reserved for the right, and vice versa. Why? Try playing this passage (mm. 1–23) in the more traditional manner, with the right hand in the upper register (the melody) and the left hand in the lower and middle register (the low C and then the "accompaniment"). It's too easy, and the pedal markings make less sense when the music is played this way. But using the hands—and the feet!—as Beethoven indicated forces a pianist to take greater care with everything: it's more difficult to play a melodic line with the left hand crossed over the right, but by doing so, I take greater care, ensuring a more legato and singing tone. Similarly the right hand can make the sixteenth-note accompaniment very light, just barely present, if great care is taken. But perhaps the most important aspect is linking the low C to the top G, the same low C that began the first movement and is now an important aspect of the melodic line (not the accompaniment). More conventional disposition of the hands is assumed when Beethoven has the top line of the theme in octaves (m. 31). But still, the first note—the C—is indicated as belonging to the main line, for it is consistently detached from the remaining three sixteenth-notes of the first beat:

The pedalings designated by Beethoven at the opening of the Rondo, the very particular use of the hands, the *pianissimo*, the expansive harmonic rhythm, and the slightly raised dampers all make for extraordinary music. Removing any of these elements undermines the entire concept, a delicate and evanescent edifice that contributes mightily to the expressive revolution embodied within this work.

Whereas the first movement progressed quickly away from C major, the Rondo stays firmly embedded in this key for quite some time. At the third iteration of the theme in immediate succession, the feeling is of overt brilliance rather than of quiet reflection, for the dynamic is *fortissimo* with a trill under the top of the theme. I play the trill with the fingering 1–2 and use 4 and 5 for the notes of the theme.

This Rondo, Allegretto moderato, is among Beethoven's most sophisticated, with sonatalike development and modulations, and careful and thorough markings. The two explosive middle episodes are in minor keys closely allied with the C major tonic—A minor (the relative minor) and C minor (the enharmonic minor). The leisurely pace suggested by the indication Allegretto moderato is in contrast to the driving pace of the first movement and the sense of inevitable forward motion generated by the descending chromatic bass—although slow—

of the Introduzione. The Allegretto designation also allows for the prestissimo coda—in which the Rondo theme is further developed—to contrast greatly in pacing, for prestissimo is the fastest possible. The brilliance of this coda, replete with octave glissandos and luminescent trills, is unprecedented.

To guard against higher levels of dynamics in the quasi-development section that follows the second episode, Beethoven wrote six *pianissimo* indications, four *sempre pianissimo* indications, and one *sempre più pianissimo* indication—all in a span of only sixty-one measures (mm. 251–312). While there is in fact one *forte* outburst (m. 285)—a bluff on the dominant that hints deceptively at an immediate return to the main theme in the home key—the *pianissimo* along with the pedal markings suggest that the character of the theme is quietly, perhaps introspectively, undergoing a series of transformations; it will eventually emerge triumphantly, *fortissimo* (m. 313).

I allow the tempo of the Prestissimo coda to be dictated by the speed required by the octave glissandos (m. 465); the tempo therefore is necessarily very fast. The harmonic motion here is actually quite slow, and we have heard the theme many times by this point in the piece. A very fast surface tempo to conclude the work is brilliant and rousing.

There is one unusual marking left. The last two chords are only *forte*, not the *fortissimo* level of the three preceding chords. Should not the last two chords in an ending like this be the loudest? What defines the end of a piece? The last dominant-to-tonic cadence actually resolves—*fortissimo*—in m. 529, fifteen measures before the end. These last fifteen measures, therefore, are the final affirmation of the home key of this work (C major), and the pedal marking from m. 529 with no end allows for this tonality to resonate undisturbed through the final fermata. The chords in mm. 540–541 are *fortissimo* because they invoke the G–G–E of the Rondo theme one last time within this resonance. The final two chords are only *forte* because they are not part of the thematic motive; they simply conclude the resonance that had indicated the end of the work with the *fortissimo* Cs in m. 529. My perspective is not that the last two chords are softer than the preceding ones, but rather that the last two chords are indeed strong, fully resonant, and those immediately preceding are sonorous to an extreme (just as the tempo here is extreme). I find that this subtle distinction works well, particularly when the pedal is held all the way through the fermata.

PROGRAM 2

Sonata in A major, Op. 2 no. 2 (1795)

Sonata in E major, Op. 14 no. 1 (1798–99)

Sonata in G major, Op. 14 no. 2 (1798–99)

Sonata *quasi una fantasia* in C-sharp minor,
Op. 27 no. 2 ("Moonlight") (1801)

While the first program featured four sonatas selected for their stylistic diversity, this one focuses on four sonatas composed within six years of each other, 1795–1801. Beethoven's development of thematic motives had not yet reached the level of concentration first expressed in Op. 78, and the registral range of the piano was more restricted than in the "Waldstein" Sonata. Regardless, the four sonatas on this program contrast vividly with one another, and all are engagingly inventive.

Sonata in A major, Op. 2 no. 2, is a gentle and graceful work, the most playful of the three in this opus. From the beginning of the opening Allegro vivace, I use a light touch and clear articulation (well-rounded fingers!) as the opening interval (A–E) is manipulated to motivate the entire first theme area. The swirling counterpoint gives the impression of frisky new voices constantly being added, and the tempo can be quick enough to give a sense of urgent direction to the ascending lines, for the triplet thirty-second-note figures are not difficult to play fast. However, I believe that the *espressivo* marking in mm. 58–59 implies a lessening of tempo as well as a deeper quality of sound and touch. (The Sonata Op. 109 Prestissimo has two occasions in which *espressivo* is followed four bars later by *a tempo*.) Here, the beginning of this phrase marks the start of the second theme area, which contrasts with the first theme in mood (now somber rather than jaunty) as well as mode (now minor), and in articulation (primarily legato) and registral disposition (confined to the middle range of the piano). To lead to the *espressivo*, the rallentando extending from mm. 48–53 is gradual, resulting in a slower tempo for the cadential prolongation and in heightened feelings of anticipation in mm. 54–57 (Example 39).

Contrasts in touch help convey the differences in feeling between the first and second theme areas. Whereas the lines of the first theme area are tossed

Example 39: Sonata Op. 2 no. 2, first movement, mm. 47–60. The rallentando leads to a slower tempo for the second theme.

back and forth playfully between the two hands, the second theme, a single melodic line in the treble area, has a heavier, singing tone. The left hand accompanies and can play more lightly than the right, increasing in intensity as it ascends. Since I take Beethoven's fingering indications in the cascading octave triplet arpeggios (mm. 84–89) to indicate a smoothness of line as well as a display of brilliant virtuosity, I make sure not to rush the tempo in these measures and in those immediately preceding. However, to make a smooth transition back to the beginning of the exposition for the repeat (and to the beginning of the development after the second time through) I increase the slower tempo of the second theme area gradually over the next several measures, beginning with the scalar triplets in m. 92 that hark back to the music from m. 32.

The surprise move to C major to start the development is accentuated by the *forte* dynamic, but the *fortissimo* that follows in m. 129, helping force the chromatic shift to A-flat major, is even more dramatic. I wait a fraction of a second before playing the *fortissimo* G octaves at this point, allowing the dip into the lowest register of the bass of Beethoven's piano to be unexpected. While the right hand plays the Alberti figures first heard as the accompaniment to the melodic second theme, the left hand develops—works out—the opening motive (m. 1–8) in a series of different harmonic contexts. Each starts *fortissimo* anew, implying a natural diminuendo as the top line descends, the left hand crossing over the right.

The second part of the development is devoted to a working-out of the thematic motive first heard in mm. 9–16. I play the light-ink grace notes (m. 181 on) virtually together with the top note in the right hand, continuing the counterpoint of the middle voice in each case. At the end of the development, the four measures (mm. 220–223) are calando (dying away, both in volume and in speed), *pianissimo,* and legato, even though yet eighth-note chords are separated by rests. The touch here can be gentle and somewhat sustained by pedal, creating the impression that each chord is hovering, suspended in air until the next one sounds. Then the familiar music of the recapitulation breaks in, *forte*. The last measure of the movement—the rests held by the fermata—helps continue the feeling of resolution achieved by the final chords; as the fourth bar in the last phrase, the last measure is crucial to the four-bar phrase structure that pervades the movement.

The characterization of the slow movement of Sonata Op. 2 no. 2—Largo appassionato—is highly individual. Usually passion is associated with faster music, but here the slow and dignified music is of an ardor sincere and ingenuous. The detached bass is the line with the greatest amount of motion. (Such a detached bass—pizzicato—was used by Brahms in his own Sonata for Cello and Piano in F major, Op. 99.) The long, sustained right-hand chords in this movement stand in great contrast to the rapid motion of the top line of the first movement, and playing them with a weighty touch and a sense of solemnity helps create the quiet but impassioned mood. Throughout the movement, whenever the opening music is heard, the right hand is marked *tenuto sempre*; the left, *staccato sempre*. Yet even within these indications, there are enormous contrasts of touch and sound: consider the *fortissimo* D minor area in m. 58 and the *pianissimo* recurrence of D major in a higher octave in m. 68. The prolongation of the final cadence is again analogous to a long goodbye in Italian opera; a little extra emphasis on the low left-hand As, prolonging the six-four chord, heightens this feeling.

The reworking of the A–E interval that so motivated the first movement also helps to make the Scherzo frolicsome. Now it is heard only in arpeggiated fragments, ascending, played almost in an off-the-cuff manner. The longer lines of the Trio provide contrast, as does the minor mode, and the sforzando markings highlight the entrances of new implied voices. I consider the rests in mm. 31–32 to be within the rallentando of m. 29, and I resume the tempo primo only with the restart of the theme in m. 32. The rests, therefore, prolong the silent anticipation of the tonic, heightening the tension engendered by the *pianissimo* dominant chord in m. 30.

In the Rondo: Grazioso the same A–E interval is expanded over a two-and-a-half-octave span. It would have been far easier for Beethoven to write simply two eighth-notes at the end of the first beat of m. 2 (and in analogous places), but instead, the sixteenth-rest following the sixteenth-note implies a lift, a breath, helping significantly to establish the graceful disposition of this movement. Whenever the theme recurs, the arpeggio is slightly different, but a sixteenth-rest always follows.

Contrasting with the smoothness and elegance of the first part of the Rondo, the middle section starts *fortissimo*, with staccato chromatic lines accompanying forceful dotted rhythms. The music drives forward; even when the lines are legato, *pianissimo*, and back in a major mode (m. 80 on) there is an underlying restlessness that is relieved only with the return in m. 100 of the main thematic A–E interval, now fully extended over three-and-a-half octaves! Quick changes of mood, touch, and tone color are needed in the coda of this movement (beginning in m. 148) to create a microcosm in which the principal nature of each theme resurfaces.

THE TWO Sonatas Op. 14 were composed in 1798–99. Both are rather intimate works of three movements. Although each begins with a sonata-form Allegro, neither sonata has a true slow movement. The middle movement of Op. 14 no. 1 is an Allegretto minuet and trio, and the last is a gently paced Rondo, Allegro comodo. Sonata Op. 14 no. 2—the more playful of the pair—enchants us with a theme with three variations (Andante) as its second movement. Usually a scherzo is found as a middle movement in a large-scale sonata (such as Op. 2 no. 2), but Sonata Op. 14 no. 2 concludes with a Scherzo, Allegro assai.

Beethoven arranged Sonata Op. 14 no. 1 for string quartet, transposing it to F major. In a letter dated 13 July 1802 to his publisher Breitkopf und Härtel, Beethoven explained his reasons:

> The *unnatural mania*, now so prevalent, for transferring even *pianoforte compositions* to stringed instruments, instruments which in all respects are so utterly different from one another, should really be checked. I firmly maintain that only *Mozart* could arrange for other instruments the works he composed for the pianoforte; similarly *Haydn* also—And without wishing to force my company on those two great men, I make the same statement about *my own pianoforte sonatas also*, for not only would whole passages have to be entirely omitted or altered, but some would have to— be added; and there one finds the nasty stumbling-block, to *overcome which one must either be the master himself* or at least have the same *skill and inventiveness*—I have arranged only one of my sonatas for string quartet, because I was so earnestly implored to do so; and I am quite convinced that nobody else could do the same thing with ease (Anderson 1961, 74–75).

At age thirty-two Beethoven was placing himself in the company of the great masters Mozart and Haydn, at least regarding musical arrangements of original works. Notwithstanding a page in the Kessler sketchbook on which the beginning of Sonata Op. 31 no. 1 is transcribed for string quartet, no other complete sonatas were arranged for other instruments. Beethoven had proven he could make such arrangements with Op. 14 no. 1, and in his mind there was no further need to repeat the feat.

A few words about the Kessler sketchbook. Currently in the Gesellschaft der Musikfreunde, Vienna, it was given to the pianist Johann Christoph Kessler (1800–1872) by the piano maker Carl Stein, who is thought to have bought it at the auction of Beethoven's estate. This sketchbook is among the few that are still intact; no leaves have been removed. Beethoven used it from winter 1801–02 to summer 1802 (Johnson et al. 1985, 124–129).

In keeping with the smaller formal scope of both Sonatas Op. 14, their main themes in all movements are more registrally confined than are the themes of many preceding sonatas, particularly Op. 2 no. 2 (Example 40a). Accordingly the Op. 14 sonatas are more immediately "singable"(Example 40b).

The lyrical qualities of Op. 14 no. 1 are apparent from the outset as the right hand plays its ascending melodic line accompanied by the pulsating left-hand chords. I like to voice these chords slightly to the top, for the right hand compresses the ascending line made by these notes (B–C-sharp–D-sharp–E) in m. 4 to conclude the first phrase. The initially simple four-bar phrase structure is extended beginning in m. 15 as the left hand rises chromatically, and the right hand increases in intensity with the crescendo to *forte* and the staccato half-note chords. I consider the staccato markings as referring to the quality of touch and sound—sharper touch, octaves almost plucked off the keys—rather than to the duration of the sound, for the fact that these are half-notes (and not eighth-notes) indicates that the sound can be held by the pedal, creating a more pointed and resonant sonority.

The phrase extension in m. 15 hints at more adventure to follow. In fact, the second theme of the Allegro starts with a simple chromatic line, initially without harmony, along any note of which a listener expects but does not receive a clarification of harmonic context. Suspense is generated, note by ascending note, each played portato and increasing in intensity. The chromaticism of the line is broken by the F-sharp (rather than F-natural) following E in m. 24. This

Example 40a: Sonata Op. 2 no. 2, third movement (Allegretto), mm. 1–4.

Example 40b: Sonata Op. 14 no. 1, second movement (Allegretto), mm. 1–8.

skip to F-sharp heightens the suspicion that we are in B major (the dominant) for this theme, a suspicion confirmed only with the cadence at the end of the phrase in m. 30.

In the development, changing fingers frequently on the top notes of the octaves can help establish the legato sound. Perhaps a very slight slowing down toward the end of the decrescendo in mm. 89–90 adds to the harmonic preparation for the return to the home key of E major, but there is no reason to take time before the surprise *forte* entrance of the recapitulation. Careful pedaling at the end of the movement will help ensure that too much sound does not accumulate, that the dynamic level remains *pianissimo*, that the movement ends gently.

The duet in octaves between the two hands at the beginning of the Allegretto establishes this movement as essentially a lyrical one, and by the direction of the note stems Beethoven has indicated that the voicing of the chords is of great importance. The crescendo in m. 62 over an empty two-octave span is a challenge. I use the pedal to ensure a blending of the two Es, and I try to make the second grow out of the sonority of the first, even though that sonority is less on the third beat than on the first. The crescendo marking guards against making the second E softer, which would otherwise naturally be the predilection, and thus helps establish the *piano* marking in the following measure to be a *piano subito*. This *piano subito* establishes an immediate contrast between the two sections—the E minor minuet and the C major trio that follows. Although the melodic lines of both are centered in the middle register of the keyboard, the minor-key minuet has a more restless feeling, for the harmonies tend to move away from the home key of E minor (tending more toward its dominant), whereas the trio is more centered upon its local main key (C major). The short coda combines the feelings—and qualities of touch—of both the minuet and the trio to conclude this songful movement.

The tempo of the last movement is designated as Allegro comodo—a comfortable allegro—implying a speed that is not too fast. As the initial right-hand octaves remain in the same register as the music heard at the beginning of the sonata, the descending left-hand triplets need to be well articulated so that the changing harmonies of the right-hand octaves can be heard. The second theme (m. 21 on) begins with a solo right-hand line that is initially harmonically ambiguous, as was the second theme of the first movement. However, instead of playing with the increasing intensity of an ascending chromatic line, I play the second theme here with questioning playfulness. Seriousness of mood is reserved for the development section; the virtuosic right-hand triplets are accentuated slightly on the first of each group to hint at an implied line. The dynamics of this line—although within the general level of *forte*—can be shaped with the rising and falling contours of the music. With parallel treatment of the left-hand octaves, this creates the area of greatest intensity in the entire work. The lilting syncopations in the coda—more thematic abstraction—are a further element of playfulness.

I LOVE to play Sonata Op. 14 no. 2. I love the way it begins, gently creating a melody from nothing, always moving subtly forward by small harmonic changes. Even the left hand is gentle and mellifluous: no crashing chords, no full chords—in fact, no chords of any sort. This is the first of Beethoven's sonatas to begin in this way. All the previous ones have significant simultaneities at the beginning, and except for Sonata Op. 109, so do all the following ones. When in Op. 14 no. 2 a texture involving chords finally does appear (m. 26—beginning of the second theme), the feeling is of a duet in the top line, rather than chordal accompaniment. In fact, the left hand still maintains a single-line texture until m. 36. The melodic fragments that gradually accrue as the themes grow invite a sensitive and tender touch, shaped by the gently rising and falling contour of the lines. Since each of the first two melodic fragments is repeated in the right hand the question might arise about whether to play the repetition of each fragment as an echo at a softer level. Perhaps the second one could be not so much softer as more wistful, more distant in memory, particularly since the left hand plays in a higher register and the sonority is therefore somewhat thinner.

With the addition of the B-flat to the thematic melody in m. 64, the beginning of the development is plaintive but still gentle. This melody is further transformed in the beginning of m. 81, when a *forte* octave appears for the first time, heralding the thematic line in the bass. The tension is heightened even further by the right hand's playing sixteenth-note triplets against the duple sixteenths in the left, and by the sharp staccato sixteenth-notes beginning in m. 84. Whatever slight rhythmic flexibility there might have been with this line at the start of the development is now gone; the two against three, the left-hand staccato marking, the *forte* dynamic all imply a strict pulse.

There is a small notational difference between the start of the false recapitulation (m. 98) and the beginning of the true recapitulation (m. 124)—the former has a sixteenth-rest following the fermata, whereas there is no rest whatsoever after the fermata for the latter. But this small difference is significant. The rest before the false return implies a breath, a lifting of the hand and foot, a fraction of a second of silence. But the lack of a rest before the true return, coupled with a sforzando marking on the leading-tone C-sharp, implies that the first D of the true return simply melts out of the sonority of the C-sharp, with the second D (the same register as the C-sharp) helping to complete the resolution and the feeling of return. The longer, sustained lines at the end of the recapitulation (as at the end of the exposition) lead into a short coda, in which the touch of the right hand (mm. 194–195) recalls the dramatic left-hand performance of the theme in the development, before breaking off in a sudden *piano* (m. 196), setting up the final cadences.

The chordal texture of the second movement certainly makes up for any lack of simultaneities in the first. This theme and three variations are charmingly inventive; more than rhythmic, harmonic, or registral transformations of the theme, it is the accompaniment of the main line—the counterpoint—that is varied as the music unfolds. Right before the last variation, Beethoven holds us in suspense—as if we are backpedaling—as the dominant harmony is repeated for four measures (mm. 61–64). The music can seem to begin evaporating here, time suspended, the harmony static but unresolved, and the dynamic level progressively softer. Pianistic touch becomes lighter and the pulse slightly relaxed as the right-hand chords are subtly voiced to the inside chromatic descent. Time is elongated once again in the final three measures, as the pace of the theme is augmented twofold. This helps set up the final chord, but its *fortissimo* dynamic—a huge joke that jolts everyone out of complacency—is always a surprise.

Playfulness continues in the following Scherzo. Although this movement is in triple meter, the main theme starts with three consecutive duplets, and rhythmic emphasis frequently shifts away from the downbeat. The resulting lilt lends the music a metrical unpredictability. In mm. 10 and 12, for example, I avoid any hint of an accent on the downbeat; the trajectory of the line is to the top right-hand C on the second beat. Only in m. 16 does the downbeat coincide with musical periodicity; hence the sforzando and fermata. By contrast the trio theme (beginning in m. 73) is firmly embedded in the triple meter, with the separate stems in the bass of the left hand (m. 77 on) forming another layer of counterpoint to the top line. But even the trio is not immune to musical joking, for the four measures of decrescendo (mm. 105–108) are an extension of the fourth consecutive eight-bar phrase, mocking and satirical in a good-natured way. The sforzandos in the coda make even more explicit the antics of the metrical instability of the main theme, and the *pianissimo* ending in the deep bass completes the escapade.

IMAGINE HEARING the "Moonlight" Sonata for the first time. Striking is the character of the adagio first movement, its gently veiled sonorities shifting subtly, wisps of melodic fragments floating above. Most apparent to a pianist is the three-part texture: the underlying bass, the undulating accompaniment, and the sustained, legato top line. The alla breve time signature implies a pulse of two beats per measure, even within Beethoven's designation of Adagio sostenuto, which guards against the music's becoming lugubrious. The big question is how to use the pedal. At the beginning of the movement, Beethoven included two indications for *senza sordini* (without dampers): *Si deve suonare tutto questo pezzo delicatissimamente e senza sordini* and *sempre pianissimo e senza sordini* (this whole piece ought to be played with the utmost delicacy and without dampers; always very soft and without dampers). Do these mean to keep the pedal down without changing it throughout the entire movement, or to use the pedal constantly but change it whenever necessary? I think the *senza sordini* indication is intended to create a special kind of sound—nothing dry, but sound bathed in its own warmth with hints of the surrounding harmonies. While I depress the pedal only slightly, just enough to raise the dampers off the strings to allow them to vibrate freely, the character of this movement requires the pedal to be changed discretely to avoid creating harmonic sludge.

The *senza sordini* indications at the beginning of the movement, which are not followed by any *con sordini* indications, are fundamentally different from the *senza* and *con sordini* indications in the Largo of Beethoven's Piano Concerto No. 3 or the pedal markings in Sonatas Op. 31 no. 2 ("Tempest") and Op. 53 ("Waldstein"), for these others have definite indications when the pedal should be depressed and when it should be lifted again. In Sonata Op. 27 no. 2 ("Moonlight"), *senza sordini* pertains to the entire first movement as a general approach to the quality of sound, similar to the initial *sempre pianissimo* indication.

It is this first movement for which the sonata is named, but not by Beethoven or even by his publisher. Ludwig Rellstab, a music critic, asserted that the mood of the first movement reminded him of the magic of the moonlight on Lake Lucerne.

The three-part texture that pervades this movement suggests different qualities of touch and sound for each different voice. The bass octaves are soft but deep, the undulating triplets are smooth and played with an accompaniment touch (flat, light fingers, not pressing too deeply into the keys), and the top line, although *pianissimo*, sings forth in a plaintive voice. In this Sonata *quasi una fantasia*, there is no second theme in the first movement—such were expectations stretched. The triplet accompaniment assumes a more melodic role and can be shaped accordingly as it is developed beginning in m. 32 on. Tension increases as new harmonies are explored, the bass remaining insistently on the G octave (the dominant) and the top line temporarily abandoned in favor of the searching qualities of the triplets.

In the short coda the portentous dotted rhythm (𝄢 ♪. ♪ | 𝅗𝅥.) is heard for the first time in the bass (but exclusively on G-sharps) as it exchanges registral placement with the triplets. The right-hand triplets come to the fore, however, in mm. 62–63 when the crescendo-decrescendo markings are intended for the right-hand only. The situation is reversed in mm. 64–65 as the passage is repeated but with the crescendo and decrescendo markings now in the left hand. (Examination of the autograph score reveals that these crucial placements of the crescendo-decrescendo markings are, in fact, correct.) As the movement ends as quietly as it began, Beethoven wrote *Attacca subito il seguente*—an element of fantasia heard also in Op. 27 no. 1—and the second movement begins without any break in sound.

The point of connection between the two is the enharmonic change from C-sharp minor of the first movement to D-flat major of the second. That is, the pitch of C-sharp is reinterpreted as D-flat, but now within a major harmony. For the performer this transformation takes place while the final C-sharp minor chord is still sounding within the fermata: the pianist's inner ear recasts the C-sharp as D-flat in preparation for delivering the surprise of the D-flat chord to the listener who in turn hears the transformation when this first chord is played. Despite the quicker pacing of the second movement, the mood is wistful and the textures delicate. The smooth lines of the Allegretto give way to sforzando syncopations in the trio, a contrasting spot of good humor in this sonata. I like to voice the left-hand chords in mm. 45–48 first to the tenor and then to the bass upon the repeat, giving a slight weight to the chromatic lines. Although the Allegretto ends with a rest, I would think it very much in keeping with *quasi fantasia* to begin the third movement almost right away. Once again, an enharmonic change (this time from D-flat major back to C-sharp minor) is the pivot point.

This last movement—Presto agitato—is the most extended of the three, and is the most overt dramatic center of the piece. I prefer a genuinely fast tempo; although the harmonic motion is not particularly rapid, finally the surface motion can be, and a feeling of agitation is generated from both speed and clarity. From the start a three-part texture analogous to that of the first movement is established: the bass line is distinct, the upwardly climbing sixteenth-note figures are a general middle area, and the top register is reached with the punctuated eighth-note chords, sforzando, staccato, in pedal (Examples 41a and b).

The tension in the music increases as the bass line descends chromatically from C-sharp to G-sharp (mm. 1–9), and intensity of touch can be increased by making both the left- and right-hand staccatos progressively sharper, especially with the melodic compression of mm. 7–9 and the concurrent crescendo.

Even during the melodic second theme (beginning in m. 21), I believe that the intensity level remains high and therefore use pedal only sparingly so that the left hand stays clear—and more concentrated and insistent than if it were blurred—as it accompanies the only "singing" line of the movement. Because of the intentionally discontinuous barring of the eighth-notes in m. 49 on, a breath of time can be taken so that the dialogue between the incisive *forte* and the songful *piano* measures is dynamically charged.

There are two fermatas, both over bare G-sharps, which is the dominant pitch and is hence fraught with expectations of resolution—one in m. 14 and the other in the parallel place in the recapitulation (m. 115). I hold these fermatas a long time. By creating feelings of suspense, seemingly spontaneously, they are crucial to the fantasia element, as is the four-measure cadenzalike passage in mm. 163–166, just four measures into the extended coda.

There seems to be textual confusion about use of the pedal in these four measures (mm. 163–166). The first edition (Cappi, Vienna, 1802) has *con sord.*

Example 41a: Sonata Op. 27 no. 2, first movement, mm. 5–7.

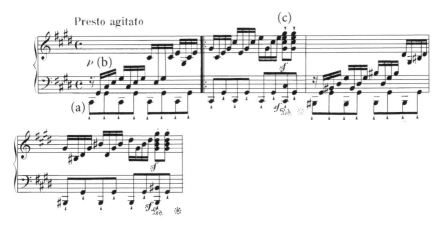

Example 41b: Sonata Op. 27 no. 2, third movement, mm. 1–4. The three-part texture (a, b, c) of the first movement is reestablished at the beginning of the third movement.

at the beginning of m. 163 (to countermand the *senza sord.* at the end of the previous measure), and *con sord.* again in m. 167. A *senza sord.* is missing. Plainly visible in the autograph, however, is this missing *senza sord.*; it is in m. 165. Thus, although the first of these flourishes is meant to be played with "normal" pedaling, the second is more intense, plays a more forceful harmonic role, and hence is played with the dampers raised. Possibly because of the deletion of the *senza sord.* marking in the first edition, subsequent editions are inaccurate. Universal Edition has no pedal markings whatsoever for mm. 163–166, but the Peters Edition has pedal markings for both flourishes, not just the second. Henle has no pedal marking for the first flourish (m. 163) but has a pedal indication for the second (m. 165), thus following the autograph score; this approach makes the most sense to me musically and seems the most expressive.

Although this sonata does not include a restatement of previous material (as did Sonata Op. 27 no. 1: the music of the Adagio was recalled at the end of the

Allegro vivace), there is a subtle hint of the spirit of the first movement in the gradual meandering descent following the trill in m. 187. For this reminiscence in shaping of line and general texture, I allow the trill to slow down to the tempo of the eighth-notes so that they follow effortlessly. Although soft and slow, the adagio octaves in mm. 188–189 begin to gather tension again, with the G-sharp octave ever so slightly louder than the F-double-sharp octave as it resolves into the final part of the extended coda. At the very end, the three-part texture finally melds into one as the sixteenth-notes and cadential chords sweep up and down the entire range of the piano. The *forte* in m. 196 (G-sharp in the right hand), the sforzando in the following measure (E in both hands), and the *fortissimo* on the first C-sharp chord are all important; by successively spelling the triad of the home key (G-sharp, E, C-sharp) they subtly help create the air of finality. Thus, after the G-sharp *forte* I would drop slightly in dynamics to reach an even more intense sforzando on the Es played by both hands, saving the most sonorous level for the *fortissimo* C-sharp chords.

The first movement of this work may be among Beethoven's best-known piano compositions. But the complete sonata, particularly the anguished drama of the last movement, offers an artistic experience so many times fuller that I would urge anyone who has played only the first movement to become immersed in the rest of the work.

Sonata in C minor, Op. 10 no. 1 (1796–98)

Sonata in F major, Op. 10 no. 2 (1796–98)

Sonata in D major, Op. 10 no. 3 (1796–98)

Sonata in A major, Op. 101 (1816)

This program is devoted to the sonatas of Op. 10 and Op. 101. Separated by some twenty years, they are pivotal to Beethoven's creative development in vastly different ways. The Op. 10 sonatas use the element of time (tempo) in more extreme ways than did the Op. 2 and Op. 7 piano sonatas that preceded it. Each sonata of Op. 10 contains either a Presto or Prestissimo movement, and Op. 10 nos. 1 and 3 include powerful slow movements as expressive centers. Op. 101 is the first of the sonatas in which the element of fugue plays an elevated role, a role it continued to play in each of the remaining last sonatas.

Beethoven worked on the three Sonatas Op. 10 simultaneously beginning in 1796, completing and publishing them all by 1798. The 9 October 1799 edition of the *Allgemeine Musikalische Zeitung* includes a review of Op. 10:

> It is not to be denied that Hr.v. B. is a man of genius, possessed of originality and who goes his own way. In this he is assured by his extraordinary thoroughness in the higher style of writing and his unusual command of the instrument for which he writes, he being unquestionably one of the best pianoforte composers and players of our time. His abundance of ideas, of which a striving genius never seems to be able to let go so soon as it has got possession of a subject worthy of his fancy, only too frequently leads him to pile up ideas, etc. Fancy, in the extraordinary degree which Beethoven possesses, supported, too, by extraordinary knowledge, is a valuable possession, and, indeed, an indispensable one for a composer, etc. The critic, who after he has tried to accustom himself more and more to Hr. Beethoven's manner, has learned to admire him more than he did at first, can scarcely suppress the wish that . . . it might occur to this fanciful composer to practice a certain economy in his labors. . . . This tenth collection, as the critic has said, seems deserving of high praise. Good invention, and earnest, manly style . . . well-ordered thoughts in every

part, difficulties not carried to an excess, an entertaining treatment of the harmony—lift these sonatas above the many (Thayer 1973, 278–279).

After having established himself with the four-movement sonatas of Op. 2 and Op. 7, Beethoven compressed the sonata to three movements in Op. 10 nos. 1 and 2. The first of these sonatas is dramatic and concise; the *forte* beginning of Sonata Op. 10 no. 1 makes audiences sit up in their chairs. The rhetorical style—propulsive dotted rhythms, abrupt dynamic changes, and C minor setting—is intense, passionate, and stormy. Music with these characteristics has been labeled Sturm und Drang (storm and stress, the latter implying an inner impulse rather than pressure), and is often associated with a Hollywood image of Beethoven shaking his fist at the heavens. The term actually derives from a German literary movement of the 1770s and was initially applied—retrospectively—to a period of Haydn's works in the late 1760s.

The opening flourish of the Allegro molto e con brio exemplifies the unambiguous manner in which harmonies are presented, as well as spanning the compass of the treble register of the pianoforte as it then existed. The tempo can be brisk, although for metrical strength and clarity, it is important to maintain a pulse of three beats per measure rather than a pulse of one. I like to make the most of the dynamic contrasts; one *pianissimo*, two *piano*, three *forte*, and four *fortissimo* markings concentrated within only the first thirty-two measures reveal an intense and fiery spirit. With a concern for unity, already characteristic of Beethoven, the right hand G–E-flat from m. 1 is transformed from a propulsive dotted figure into a gentle, even rhythm at the beginning of m. 32 (Examples 42a and b).

Example 42a: Op. 10 no. 1, first movement, opening.

Example 42b: Op. 10 no. 1, first movement, mm. 32–36.

Although the harmonic motion beginning in m. 32 is actually faster than in the first theme, the surface motion is slower, and the music flows at an ambling pace.

The long lyrical lines of the second theme contrast with the short motivic fragments of the first, but rhetorical qualities—particularly large registral spans, such as the two-and-a-half-octave leap in m. 71—are still ubiquitous. The development section is primarily *piano*, but the crescendo and decrescendo markings in mm. 125–128 ensure that the high point is the dissonant E–E-flat in m. 127, thus heightening the quiet tension here. The movement could end at the penultimate cadence (m. 281) in the coda: the home key of C minor has been reestablished; the recapitulation is complete. Therefore, I elongate the rests in that measure ever so slightly, giving the impression that the movement is indeed finished. As a result of this slight delay, the *fortissimo* final cadence becomes a surprise, consistent with the high drama throughout.

The registral leaps and juxtapositions of dynamics of the first movement are smoothed in the florid Adagio molto. I use as singing a tone as possible, with gentle but firm pressure on the keys. The quality of sound in the *forte* areas (for example, m. 17 on) is different from the *forte* areas of the first movement: the sound here is deeper and rounder. The music reaches an expressive apex in mm. 98–99 as the theme is abstracted into octaves in the top line with full harmonies and syncopation to support—here it is nice to expand slightly in time as well as in dynamics.

Throughout this second movement, the general harmonic motion is very slow, although within the most ornate figures the surface motion is rapid. The general form and operatic character of this movement resemble those of the Adagio of Sonata Op. 2 no. 1 more closely than does any other slow movement of a preceding sonata. Sonata Op. 2 no. 1 is also the only other minor-key sonata to date; perhaps Beethoven felt that this lyrical style of major-key slow movement—rather than the more declamatory slow movements of Sonatas Op. 2 no. 2, Op. 2 no. 3, and Op. 7, which are far more registrally confined—acted as more of a dynamic foil to the dramatic intensity of the minor-key first movements. In any case, this Adagio was the last such lyrical sonata slow movement Beethoven was to write; Sonata Op. 10 no. 2 lacks a true slow movement, and the impassioned Largo e mesto of Sonata Op. 10 no. 3 is Beethoven's first sonata slow movement in a minor key, a radical point of departure. Beethoven never returned to the style of a florid slow movement in a piano sonata.

The Prestissimo begins in an urgent whisper, as the terse first theme develops gradually over three statements of the initial rhythmic motive, analogous to the manner of motivic development in the first theme area of the first movement. After a long fermata, the more melodic second theme of the Prestissimo also accrues over three statements of its own motivic kernel. Registral leaps and dynamic extremes (*ff* to *p*) abound. Tension builds throughout this movement as Beethoven eschews any cadence on the home key (C minor). When it is finally attained in m. 100, the music begins to feel more like an ending. Since it stays in this key for only two measures, and to heighten the surprise of the entrance of the bass A-flat in m. 102, I wait slightly after the last chord of m. 101. The restatement of the second theme in the unlikely key of D-flat major (dominant of the relative major) is quasi-improvisatory, with flexibility of pulse; here Beethoven has specified both ritard and calando.

The flourish of a dominant arpeggio (briefly reminiscent of those of the first movement) leads into the coda, which concludes dramatically but softly with three descending statements of the opening motive. The concluding harmony is major, but the particular disposition of the final chord (right hand crossing over to play the low C, the dominant rather than tonic pitch as the highest note) makes the cadence seem not quite final. I do not slow down here. There is no ritard, only a decrescendo; the pacing of the music remains steady, and the fermata over the eighth-rest ensures the silence necessary for the drama to resolve.

WHEN I START to play Sonata Op. 10 no. 2, my feelings are completely opposite to those that I have when I start its immediate predecessor: in Op. 10 no. 2 declamation gives way to questioning, stormy weightiness to gentle playfulness. Careful articulation of the sixteenth-note triplets (as in m. 1), separating them from the staccato quarter-note that follows—as Beethoven notated—contributes to the clarity of texture and the frolicsome nature of this figure. It also allows for a marked contrast with the longer legato arched line that follows. Since the apex of the crescendo in m. 7 is actually on the B-flat (rather than on the C, the highest note of the line), the dynamics of the phrase help leave us suspended on the dominant until the next four-bar unit brings us back, although only briefly, to the tonic key (F major). The offbeat sforzandos (m. 31 on) accentuate the interplay between the soprano and alto lines in a fleeting excursion into a four-part texture before leading to the second theme area. Careful grading of dynamics also adds to the rich mosaic of thematic adventures, which reach their virtuosic zenith with the crossing of hands for the right-hand trills in the bass and then the treble registers.

The development area is rhythmically motivated by sixteenth-note triplets (first heard in m. 1); a steady pulse is of the utmost importance throughout the shifting harmonies. This pulse is abandoned with the fermata in m. 117, which leaves us hanging—in registral extremes—awaiting the recapitulation, but as a musical joke in the "wrong" key (D major; see Chapter 5 on humor). The "correct" key (F major) is reestablished, but not before a tangential hint at G minor, even further afield. The *pianissimo* here (m. 130) is the only time this theme is so soft; the dynamic markings are significant and help infuse this area with feelings of amiable questioning.

In keeping with the light-hearted character of this work, there is no true slow movement. Instead, the middle movement of Sonata Op. 10 no. 2 is an Allegretto (minuet and trio). But it is in a minor key (F minor), songful and searching in mood. The opening of this movement—initially empty octave unisons—is the longest legato line of the sonata. I use a touch to make a sound that is as smooth, bell-like, and hollow as possible, moderating only when harmonies subtly accrue beginning in m. 5—fingers well curved, wrists flexible, light pedal leading into a deeper, weightier sensation. The appoggiaturas—rinforzando—(m. 23 on) are poignant but are still played *piano*.

In playing the opening of the trio, I voice the portato chords slightly to the top but still maintain the warmth of the lower register in this new D-flat major texture. Nuances of touch, phrasing, and dynamic shading are many, particularly as the line ventures higher (m. 49) and is enriched with syncopated sforzandos and running eighth-note counterpoint (mm. 54–55 on). Avoidance of a well-established D-flat major grounding (despite the change of key signature for the trio) and a preponderance of four-bar phrases concluding in local cadences involving minor harmonies make this section seem restless as it yearns for harmonic stability. When D-flats—as hollow octaves (m. 119)—begin to be reinterpreted as the flatted-sixth degree of F minor and thereby take on a more ominous character, the sound can be direct, very soft, but portentous. Syncopations within the counterpoint of the main theme and crescendos intensify the music of the stylized minuet when it returns. This entire movement—although an Allegretto—is neither light nor playful. The tempo needs to be spacious enough to allow for both clarity of voicing and for tension in the syncopated areas.

The final movement (Presto) of this sonata, however, is lithe and jaunty. Although it is much easier to slur the groups of four sixteenth-notes into the following eighth-note, Beethoven marked them as separated, and playing them as such gives the music more of its characteristic lift (Example 43).

The *forte* heralding the change of key at the beginning of the development area comes as a surprise. This section of the piece has the most rapid rate of harmonic change, and clarity in voicing of the mock fugato gives the impression that the music is swirling all around us. In m. 87 on, although the only dynamic indication is *fortissimo*, the counterpoint to the theme—the running sixteenth-notes—can be shaped by their contour, falling in dynamic level slightly as they

Example 43: Sonata Op. 10 no. 2, third movement, mm. 1–4. In mm. 3 and 4 play as phrased, guarding against connecting the sixteenth-notes to the eighth-notes that follow.

descend, rising in level as they ascend. This concept applies to the overall shape of the thematic line as well. Since both sections of this movement are repeated and the last four measures are marked *fortissimo*, I save a little strength for the last time through, making the last cadence the most conclusive.

THE ENERGETIC opening line of Sonata Op. 10 no. 3—complete with fermata at the end—augurs a substantial work. It is, in fact, the longest and most weighty sonata of Op. 10. It is also the first Beethoven sonata with a slow movement in a minor key—no small matter, since slow movements by Beethoven as well as by his classical predecessors Haydn and Mozart were generally in a major mode. This movement, Largo e mesto, is the expressive center of the work, unrivaled in stature and emotional depth until the Adagio sostenuto of Op. 106, composed more than two decades later.

Clear articulation of the sonata's opening line is of utmost importance not only for the beginning but also because this line recurs in many different ways, with contrasting articulation, throughout the entire work. The first four notes are taken up and reinterpreted immediately, legato, beginning in mm. 4–5. They are played in a different guise beginning in m. 53 and form the basis for the four-note motive that permeates the rest of the exposition, starts the development, and ushers in the coda. The very first interval of the Presto also serves as a starting point and expressive source for the Largo e mesto. And the main theme of the last movement—Rondo: Allegro—is a reinterpretation of the next three pitches of the Presto's opening line.

As the opening line rises and increases in intensity, it is natural to increase the dynamics slightly. I also make the staccato notes a bit sharper as the line ascends. But the real crescendo should be saved until m. 18, where the line is syncopated and its trajectory leads beyond the A of m. 4 to F-sharp, *fortissimo*. This trajectory sets up the second theme, where a more languid touch conveys the contrast in character (now melodic) and mode (B minor, relative minor of the home key of D major). Frequently throughout the exposition, as fragments or elements of the main theme reassert themselves, often starting from a gentle, *piano* texture, careful pedaling is necessary to ensure signature staccato characteristics.

As the development begins by changing the familiar four-note motive from major to minor (m. 124–125), I would warn against taking any special time for the F-natural. Doing so would be too obvious; I would suggest instead a subtle change in touch from confident and assertive (though *pianissimo*) to questioning and introspective, as if wondering where the music could go from here. The establishment of the B-flat major harmony in m. 133 increases tension, and even though the theme is heard for the first time not in octaves or single notes but harmonized in thirds and sixths, the dynamic level should drop right away to *piano*, which makes the *fortissimo* in m. 141 all the more dramatic. Since the recapitulation begins *piano*, I hold the fermata of the preceding sforzando dominant chord (m. 184) until the sound has diminished sufficiently. The exploration of different harmonies in the coda (m. 306 on) can be as quasi-improvisatory as the beginning of the development, but the end of the movement is rousing and exciting.

In the slow movement—Largo e mesto (slow and sad)—the descending minor second of the initial theme (D–C-sharp) is transformed into a monument of expression. The meter and pulse is six beats to a measure, the chords are sonorous, and the top line sings mournfully above. Even though the music is slow, thirty seconds of music here must be infused with as much drama as thirty seconds in the first movement, although far fewer measures will be played. I like to make sure that the rests in the right hand beginning in m. 36 are felt; they are sighs, gasps (analogous to those in the restatement of the Arioso dolente in Sonata Op. 110). Even though the bell-like tolling continues in the bass, if the rests are not heard interrupting the top line, they lose their significance. Rests assume an even greater significance before the main theme recurs, when they are prolonged significantly, increasing tension silently (mm. 41–42). I know that there can be a tendency to rush a bit beginning in m. 65, particularly as the density of notes increases in the right hand as the line rises and the harmonies become more urgent, but I believe a steady tempo actually heightens the drama. In mm. 84–85 I voice the inside notes of both hands slightly while still keeping the outer Ds of each chord ringing clearly, and then play the ending two appoggiaturas with more tension on the C-sharp and less on the D. The final Ds are indeed very soft, barely resonating, and not held longer than their indicated values. The movement ends in silence, as the last rest is maintained by a fermata.

Believing that the tempo of a trio is basically the same as for the surrounding scherzo or minuet sections, I take the cue for the speed of the next movement from the triplets of the Trio. They are the fastest surface motion; their maximum speed determines the overall tempo for the Trio and the Menuetto as well. As an emotional foil to the inner turbulence of the Largo e mesto, the Menuetto is simple and uncluttered; careful voicing and phrasing keep it elegant. The Trio is more boisterous, with its crossings of hands and a *fortissimo* outburst in the middle.

The Rondo opens with a three-note motive, a transposition of the fifth, sixth, and seventh pitches of the Presto's main theme. Just as the first four notes of this figure play such a consuming role in the first movement, so do the next three notes now serve to motivate and indeed permeate the Rondo (Examples 44a and b). Instead of being staccato, they are now legato, but the staccato octaves from the opening theme of the Presto return in mm. 10–12. This is a playful movement, with many changes of direction and mood.

In m. 92 on, both the three-note and the four-note motives are played consecutively again, but the order is "wrong"—the three-note motive is first. Hence, the sforzando at the start of each four-note group is important to accen-

Example 44a: Op. 10 no. 3, first movement, mm. 1–4. Note that C-sharp–D–F-sharp are embedded (as the fifth, sixth, and seventh notes) in the opening motive.

Example 44b: Op. 10 no. 3, last movement, mm. 1–2. The opening motive is a transposition of C-sharp–D–F from the first movement.

tuate, for it helps point out the "mistake." The greater one's musical memory—recalling even subliminally the initial ordering of these pitches—the greater the joke. When the right hand emerges from the D octave in m. 106 to play its nearly chromatic scale up and down the keyboard, the inverted three-note motive in the left hand should predominate even in *piano*; the right should not obscure the left. The last note, the low D, is only a quarter-note, not longer; once again, as with Sonata Op. 10 no. 1, the fermata over the last rest ensures that the piece concludes in silence.

ALTHOUGH the first movement of Sonata Op. 101 is quiet, textures are smooth, and the tempo is spacious enough for a pulse of six eighth-notes per measure (not "in two"), feelings of unrest and even of yearning are engendered by avoidance of the tonic throughout. Intricate subtleties of voicing, dynamics, and phrasing are part of the master plan; not a stroke of the pen is wasted, nor is anything lacking. The music breathes initially in two-bar phrases, but it is continually propelled forward in search of a restful cadence. The character of the second theme area is even more concentrated than that of the first theme, with Beethoven forging a new phrasing indication in m. 16—a double slur and a staccato mark—to reveal a new level of expression:

(Years later, Brahms also used this combination of markings in some of his piano works.) I play each grouping as a single unit, with the most weight on the first note, which is connected as smoothly as possible to the second note, then a slight lifting of the finger before and after the third note. The dotted quarter-note that follows, although obviously held longer, is not necessarily heavier; too much weight would spoil the delicately constructed questioning spirit of the group.

When the line opens up in its largest registral span yet (m. 24), placement of the sforzandos is different for each hand (third beat for the left hand, fourth for the right). The left hand is syncopated; the sforzando sound is a quick accent, initially sharper than the rounder accentuation of the right-hand G-sharp. The high point of the line—the B that follows—is not accented, although it is the apex of the crescendo. Although this might seem contradictory, it isn't, for the sforzando suggests a quality of sound within the crescendo, which refers to quantity of sound. I like to take a brief moment before the *piano subito* B-seventh chord, which is in fact separated from the crescendo line by a break in the barring. At this tempo and with only one firm downbeat, six measures (mm. 29–34) are a long time to maintain a feeling of syncopation. Yet doing so is crucial to the ethos of restless yearning for a tonic (even a local tonic) cadence. The syncopations keep E major from feeling too firmly established, and keeping a strict pulse of six beats per bar will help maintain the feelings of syncopation.

The *molto espressivo* indication (m. 52) for the series of carefully voiced chords before the false recapitulation (in A minor) implies a slight lessening of the tempo and a deepening of touch. (So do *espressivo* indications in Sonatas Op. 2 no. 2 and Op. 109.) I regain the primary tempo in m. 58.

Syncopated chords, analogous to those of the exposition that led into the development, return in m. 81, and although A major (the home key) is attained, albeit in an indefinite manner, the crescendo on the tension-filled ninth chords that wrest away from A major leads into a coda. Although a feeling of arriving at a home key is gradually induced, none of the arrivals on the tonic chord are on strong beats. Even in the last measure, it is the dominant harmony—not A major—that is on the downbeat. The ending of this movement intentionally—courageously—leaves us hanging, waiting for a stronger resolution. The A of the final chord is immediately reinterpreted as the third of F major with the *attacca* start of the second movement.

In this intentional harmonic ambiguity and in several other dimensions as well, Sonata Op. 101 bears likeness to the two Op. 27 sonatas. The first movements of all three sonatas are of a pace slower than allegro, and reinterpretation of final pitches of one movement to beginning a following—generally without a distinct pause—is a defining element of a fantasia. In Sonata Op. 101 opening strains of the first movement are quoted explicitly to lead into the last movement; the only other instance of a reminiscence of this sort within a Beethoven piano sonata is in Op. 27 no. 1, in which the Adagio returns at the end of the last movement to lead into the coda. Sonata Op. 101 is also spiritually akin to the Sonata for Cello and Piano Op. 102 no. 1, which was composed about a year before Op. 101. The two works share special formal characteristics: a gentle Andante opening in 6/8 meter, leading to a lively movement in a 4-meter, and a recurrence of the music of the opening before concluding with a fast-paced movement in 2/4 meter. This general scheme is certainly not that of a typical classical sonata, and in fact, on the title page for Op. 102 no. 1, Beethoven wrote *Freie Sonata* (free sonata). The same could apply to Op. 101.

Beethoven began using German—along with Italian—for movement programmatic and character indications with Sonata Op. 81a and continued exclusively in German for the movement headings in Sonata Op. 90. With Sonata Op. 101 Beethoven again used both German and Italian. However, Op. 101 is the first sonata for which Beethoven, in a letter dated 23 January 1817 to his publisher Steiner, requested at once that on the title page "hereafter . . . in place of pianoforte, 'Hammerklavier' be printed" (Thayer 1973, 668). This change necessitated reengraving the title page, for the sonata itself was already in the hands of the printers. Furthermore, Beethoven was unsure about whether "Hammerklavier" was indeed correct, and suggested consulting a linguist about whether Hämmerklavier or Hämmerflügel might be better. He also volunteered to pay for a new title page himself, suggesting that the already engraved one could be used for a future sonata. Only Op. 101 and the next sonata, Op. 106, were indeed published as "für das Hammerklavier," even though this designation also appears on the autograph of Op. 109 and on a corrected copy of Op. 110. That "Hammerklavier" has become associated exclusively with Op. 106 seems to be a quirk of history.

The first movement of Sonata Op. 101 was designated by Beethoven as Etwas lebhaft und mit der innigsten Empfindung; Allegretto ma non troppo. The German (somewhat lively and with the innermost feeling) adds significantly to the more traditional Italian terms. The same is true for the other movements. In published editions the second movement is Lebhaft. Marschmässig (Vivace alla marcia), but in the autograph Beethoven added the word *Ziemlich* (rather) before *Lebhaft*. The third movement is Langsam und sehnsuchtsvoll (Adagio, ma non troppo, con affetto). Here the term *sehnsuchtsvoll* (longingly) applies directly to the character of the music, not simply to the tempo. The designation for the final movement—Geschwind, doch nicht zu sehr, und mit Entschlossenheit: Allegro (fast, but not too much so, and decisively)—reveals that the two languages are meant merely to complement one another.

The marchlike feeling of the second movement derives from the ubiquitous sixteenth-note dotted rhythms. Often the feeling of lift is generated by sixteenth-rests on the second half of the beat. But too fast a tempo—or an inaccurate pulse—can obscure all this and lead instead to a feeling of three divisions per

beat (rather than four) if the final sixteenth-note of each beat is too slow relative
to the quarter-note pulse. Therefore in addition to the quarter-note pulse, I try
to feel a very quick pulse of four within each beat to ensure that the sixteenth-
notes are not elongated into triplet eighth-notes.

An element of whimsy is introduced by the long pedal marking beginning in
m. 30, gently blending together harmonies, *piano*, very unmartial, over a low D-
flat pedal tone. I use a delicate touch here, taking a bit more time but still maintaining the impetus of the dotted rhythms. With the bass descent to C, the pedal
is released, and when the left hand accompanies in triplets beginning in m. 36,
I distinguish between the right- and left-hand rhythms so that the music gradually, over the ensuing six measures, returns to its true marchlike character.

The wonderful contrast between the scherzo and the trio involves the
smoothness of line and the canonical imitation in the latter. If there is a slight
relaxing of the pulse in the trio, I try to make sure that it becomes strict again in
m. 84 and remains so, enabling the scherzo to reenter smoothly.

The mood of the next movement is established by the feeling of the first
chord—Mit einer Saite; sul una corda (therefore with the left pedal depressed,
pianissimo)—as a stark contrast to the exuberance of the second movement.
This slow section, heard retrospectively as an interlude before the finale, is the
slowest movement of the work and its most reflective and contemplative area.
Just as the first movement deliberately avoided definitive tonic cadences, so too
does this section. To help preserve the arch of the sixteenth- and thirty-second-
note figures. I avoid an accent on the third sixteenth of the beat:

And I play all the grace notes beginning in m. 12 before the beat. As the slow
pirouette of m. 20 unfolds, the harmony (E major) seems to become more and
more established as a local tonic. This, of course, is soon revealed not to be the
case, for the opening phrase of the piece sneaks in, and although centered on E,
the figure is not sanguine about it. The fermata over the eighth-rest is held long
enough to allow this recollection to sink in, and to allow a listener sufficient
time to wonder what might come next. As more thematic fragments are played,
they gradually turn into a whirlwind presto run which leads to three trills. I
begin the first one (D) slowly, increasing speed until it's very fast, then keep this
fast speed for the second trill (D-sharp) as well. The crescendo begins only with
the final trill (E) and does not reach *forte* until the upbeat to the main theme of
the last movement.

In his commentary on Op. 101 Heinrich Schenker described the designation
for the left hand and the disposition of the phrasing in mm. 16–17 of the first
movement as a result of Beethoven's "tief gesunkenen Ohr-Kultur" (deeply embedded inner hearing) (Schenker 1970, 23). This grouping is special not only for

the first movement of Op. 101 but also, with a small rhythmic modification, as part of the main theme—and fugue subject—in the last movement (Example 45).

Example 45: Sonata Op. 101, first movement, mm. 16–17, a grouping transformed into the main theme (and fugue subject in mm. 91–92) of the fourth movement of this sonata.

Beethoven was concerned in varying degrees with fugue in each of his late piano sonatas, beginning with Op. 101. The entire development section of the final (and longest) movement of Op. 101 is a fugue. The last movement of Op. 106 is an epic fugue. The fifth variation of the last movement of Op. 109 is a fugato, and the last movement of Op. 110 encompasses a fugue that returns with the subject explicitly inverted. Sketches of the opening diminished seventh motive of the first movement of Op. 111, which date some fifteen years prior to the actual composition of the sonata, are evidence that Beethoven considered this motive a possible fugal subject, and the development of the first movement is a fugato. That the main theme of the last movement of Op. 101 should bear such a close resemblance to a seminal grouping in the first movement is not coincidence. It reaffirms that this music exists on its own singular terms, that it is highly self-referential, and that minute musical details determine not only local expression but also global events.

The character of this movement is triumphant; tonal restlessness and searching have given way to unambiguous harmonic confidence and strength. Still, a part of the main theme of the last movement of Op. 101 is transformed into a terse, rhythmic figure in the alto and tenor parts under the only melodic line of the movement (mm. 33–44, leading to the second theme). This alto and tenor duet foreshadows the viola and cello interplay in the Presto movement of the String Quartet Op. 131 (Examples 46a and b). In both cases, the particular kind of writing creates a propulsive current beneath the longest line of the movement.

In addition, the relationship between the energetic first theme of this movement and the concentrated stillness, though *dolce*, of the second theme foreshadows a similar polar relationship between the first and second themes in the first movement of Sonata Op. 111.

After the second ending of the exposition, a sense of focused tranquility returns, *pianissimo*, beginning the transformation in mood to the foreboding

Example 46a: Sonata Op. 101, fourth movement, mm. 37–47. Note the
alternation between the alto and tenor lines.

Example 46b: String Quartet Op. 131, fifth movement, mm. 66–75. Note the
alternation between the viola and cello.

character of the fugue subject, initially in A minor, *pianissimo*, in the lowest register of the piano. The development section of this movement is a four-part
fugue in the enharmonic minor. (The entire last movement of the Sonata for
Cello and Piano Op. 102 no. 2 is also a fugue; sketches for both appear in the
Scheide sketchbook of 1815–16.) The climax of the fugal development section
of Op. 101 is a statement of the entire subject in the bass, rhythmically augmented by a factor of four. By 1816 the compass of Beethoven's piano extended
to the low E almost 3 octaves below middle C. Beethoven made dramatic use of
it here, and to ensure that no one would reproach him for erring (for many

pianos still extended only to the low F), Beethoven wrote *contra E* in the score. In a letter from January 1817 to Tobias Haslinger (Beethoven's primary contact at the publishing firm of Steiner), Beethoven also specified that he wanted all the chords with the low E to be expressly spelled out in the printed edition (Anderson 1961, 660):

E	E	E	E	E
A	F♯	G♯	A	B
E	E	E	E	E

This insistence on the low E also ensures that Op. 101 could not and would not be played on earlier, less encompassing pianofortes. Although the notes in today's printed editions are correct, the complete spelling that Beethoven so carefully requested has not been carried over, but his indication for *contra E* has survived.

This low E ushers in the return to A major for the recapitulation, for the E is the starting point of a dominant arpeggiation spanning virtually the entire keyboard. A coda, starting with a false hint of fugue in D minor to balance the A minor fugal development, is essentially calm and quiet, even throughout a not-quite-tonic (G-sharp–A) tremolando in the bass beginning in m. 319. (This measure number assumes m. 1 as the first measure of the movement marked Geschwind, doch nicht zu sehr . . . : Allegro. For editions in which measures are numbered consecutively from the beginning of the slow movement, add twenty-eight to these numbers.) The tonic is finally affirmed by *fortissimo* chords beginning in m. 331. I make the second, third, and fourth chords of this measure louder than the first, a treatment suggested by the filling in of these chords in the bass with C-sharp and E and by the augmentation of the characteristic rhythmic pattern (♪♪♪ ♩) of the main theme. From its quiet, lyrical, searching beginnings, Sonata Op. 101 draws to an exultant close.

Sonata in E-flat major, Op. 7 (1797)

Sonata in G major, Op. 31 no. 1 (1802)

Sonata in E minor, Op. 90 (1814)

Sonata in C minor, Op. 13 ("Pathétique")
(1798–99)

*T*he wide diversity of character among these sonatas is a defining element of this program. Dating from three different compositional periods, they range in disposition from the large-scale grandeur of Op. 7 to the good-natured humor of Op. 31 no. 1, from the searching intimacy of Op. 90 to the pathos of Op. 13.

The 7 October 1797 edition of the *Wiener Zeitung* announced the publication of Op. 7 by Artaria (Thayer 1973, 198). Its four movements, both individual and collectively, are on a larger scale than its Op. 2 predecessors, and it is the first work that Beethoven entitled "Grand" Sonata. Although Op. 7 contains a profusion of musical ideas, a basic and striking aspect of the piece is the overt presence of repeated notes in the first, second, and fourth movements and their more subtle presence in the trio of the third movement (Examples 47a–d). These repeated notes help create the impression of underlying motion even within a static harmony, lending qualities of both tension and ebullience to the work.

Although *piano*, the beginning is clear and direct in establishing the home tonality (E-flat major) and phrase structure (four-bar units). The movement heading (Allegro molto e con brio) implies a brisk tempo, but the unit of pulse should remain the eighth-note to ensure a pulse of six per measure. This will imbue the music with more palpable feelings of inner drive and direction than would be possible by playing the movement in two. Because of the length of the opening chords and slightly falling contour within each two-bar unit, the musical shape is an implied diminuendo from m. 1 to m. 2 and again from m. 3 to m. 4 (Example 48).

The rising and falling contour and the increasing sweep of the legato lines that follow give the impression of moving forward, although they are still in

143

Example 47a: Sonata Op. 7, first movement, mm. 1–4.

Example 47b: Sonata Op. 7, second movement, mm. 78–82.

Example 47c: Sonata Op. 7, third movement, mm. 95–99.

Example 47d: Sonata Op. 7, fourth movement, mm. 1–2.

strict tempo. I like to make a big contrast between the stentorian *fortissimo* measures (mm. 25 and 29) and the questioning *pianissimo* bars that follow (mm. 26 and 30). Each rhetorical outburst is a harmonic surprise; I stress the bass register and play deeply into the keys with plenty of pedal. The higher chords are within the same harmony; I voice slightly toward the top, with a light staccato touch, with small amounts of pedal only in the driest of acoustical situations. The buoyant character of the music suggests taking a little time for the large registral leaps (mm. 51, 53) and setting up the sforzandos. Of course the left hand doesn't need time here at all, so in order for the hands to remain to-

Example 48: Sonata Op. 7, first movement, mm. 1–4.

gether, the right cannot afford to take too much time, and the left needs to be just a little flexible.

Contrasting with everything that came before is the choralelike texture of the second theme (m. 59 on). The hands are still, quiet, and as smooth as possible. Repeated notes gradually creep back in, as the animated qualities of this movement again rise to the surface. In the close of the exposition, the rapid sixteenth-note tremolandos in the right hand create hints of minor harmonies for the first time in this work, and as they need to be clear the pulse of six should be maintained. I find that the basic tempo of the movement really derives from the maximum speed of this area.

The development takes the hints of minor keys and makes them overt. Even though the first four-bar phrase here (transposition of the very opening) is *fortissimo* and there are no further dynamic markings until the crescendo in m. 151, I drop to *piano* for the start of the left-hand scalar figure in m. 141. This allows for dynamic shaping within the contours of the phrase and is implied in any case by the crescendo in m. 151. I also make sure the sforzandos that follow are truly incisive. The touch for the *pianissimo* transformation of the opening chords (m. 169 on), in the surprise key of A minor, is much more gentle than that of any other occurrence of this material, and the repeated notes are, in fact, subtly under tempo.

In mm. 351–354 of the coda, the chords of the opening theme are displaced by one measure, eventually allowing for the compression to two chords per bar and then to two dominant-tonic resolutions to conclude the movement. This displacement makes for a bit of tension, as it creates a syncopation within the four-bar unit of phrase, particularly if the low bass E-flat is played a bit more sonorously, even within the crescendo from *pianissimo*. Rather than the longer right-hand chords being aligned with the stronger left-hand bass, they are now out of synchronization. This rhythmic tension helps make the resolution even more of a psychological relief.

The contrast between the first and second movement is startling in several dramatic dimensions. The remarkable change of key from E-flat major of the first movement to C major of the Largo con gran espressione is only the first surprise. So strong is the V–I, V–I impulse from the first movement that the immediate move from the tonic to the dominant seventh (C to G-seventh) in the first two chords of the Largo is a shock. So is the long beat of silence (quarter-rest) that follows. (The longest rest in the first movement was an eighth-rest within the rapid 6/8.) This silence helps define the *con gran espressione*. Like the first movement, this one also begins with four chords, but their dynamic shaping contrasts with that of the four which opened the Allegro (Example 49).

Example 49: Sonata Op. 7, second movement, mm. 1–4.

Voicing of the chords becomes important, especially in m. 7 with the introduction of a specific alto line and a poignant A-flat appoggiatura. This chromatic interplay, initially seemingly small (although marked with its own specific sforzando), gradually assumes larger roles in the course of the movement. Following the songful second theme (starting in m. 25), the music pauses on empty octaves in both hands: initially G and F-sharp in mm. 37–38 and then incorporating the A-flat (sforzando) in mm. 39–40. In the concluding measures of the movement, this chromaticism grows to an entire descending bass line extending from m. 86 to m. 89 (C–B–B-flat–A–A-flat–G–F-sharp–F), harmonizing the original right-hand chords of the beginning of the movement in new ways that cause them to be heard afresh, all leading to the final dominant-tonic (G–C) cadence. Hence the first A-flat appoggiatura is really of prime importance; I take a little time to set up the sforzando and to infuse the surprise of its presence with dramatic tension.

In the second theme area, the *sempre tenuto* marking for the right hand contrasts with the staccato left hand. This simultaneous opposition of touches is not easily achieved. It is tempting to use pedal to help connect the right-hand chords, but this would interfere with the detached left-hand notes. I try to use a touch in the right hand that produces a deep, singing tone, and I change fingers as often as necessary on the top notes of the chords to achieve a sense of smoothness. If pedal is used, it should be used only sparingly.

When the music of the opening theme recurs beginning in m. 65 and for the first time the rests on the third beat of each measure are filled in with embellishments, I play the first of these embellishments as if improvising, for by now we have all come to expect silence on the last beat. The new notes there are a surprise, but they mark the beginning of the end; no longer is the third beat a time of repose; instead it is beginning to lead on ahead.

The tenor line is voiced as the most prominent one when it plays the second theme beginning in m. 74. Repeated notes recur—as a stasis—beginning in m. 78, leading to the final restatement of the opening theme as the music offers the many stylized operatic goodbyes now familiar from the slow movements of the three previous piano sonatas.

I like to begin the Allegro minuet with a very sweet tone, softly, giving the impression of emerging gradually from the great stillness of the slow movement's end. When the first section of the minuet is repeated I play with a slightly fuller sound, contours more chiseled, staccatos somewhat sharper. It is important to give the measure of rest (m. 69) its full due—how unusual it is to have a full measure of silence in the midst of a piece! This measure keeps us in suspense (completing the eight-bar phrase), awaiting a harmonic resolution that arrives in the form of solo B-flats, repeated notes once again. That Beethoven included a full measure of silence—a relatively long cessation of musical movement—is in character with the expansive nature of this work: the minuet/trio is the longest such movement in all the Beethoven sonatas.

The incessant triplets along with the *ffp* indications within a *pp* dynamic contribute to the focused intensity of the minor-key trio. I use only light pedal here, allowing the upward motion of each triplet group to be evident, even within the areas that lack any overall larger motion (when the same triplet is repeated). This endows the trio with a sense of urgency throughout, relieved only by the return to the minuet.

The willowy and flowing character of the last movement (Rondo: Poco Allegretto e grazioso) contrasts from the brilliance of the first movement, the spaciousness of the second, and the alternating amiability and agitation of the third. I use a very singing tone in the right hand for the first part of the Rondo theme and a more rhetorical contrast of touches in the left hand for the second part (m. 16 on). The final Rondo movements of the three predecessors of Sonata Op. 7 (the three Sonatas Op. 2) all include middle sections that contrast in musical character and pianism. This type of contrast continues in Op. 7, hence the C minor section that begins in m. 64. Sharp staccato chords played against strong arpeggiated thirty-second notes give this area a dramatic mood, perhaps anticipating the Sturm und Drang that pervades the following sonata (Op. 10 no. 1, also in C minor). An even tempo and good articulation will help maintain the inner intensity here.

A surprise chromatic modulation from B-flat to B major (mm. 154–155) demands time on the fermata of m. 154, and I like to let the B major octave sneak in as softly as possible in m. 156. Similarly in m. 161 the *ffp* chords necessary to return chromatically to B-flat major need a little extra time to reverberate before the following notes are played. In the coda the terse thirty-second-note figures from the C minor middle section are transformed into a flowing accompaniment. The very ending of this movement is simple and elegant—no virtuosity, no drama, just reverberation of the final cadence.

Sonata Op. 31 no. 1 is a genuinely funny piece. Before starting it I try to put myself into the frame of mind of a pianist—perhaps a nervous pianist—who cannot seem to play chords together: the right hand anticipates the left by a sixteenth-note. This "problem" is brought to the musical forefront by Beethoven's gentle mocking humor (Example 50).

Example 50: Sonata Op. 31 no. 1, first movement, mm. 1–7.

The second movement is a good-natured parody of Italian lyric opera, in which the "diva" goes off on extraordinary runs and trills, leaving the "accompanist" wondering what to do. The third movement continues with long, flowing lyrical lines alternating between the two hands, which assume ridiculously funny extremes of tempo and dynamics in the coda.

In ironic contrast to the humor in this music, the publication of this work in 1803 (along with the other sonatas of Op. 31) was fraught with an unusual degree of turbulence. Although the composer had promised the three Sonatas Op. 31 to the publisher Nägeli in Zurich, Beethoven's brother Carl (Caspar), who frequently meddled in his affairs, wanted to sell them to a Leipzig publisher. So intense was the disagreement between the two brothers that they actually came to blows. However, Ludwig prevailed. Having given his word to Nägeli, he wanted to keep it, and the sonatas were sent to Zurich. The first two sonatas of Op. 31 were published in spring 1803 in Nägeli's *Répertoire des Clavecinistes* as Cahier 5; the third followed a year later (paired inexplicably with Sonata Op. 13) as Cahier 11.

The argument between the brothers Beethoven was only the beginning of the problems regarding the publication of Op. 31 no. 1. It seems that proofs of the first edition were not sent to Beethoven, and Nägeli published this work without giving Beethoven a chance to offer corrections. When the obligatory complimentary copy arrived at Beethoven's home, he was in the midst of composing, as Ferdinand Ries relates:

"Play the Sonata through," he said to me, remaining seated at his writing-desk. There was an unusual number of errors in the proofs [here Ries is incorrect; this was the first edition], which already made Beethoven impatient. At the end of the first Allegro in the Sonata in G major, however, Nägeli had introduced four measures—after the fourth measure of the last hold:

When I played this Beethoven jumped up in a rage, came running to me, half pushed me away from the pianoforte, shouting: "Where the devil do you find that?" One can scarcely imagine his amazement and rage when he saw the printed notes. I received the commission to make a record of all the errors and at once sent the sonatas to Simrock in Bonn, who was to make a reprint and call it *Edition très correcte* (Thayer 1973, 318–319).

Following its removal from the presses of Nägeli, Sonata Op. 31 no. 1 was indeed published by Simrock to Beethoven's satisfaction.

Sonata Op. 31 no. 1 is inherently a thoroughly well-crafted and even forward-looking work. Following the initial G-major statement of the main theme of the first movement (Allegro vivace), this theme is repeated immediately in m. 12 but in F major rather than in the expected dominant. The *forte* dynamic here is important; it is integral to the daring harmonic surprise, the first instance of this sort in the piano sonatas. Perhaps it paves the way compositionally for the more overt descending line of the thematic motive of Sonata Op. 53 ("Waldstein"). Once the hands are back together again (m. 26), Beethoven enjoys having them not just casually together but virtually locked together as they cascade up and down the keyboard an octave apart in runs and arpeggios, ending defiantly together with the sforzando D (dominant pitch) with a fermata—one that is held a long time—in m. 44. By now the pianist has gone to great lengths to show that he can indeed play with his hands together, only to have the initial "problem" recur immediately after the triumphant D, as the opening theme begins again in m. 46.

This time, however, we are led to a second theme that contrasts not only in character but also greatly in key. It begins in B major, mediant of G major, rather than the expected dominant. (This surprising choice of key for the second theme is another foreshadowing of the "Waldstein" Sonata Op. 53 in which the second theme of the first movement is also in the mediant.) Here the problem of playing with the hands together seems to have disappeared, but the offbeat syncopations and the alternation of the main line between the two hands main-

tain the lively character of the music. In mm. 93–95 I voice the right hand carefully to allow the two voices to be heard independently. This means playing the
longer notes with slightly more weight, implying a shifting of pressure from the
top of the hand (fifth finger) to the inside (thumb), and making the sixteenth-
notes transparent enough so that the held note is heard for its full duration.

Although the development area is almost devoid of dynamic markings from
the *forte* m. 126 until the *forte* m. 170 (except for several sforzandos, mm. 140
and 148, and then mm. 158–161), the contour of the lines and changes of harmony imply the nature of dynamic shaping. With each new harmony—corresponding to the top of each new line—and the associated feelings of tension, I
play more strongly. As the lines move downward, I tend to shape the level of
dynamic downward as well. The sforzandos in mm. 158–161 emphasize the
feelings of urgency of the arpeggiated dominant seventh chords, particularly
since they occur on the weaker of the two beats of the measure.

A new twist is added to the problem of the hands yet again at the end of the
development: if the hands still can't play together in the normal position, they
certainly cannot when the left crosses over the right. Real trouble. The development area thus evaporates in a questioning mode, *pianissimo*, the left hand not
really knowing what to do or in what register to play. In a magnificent attempt
to line up the hands, the main theme comes back *fortissimo* (mm. 193–194),
but alas the hands are still not working properly. This problem is summed up in
the coda, with attempts made at all dynamic levels (*pianissimo*, crescendo, *fortissimo*) to get the hands to play together. Finally they do at the most unexpected
spot—the last two chords, *pianissimo*.

Throughout this movement, dynamics, touch, and character of playing are
crucial to conveying the humor. For example, playing the sixteenth-note difference between the two hands accurately but in a way that seems to yearn for
correction, and waiting the full measure rest before the last two chords but playing them in an understated way, will convey both the frustration and humor of
not being able to play with the hands together for virtually the entire movement
and finally the ease and aplomb of having the hands work properly.

The Adagio grazioso is the only slow movement of the piano sonatas to start
with a trill. A stylized vocal soloist-accompanist texture is immediately established, and when the "baritone" enters in m. 9 with a trill as well, the "soprano"
responds with a virtuoso figure extending throughout the treble range. It thus
becomes important to keep the three parts (two solo "singers" and "accompanist") separate and independent. Sometimes I allow the "singer" hand to take
additional freedom of time, which means that the other hand must comply with
flexibility in accompanying. In m. 26 when the trill under a fermata extends
into a cadenza, I try to shape it as a vocalist might, both in dynamics and speed:
starting the figure by allowing it to grow out of the trill, shaping upward to the
high F and then gradually down away from it. Sheer speed is not important

here; the musical point is to increase the speed slightly as the line curves upward, and then gradually and smoothly to bring it back down to the C trill of m. 27.

In the contrasting middle section, using pedal to connect the right hand would interfere with the staccato feeling of the left. If pedal is used at the beginning of each left-hand figure, it should then be lifted for the detached notes, and the right hand can be connected by judicious changing of fingers on the octaves. Although this movement is the longest of the sonata and its breadth exceeds that of previous slow movements, there is no need to rush at any point. The tempo should remain the same throughout the middle sixteenth-note section, allowing the rhetorical qualities their full due.

With the return of the trill theme in m. 65, the accompaniment touch needs to be light and airy to keep the sixteenth-notes from interfering with the main line. And in the coda a little time may be taken for clarity when the main line dips down into the lowest register of the instrument (low A-flat, sforzando).

The movement could end with the cadence in m. 115. But Beethoven chose to have the music say goodbye another time, more softly, in m. 116. To all of us listening, this seems surely to be the end; keep the silence for its full value. So when m. 117 enters—as a surprise—slightly higher with a crescendo, we are no longer really sure where we're going. The line continues, aided by the sforzando in m. 118. Finally, I voice to the top of the two chords of the last cadence so that the line that emerges in the penultimate measure continues all the way to the end.

The last movement of Sonata Op. 31 no. 1 (Rondo: Allegretto) is not passionate, nor is it overtly brilliant. It is, however, charming and graceful, demanding finesse, and understated in its pianistic challenges. The long-held bass notes—although *piano*—give the piece a bucolic flair. When the main theme is played in the bass (mm. 16–17), the right-hand accompaniment can be soft, shaped, and flowing, with carefully articulated fingers held close to the keys and with a minimum of pedal. As thematic fragments are tossed back and forth between the hands (m. 30 on) so do the dynamics alternate, the accompaniment always supportive beneath the surface. In the development, as minor-key versions of the theme are explored and a fugato established, the intensity of touch increases, and the theme is played *forte* for the first time.

In the coda, elements of the theme are reconsidered in different tempos— Adagio alternating with tempo primo—and I use different qualities of touch for different contexts. The Adagio measures suggest a fuller sonority, not just because the second is marked *forte* (but the first is not), but also because of the slower tempo and fuller chords. The bass trill that begins in m. 241 is a recollection of the Adagio grazioso, and the Presto that begins shortly thereafter reverses the initial figure of the first theme of the last movement (D–C-sharp–D–E has become E–D–C-sharp–D). The tempo here is quick, but not so fast as to obscure in any way the syncopations implied by the right hand in m. 252 and made explicit by the left in m. 256. These hint at the humorous music of the Allegro vivace, in which the two hands were not able to play quite together. In fact, this "problem" recurs in the closing measures of the piece, with the left hand now preceding the right. (The right had always preceded the left in the first movement.) As the dynamics and the registers both become lower, the hands are finally together on the last chord. But this chord is on a weak beat of the measure and leaves us hanging with a full measure rest under a fermata. The end of the piece smiles, and we smile back.

BEFORE BEGINNING to play Sonata Op. 90, I hear in my mind not only the notes and character of the first several measures—specifically the brusque, declamatory opening *forte* line G–G–F-sharp–E–A, complete with E minor harmony and rhythm—but also the *dolce* E major beginning of the second movement, a gesture of opening one's soul. Although we often wish to play as if spontaneously, in reality we know what lies ahead. But by hearing internally these two phrases that reflect the basis of contrast between the two movements of Sonata Op. 90, I can better prepare to define—as though spontaneously—the characteristic elements of each. The importance of a phrase lies not only in its local area, but also in its implications for more global trajectory. One can hear the beginning of the first movement not only as the first phrase of the piece, but also as representing a defining element with which the entire second movement contrasts. After vividly imagining in my inner ear the feelings that the two first phrases conjure, I then rehear the opening of the first movement, setting the mood internally, and begin to play.

The placement on this program of Sonata Op. 90 after the large-scale Op. 7 and the playful Op. 31 no. 1 highlights the wide range of differences of expression, compositional style, formal bearing, and pianism—all, of course, interrelated—among the sonatas. Op. 90 is serious in nature and forward-looking in style although only a two-movement work, and the second movement augurs a new kind of lyrical pianistic voice.

Five years elapsed between the composition of Sonata Op. 81a in 1809 and Sonata Op. 90 in 1814, and the latter is like nothing ever composed before. The most dramatic personal events during the five years that Beethoven did not write for the piano are the letter of extraordinary intensity of 5–7 July 1812 (Thayer 1973, 534) to an "*unsterbliche Geliebte*" (eternally beloved) and an attempt to starve himself in 1813 (Solomon 1977, 220). Even though he composed the Seventh and Eighth Symphonies in 1811–12 and the "Archduke" Trio in 1811, and revised *Fidelio* in 1814, Beethoven was plagued by serious concerns (including financial instability) that slowed his work to a relative trickle during the years 1810–1814. The decision to compose again for the piano originated with a loan that the publisher and piano manufacturer Sigmund Anton Steiner extended to Beethoven's brother Carl in 1813. Repayment of the loan eventually became Beethoven's own responsibility, and Steiner offered to grant an extension if Beethoven would provide him with a new piano sonata to publish. (Steiner eventually published a large number of Beethoven's works.) The resulting work—Sonata Op. 90—marked a compositional turning point; in returning to the piano, Beethoven established a trajectory that carried him forward to his last works. Immersing himself in new stylistic ideals may have helped him out of his own paralyzing turmoil.

Sonata Op. 90 is based on the interval of the third. In the probing first movement, it is the falling minor third (G–E); in the contrasting and affirming second movement, it is the ascending major third (E–G-sharp). While the concept of one interval motivating a work is not new (we heard it first in Sonata Op. 2 no. 2), the concentrated manner in which this motivation is manifest is unprecedented in Op. 90 and points forward to Op. 106, which is motivated by the same interval. The two-movement major-minor format, with the terse first movement more tumultuous than the lyrical second, may have paved the way for Sonata Op. 111, which is of the same dramatic scheme.

The use of exclusively German character indications for the movement headings of Op. 90 is significant; Beethoven felt that the conventional Italian terms no longer conveyed a precise enough meaning. In fact, the German phrases used for the movement headings of Sonata Op. 90 are the longest such phrases in the piano sonatas: Mit Lebhaftigkeit und durchaus mit Empfindung und Ausdruck (with liveliness and throughout with feeling and expression) and Nicht zu geschwind und sehr singbar vorzutragen (not too fast and played in a very singing manner).

Subtleties of notation reflect Beethoven's subtleties of expression. The first chords are *forte*, and all except the first two beats of m. 1 are detached eighth-notes with eighth-rests. There is a quality of gruffness to the rhetorical opening. The answer to the question posed by these chords is *piano*, beginning with the last beat of m. 2. The chords are more registrally confined, giving a smaller sound, and the beats that had previously been detached eighth-notes with eighth-rests are now quarter-notes. This change gives a more lyrical flow, particularly with the gently detached portato quarter-notes that conclude the answer, sounding like soft gasps. The interplay between gruffness and lyricism continues with lyricism winning out; the line begun with the last beat of m. 8 is the longest of the movement. I relish the beguiling way this line begins, particularly with the chromatic left hand (E–E-flat–D) in mm. 10–11, and make it as smooth as possible.

Feelings of resignation are conjured by this movement. The large registral leap down from E to F-sharp (mm. 18–19) contributes to this within a crescendo; so do the fermatas (m. 16 and m. 24) at the end of the first and second phrases, for the registral transfers down almost two octaves feel very different from dynamic leaps upward, and the halting at the ends of phrases makes for feelings of hesitancy. Scales that tumble down the keyboard beginning in m. 29 more than fill in the interval of the two previous registral leaps down, but these scales are not of the virtuosic character of figurations in Sonata Op. 7. Here they are less sparkling, more into the keys, more introverted. When the B-flat of m. 39 changes enharmonically to A-sharp in the next bar, I like to voice the chord slightly to the top, allowing the mystery of the B-flat–A-sharp duality to continue as long as possible.

Whenever I play this piece I am amazed that Beethoven could construct so much with so little. The second theme, which feels so different from anything before it, is actually a reinterpretation of the ascending empty octaves in mm. 24–28. However, in B minor (the dominant) context (m. 55 on) and a different metrical format with a left-hand accompaniment, the octaves are transformed into what seems like a new theme. They are further abstracted in m. 61, with the eighth-rests as sighs between the melodic fragments. The music is reduced to a slow pulse on a single repeated *pianissimo* B—which cannot be rushed—before the main theme returns, ascending and with increasing tension, in the development area.

Distinctions between melody and harmony become blurred after the left hand plays the long melodic line beginning in m. 113 (which was initially heard beginning in m. 8); by m. 120 a listener is not sure whether the right hand is accompanying the left or if it has the main line. The answer, of course, is that both hands are of equal importance here, with this equal billing continuing through the rhythmic interplay of the opening G–F–E interval (mm. 133–143). Here this primary interval of the work is portrayed in its most bare and intense form. The canon—particularly mm. 141–143—leaves the listener suspended in a monochromatic harmony that blends horizontal and vertical music. Out of this harmonic veil the main theme recurs to begin the recapitulation.

In the short coda the only phrasing slur in mm. 232–237 is over the left-hand G–F-sharp–E of m. 236, making explicit—for the last time in the movement— the longing, lyrical quality of the descending third that so motivated the piece. I would voice m. 236 with a little extra pressure of touch on the left hand to help bring this to the fore.

There is a fermata over the last rest of the first movement, and I do not pull back from the keyboard when the music stops. Rather I focus on preparing to begin the second movement without any interruption, allowing its first sounds—the ascending major-third E–F-sharp–G-sharp—to emerge from the pool of silence into which the last E minor chord of the first movement dissolved. The warm and enveloping manner of the ascending E–F-sharp–G-sharp, in the mellifluous middle register of the keyboard, *piano*, *dolce*, legato, is opposite in character to the opening descending minor third of the first movement. I use just enough pedal to enhance the sound of the top singing line without blurring the inner voice. From the start this contemplative second movement sets forth long melodic lines over a subtly shifting undulating accompaniment. There is no exuberance here, no humor, no heaven-storming drama, simply a warm song (perhaps setting forth musical ideals Schubert was to espouse) played with open but unsentimental expression. Even so, I would begin the second movement in tempo—avoiding a possible temptation to begin the first several notes slower, reaching the main tempo with the first full chord—simply because Beethoven marked *teneramente* (from *tenerezza*—tenderness) when the opening music returns in m. 24. The interpretive implication is to save the idea of beginning the phrase slower until the specific indication: doing something once is expressive; twice is a mannerism. In each of the three large thematic areas, the *teneramente* marking returns for the second hearing of the thematic melody (m. 93 and m. 163), which enters via contrary motion, the left hand playing G-sharp–F-sharp–E to the right hand's E–F-sharp–G-sharp.

In m. 60 (and similar places) where the music seems to slow down as the bass changes from four sixteenth-notes per beat to three triplets, keeping a steady and consistent pulse is important, avoiding the tendency to rush. Following the first return to the main theme, the music takes an unexpected turn toward E minor (m. 103), and accordingly it is nice to voice the inner line (G-sharp–G) with a special legato tone as Beethoven indicated with the slur mark. Tension builds as the right hand ascends (beginning in m. 107) and the left descends, but grading the crescendo and eventual *forte* differently in each hand, with less strength in the bass, will allow the top to be heard all the way through, particularly the long D–F chord (mm. 110–111, as the dominant of C major).

Shortly before the coda begins with the theme in the tenor range (m. 230), a melodic fragment of the theme is isolated and developed into a canon with a hint of chromaticism. This is the only area (beginning in m. 212) of real harmonic tension in the movement, and it is *pianissimo* throughout. Beethoven even wrote *sempre pianissimo* in the measures of enharmonic changes (mm. 216–218) to guard against an increase in dynamics. Then tension is achieved by a penetrating quality of touch and by perhaps taking a little extra time.

Plasticity of the theme is saved for the end of the movement, at which point our perceptions of time and dynamics become very concentrated. A diminuendo corresponding to a ritardando (slowing down gradually) is followed by a crescendo and accelerando back to *piano* and *a tempo*—all within eight measures (mm. 282–289). The final measure—before which I take a short breath of time—is legato, *pianissimo*, and the simplest of cadences: no ritard, no fermata, no chords for finality. We are left hanging as the music comes to a stop. Sonata Op. 90 is played less frequently than are many others, possibly because its intimacy does not encourage an audience to leap to its feet with wild applause. But the communicative expressive power of this work is immense, and I consider it to be the first in the group of the six late, transcendent Beethoven sonatas.

THE FIRST CHORD of Sonata Op. 13 ("Pathétique") conjures a different sonic world; that Beethoven himself designated the sobriquet "Pathétique" indicates that he fully intended for others to appreciate the dramatic content. C minor was Beethoven's Sturm und Drang key. His three piano sonatas in C minor—Op. 10 no. 1, Op. 13, and Op. 111—are all infused with extraordinary intensity. It is unique that Beethoven should use the same key (C minor) for two sonatas, Op. 10 no. 1 and Op. 13, that were composed so closely together. Sonata Op. 10 no. 1 is concentrated and concise. Sonata Op. 13, composed less than two years afterward, uses the same key scheme for its three movements (C minor, A-flat major, C minor) but is more expansive in conception. The Grave as slow music *before* the Allegro is unique in the canon of Beethoven sonatas published at that time, but Beethoven himself actually experimented with a similar concept of integrating slow dramatic phrases within the framework of an allegro first movement in his Sonata in F minor WoO 47 that he composed in Bonn as a young man of thirteen (Example 51). Beethoven was likely also familiar with a Dussek piano work of 1793 in C minor entitled *The Sufferings of the Queen of France, A Musical Composition Expressing the feelings of the Unfortunate Marie Antoinette During her Imprisonment, Trial, Etc.* This work also begins with a slow introduction and consists of ten descriptive sections, more along the lines of a fantasy.

Fp is the first marking of Op. 13: what does it mean? how is it played? The idea is for the chord to be heard *forte* initially, then rapidly dying down to *piano*. This is fundamentally different from an accent within a *piano* context and from the sforzando marking first encountered here in m. 4. Beethoven could also have notated the first chord as *forte* and then placed a *piano* marking under the second chord, implying that the dynamic level naturally decays from *forte* to *piano*. To achieve an effective *fp*, the pianist simply depresses the keys rapidly, creating the *forte*, then immediately allows them to rise so that the sound is damped almost instantaneously. Depressing the keys immediately once again so that the dampers rise quickly allows the strings to continue to vibrate but now with considerably less energy, *piano*. All this takes only a small fraction of a second but sets the stage for the drama that unfolds throughout the piece.

The tempo of the Grave is slow enough so that the sixty-fourth note groupings (and also 128th-notes) are clear but not so slow as to be ponderous. Dynamic contrasts and long rests are integral to the drama. The Allegro molto enters without interruption, and here, since the harmonic motion is basically slow, I play at the fastest tempo that allows for the bass tremolandos—which add mightily to the overall tension of the movement—to be transparent with only subtle pedaling. I try to resist the temptation to make a crescendo in mm. 11–14 as the right-hand line rises, and find that although the piano dynamic of m. 11 lasts until the crescendo in m. 15, a slight shaping upward of the line is inevitable, such is the forward momentum of the music. But keeping these

Allegro assai

Example 51: Sonata in F minor WoO 47, first movement, mm. 1–16.

measures generally soft does in fact add to the agitation and drama. The touch on the staccato half-notes (m. 15) is light, and the chords are separated but not sharply detached. I do not see any reason to slow down for the second theme (m. 51 on) but rather use a more singing tone and legato qualities of touch. I play all the mordents (m. 57 on) starting with the main note, on the beat.

Although the repeat of the exposition in the first movement of the F minor Sonata WoO 47 includes a rehearing of the opening slow music, that of Sonata Op. 13 does not. The repeat sign at the end of the exposition takes us back to m. 11, the beginning of the Allegro molto. But following the rehearing of the exposition, four measures of the music of the Grave do in fact return, and the initial effect is startling: since the slow music returns here, no longer can we consider the Grave merely as introductory, and we are left wondering what is going to happen next. Portentous, weighty chords lead from the home key of C minor to E minor, rather than the dominant (G minor) which would be more expected. As the Allegro molto reenters in m. 137, we realize that we have been ushered into the development area. Crescendos that were withheld from the ascending right-hand line in the exposition are present and give the impression that the line is pushing forward even though the tempo remains steady. For the first time the left hand has the melodic fragments under right-hand tremolandos (beginning in m. 150) which should remain vibrant as they descend chromatically, leading eventually to the long-awaited dominant (m. 167). Here the tremolandos are back in the left hand, and the feeling is an unsettling combination of G major within a larger framework of C minor.

There is a story behind the repeat sign in m. 11 of the first movement. The first editions—Eder (1799) and Hoffmeister (later the same year)—both place the repeat sign in m. 11, as do all responsible modern editions. In a reprint of Op. 13 done by Haslinger (1828), the repeat sign in m. 11 is missing. It is also missing in the first complete works edition (Breitkopf und Härtel, 1864–67), but that edition is widely recognized today as containing many inaccuracies. I consider this to be an error of omission rather than an indication to begin the repetition of the exposition in m. 1, since the early editions brought out during Beethoven's lifetime have the repeat sign in the same place (m. 11) and there is no correspondence from Beethoven about changing it.

Just to be sure, I have tried playing the piece both ways. I find that going back to m. 11 heightens the surprise, contrast, and drama in the recurrences of the slow music after the exposition is complete and later in the movement. But repeating the exposition from m. 1—and therefore hearing the entire Grave twice—lessens the impact of these recurrences.

Unlike the earlier F minor sonata, the recapitulation of which is more literal and includes the slow music from the opening, the recapitulation here does not include music from the opening Grave. But the coda does. Beginning in m. 295 the *fp* chords are replaced by rests; three groups of dotted-rhythm chords ascend with increasing tension to the longest smoothly descending—and poignant—line of the movement (D-flat down an entire octave—mm. 297–298) which sets up the final reiteration of the main theme of the Allegro molto. The ensuing crescendo, once again delayed until after the right-hand ascending chords, leads to the final definitive cadence.

After the contrasts of tempo of the first movement and its interruptions of phrases, its staccato notes, and its inner tension, the long, singing phrases of the second movement appear as welcome comfort. The Adagio cantabile is unabashedly lyrical with a three-tiered texture. The undulating inner accompaniment gently leads the motion forward, with the bass as a solid harmonic grounding and the top line soaring lyrically above. Each line requires a different quality of sound, a different touch—flat fingers playing lightly for an accompaniment touch; slightly heavier, more rounded fingers for a singing tone. I believe that shaping the dynamic contour of the line as it rises and falls is natural; the *piano* indication simply sets the general dynamic level. The slurs guard against overly square phrasing by suggesting more or less weight on their beginnings and ends, which are occasionally drawn where one might not usually expect to find them.

Each of the two episodes concentrates on a different musical character. The stillness of the repeated bass and questioning character of the top line of the first contrast with the introspective conversant qualities of the second. When the theme returns for the last time (m. 51) the accompaniment continues the triplet motion begun in the second episode, but it is important not to push the tempo ahead at this point and to maintain the repose of the character of the theme. Beethoven is specific about the apex of the crescendos in m. 67 and m. 69: the A-flat in the right hand is the loudest point, after which the line recedes. Although the top note (A-flat) remains the same for the last three chords, the bass descends an octave, and additional pitches in the right hand complete the tonic triad. Without sacrificing the top note, I like to voice the right-hand chords to bring the descending E-flat–C to the surface subtly while the bass A-flat rings softly beneath. This iteration of the home triad as the voices accrue over the last measure allows the last chord (surprisingly without an E-flat) to resonate deeply and peacefully.

An interpretive decision for the last movement concerns its fundamental character. Is it tempestuous and headlong like the first movement, or is it more restrained, more held back? I believe the latter is the case. The only marking is Rondo: Allegro; there is no *molto* or *con brio* as there is for the first movement. The harmonic and metrical stability of the bass eighth-notes—as opposed to the tension inherent in the bass tremolandos of the first movement—adds to the resolute nature of the theme. Although this movement is alla breve, I play it less fast than the first, at a speed that allows the lyricism of the top line to be felt in all its poignancy. Noting that the main theme is a reinterpretation of the second theme of the first movement could suggest that one might play the C minor statement of the second theme with just a little more import than previous statements (Examples 52a and b).

Example 52a: Sonata Op. 13, first movement, mm. 237–241.

Example 52b: Sonata Op. 13, third movement, mm. 1–2. The G–C–D–E-flat from the first movement form the beginning of the main theme of the last movement.

To preserve the tempo and for inner strength where the triplets begin (m. 33), I find a pulse of four beats per bar—rather than simply two—is helpful. Openness of tone—even within a dynamic of *piano*—is generally the rule in major key areas such as m. 44, in contrast to the soft intensity of the C minor theme. Following alternations of character between the two statements of the main theme and two major-key episodes, the primary intensity is distilled to a single chromatic descending line beginning in m. 167 before the final, most poignant statement of the theme. The bass line continues in groups of four eighth-notes in m. 179 rather than breaking with this pattern as in all previous thematic statements. This continuity, along with the right-hand eighth-notes and the crescendo, imbues the music with even greater urgency, sending it forward into the coda. Toward the end, the previous two movements are briefly recalled: mm. 203–206 are briefly in A-flat major, reminiscent in register and texture of the Adagio cantabile, and mm. 207–208 recall the first movement with its upward motion to augmented sixth and 6/4 harmonies of C minor. The last measures bring us back to the last movement, for the cascading triplet figure was heard twice before. But a C minor cadence is achieved only with this final flourish.

A brief story about the "Pathétique" illustrates the polar extremes of response that it generated. In his introduction to the English edition of Schindler's *The*

Life of Beethoven, the trustworthy pianist and composer Ignaz Moscheles (1794–1870) relates that as a young boy, he had been placed under the tutelage of Dionysius Weber, the director of the Prague Musical Conservatory. Moscheles

> learnt from some school-fellows that a young composer had appeared in Vienna, who wrote the oddest stuff possible—such as no one could either play or understand; crazy music, in opposition to all rule; and that this composer's name was *Beethoven*. On repairing to the library to satisfy my curiosity as to this so-called eccentric genius, I found there Beethoven's *Sonata pathétique*. This was in the year 1804. My pocket-money would not suffice for the purchase of it, so I secretly copied it. The novelty of its style was so attractive to me, and I became so enthusiastic in my admiration of it, that I forgot myself so as to mention my new acquisition to my master, who reminded me of his injunction [to study no composers other than Bach, Mozart, and Clementi for three years], and warned me not to play or study any eccentric productions until I had based my style upon more solid models. Without, however, minding his injunctions I seized upon the pianoforte works of Beethoven as they successively appeared, and in them found a solace and a delight such as no other composer afforded me (Thayer 1973, 242–243).

Although Sonata Op. 13 was an immediate public success, it did indeed engender criticism from conservatives. But Beethoven seemed not to be concerned with adverse responses. "Let them talk," he wrote in a letter to the publisher Hoffmeister under the date "15 January (or thereabouts) 1801": "By means of their chatter they will certainly never make anyone immortal, nor will they ever take immortality from anyone upon whom Apollo has bestowed it" (Anderson 1961, 48). Beethoven could undoubtedly have continued producing works affecting in the same manner as the Sonata "Pathétique," easily amassing adulation and wealth, but the path he chose instead is revealing about his artistic motivation: having successfully composed such a work, he moved on to other musical challenges.

Sonata in G minor, Op. 49 no. 1 (1798)

Sonata in G major, Op. 49 no. 2 (1796)

Sonata in E-flat major, Op. 31 no. 3 (1801–02)

Sonata in F major, Op. 54 (1804)

Sonata in F minor, Op. 57 ("Appassionata") (1804–05)

*A*lthough the sonatas on this program are close to one another in opus designation, they are varied in mood and in compositional mission. The Sonatas Op. 49 date from the last years of the 1790s and are charming in their brevity. Sonata Op. 31 no. 3, the last of the pre-Heiligenstadt sonatas, concludes Beethoven's second period of piano sonatas (1801–02), a time of formal experimentation. Sonata Op. 54 and Sonata Op. 57 ("Appassionata") postdate Heiligenstadt. Although outwardly different, they are conceived from similar musical material. Following their completion, Beethoven wrote no further piano sonatas for four years, his longest absence from the genre to date.

The two Sonatas Op. 49 are both small pieces of two movements; their very intimacy is their greatest challenge to the performer. Their brevity, the succinct qualities of their themes, their limited registral range and scale of dynamics—all are smaller in scope than those of any sonata that Beethoven had composed previously (including even the three very early ones, WoO 47, that Beethoven did not publish). Yet they are impeccably crafted and demand pianistic control, particularly finesse in voicing and dynamics.

The first sonata is the more somber of the two. The pacing of the first movement, in G minor, is gentle and ambling (Andante); the sobriety of character can easily be weakened by playing too fast. At the very beginning of the piece, I make a distinct dynamic differentiation between the songful, plaintive melody and the accompanying chords, but nevertheless voice the left-hand legato chords slightly to the top. The sixteenth-note accompanying figures in the second theme are then softer, more in the background, which helps to enhance the contrast in texture and character between the first and second themes. The loudest sustained part of the short first movement is the *forte* opening of the development area with the trills in both hands, but this fades back to *piano* by the fourth measure, the cadence on E-flat major. Although no dynamic is indicated, I make a subtle crescendo in mm. 62–63 (Example 53).

Example 53: Sonata Op. 49 no. 1, first movement, mm. 61–63. I make a slight crescendo in mm. 62–63.

Tension builds in these measures as the right hand ascends chromatically, preparing—as we hear retrospectively—for the main theme to reenter as a surprise, *piano subito*, in m. 64. I take a bit of time at the beginning of the last eight-bar phrase—the coda—as B-natural is introduced (m. 103) to change from G minor to G major. But tempo primo is resumed almost right away and the piece ends quietly, in tempo, without a ritard, leaving us hanging, waiting for the next movement.

The ensuing Rondo: Allegro is lively, but the pulse is six eighth-notes to the bar, not in two, and the tempo is determined by the speed of the sixteenth-notes, not the eighth-notes. The opening theme is confined to the middle register, as is the first theme of the Andante, and the weighting implied by the slur over the B–G is a subtle way of showing the change in character from the minor interval B-flat–G of the first movement. The light character of the Rondo's opening becomes slightly more intense with the second theme, which is back in G minor and includes crescendos to *forte*. Clear portrayal of mood among the alternating themes in this Rondo is among the most important aspects of the piece, particularly since the themes are so concise. In the area of greatest profusion of dynamic indications (beginning in m. 135) the motivic unit of the main theme is tossed playfully back and forth between the two hands in different registers before the coda concludes with the theme safely back in the right hand and two *fortissimo* cadential chords.

SONATA Op. 49 no. 2 provides a challenging opportunity to consider one's understanding of Beethoven's early compositional and performing style, for there are no dynamic markings whatsoever in the first edition (Bureau d'Arts et d'Industrie, 1805). Modern editions are based on this first edition since the autograph has been lost, and any dynamic markings are simply editorial. In performance, therefore, to judge appropriate dynamics, one applies one's own understanding of Beethoven's style of this era, of how he integrated the musical elements: tempo, character of themes, harmonic and metrical relations, nature of pianism. I begin the opening of Sonata Op. 49 no. 2 with feelings of confidence, aplomb, and a touch of bravura, *forte*. Rather than dropping to *piano* in m. 2 with the start of the slur (as is the case in some editions), I prefer to carry on in *forte* until the phrase winds down in m. 4, at which point I make a slight decrescendo, only to begin the repeat of the theme *forte* again. The quiet and more registrally confined second theme, which begins at the end of m. 20, can be *piano* until m. 36, which is again more brilliant. The development also begins *forte*, but then I drop immediately to *piano* for the triplet in the second half of m. 53. This contributes to feelings of surprise and anticipation, for the mode is minor for the first time and there is some question as to where the music is leading. Aside from the next *forte* motivic half-note (m. 56)—which is now in A minor—I like to maintain the level of *piano* for the remainder of the development, but the arrival of the main theme back in G major back is *forte*.

The second movement is marked Tempo di menuetto. The only other piano sonata movement Beethoven marked similarly is the first movement of Sonata Op. 54. The minuet theme is the basis for the theme of a similar movement (Tempo di menuetto) in the Septet for Winds Op. 20. The theme in the piano sonata is basically *piano*, and the two contrasting episodes are *piano* and *forte* respectively. The ways in which each episode leads back to areas of the main theme are simple, elegant, and balanced: the first via the right hand, and the second via the left (Examples 54a and b).

The coda, beginning in mm. 107–108, introduces rests into the dotted figure of the main theme which, as the line descends, make it feel both more airy and

Example 54a: Sonata Op. 49 no. 2, second movement, mm. 44–48. The connection back to the main theme is made by the right hand.

Example 54b: Op. 49 no. 2, second movement, mm. 85–88. The connection back to the main theme is made by the left hand.

more resigned. One could build drama with a crescendo as the line then ascends, but I think it is most in keeping with the intimate, impeccably crafted nature of these two "brother" works to end the last chords softly, foregoing any temptation toward a more brilliant *forte* ending.

AN UNEXPECTEDLY delightful aspect of performing Sonata Op. 31 no. 3 is the good-humored, quizzical, unsettled sensation created at the very beginning of the work: the music starts, the harmonies are ambiguous, and the music slows down and stops after a crescendo on an unstable second inversion chord—all this in only the first six measures. Although the home key (which we have no reason to recognize as the home key) of E-flat major is touched in m. 8, the music rapidly moves away from this tonality and reiterates the opening measures in a higher, more questioning register.

The publication of the Op. 31 sonatas in 1803 was not without turmoil, as we saw in Program 4. But Sonata Op. 31 no. 3, the only four-movement work of this opus, is an ebullient piece. The first movement combines the good humor of Sonata Op. 31 no. 1 with the improvisatory qualities of Sonata Op. 31 no. 2. However, unlike its brethren, Op. 31 no. 3 lacks a true slow movement, for the middle two movements are a lively Scherzo and a songful Menuetto. The last movement is playful and in sonata-allegro form.

The striking opening chords of the Allegro and the ensuing ritard and fermata are not merely introductory: they include the primary motive

and constitute the first theme, and they are developed as such. Voicing the chords slightly to the top and using the sonic characteristics of each register of the piano to the fullest (for example, mm. 12–13 contrasting with mm. 14–15) helps maximize the expressive nature of the writing; so will matching the dynamics to the rising and falling contour of the line in mm. 25–31. Careful shaping of the crescendos and decrescendos in the measures that follow add to the hesitant, rhetorical qualities in mm. 35–42. These in turn lead to the mighty stentorian cascade of *forte* Fs (mm. 44–45) through all the registers of the piano, setting up the second theme. Throughout the exposition, the true tonic key of E-flat major is never firmly defined. This flirting with and dancing around the tonic key give the work an improvisatory and playful air.

The mood of the second theme immediately contrasts with everything heard previously, for it is more fully harmonically grounded, and the music progresses without interruption by ritardandos or fermatas. Although played with a more definite sense of direction, the cadence at the beginning of m. 53 goes off on an improvisatory flourish as the music winds its way to a higher register. The metrical sense—a pulse of three beats per measure—begins to evaporate with the chain of trills in m. 68, as local cadences occur on weak as well as on strong beats of the ensuing measures, and vanishes altogether with the arpeggios beginning in m. 72 (Example 55). This makes the music hover as if being played with unfettered abandon, until a sense of meter is reestablished in m. 82.

Example 55: Sonata Op. 31 no. 3, first movement, mm. 72–75. The placement of the arpeggios that descend through an octave give the sensation of the meter's dissolving.

Intentional ambiguity of harmony returns to herald the development area and the recapitulation. In the former, tension is heightened by the chords (the same type already heard in the opening) that lead to diminished chords in mm. 92–93 (spelled with F-sharps rather than G-flats as in m. 4) and by the crescendo within the ritard. I voice the right-hand chords slightly to the top to weight the chromatic ascending line, further increasing the drama. Thematic elements from the exposition are heard in close juxtaposition in the development, and as the main theme returns to usher in the recapitulation (m. 137), the E-flat from the "opening" chords is omitted, and the key of F minor is temporarily invoked. The tonic key of E-flat is studiously avoided throughout the development section and first part of the recapitulation until the return of the second theme (m. 170). Hence, the bass line in mm. 169–170 (B-flat–A-flat–G)—all in the lowest register of Beethoven's piano—is important in setting up this theme and in imbuing its arrival with a sense of finality. (This line was not present in the parallel place in the exposition.) I take a little time to allow these notes to sound fully, and then proceed back in tempo primo. The final eight measures of the coda finally firmly establish E-flat major, but the *piano* dynamic of the ascending staccato sixths and *forte subito* for the last two chords still maintain the element of good-natured surprise which is so much a part of this movement.

Next in this sonata is not a slow movement, as might ordinarily be expected, but rather an exhilarating, joyful Scherzo: Allegretto vivace. It retains some of the playful and improvisatory elements of the first movement: lilting sforzando markings abound, and poco ritard indications on repeated notes before cadence points (for example, mm. 14–15) allow the music to hover before regaining momentum. The tempo, while fast, is ultimately determined by the quickness of repetition of the piano action, for it is important to hear the quickness of the repeated thirty-second-note chords (m. 43 on) slipping in between the right-hand sixteenth-notes. If the tempo is too fast, this differentiation will not be heard; too slow and the music is not up to full exuberance. I like to make the dynamic contrasts (mm. 90–95) between the higher register *piano* figures and the more gruff lower register *fortes* as dramatic as possible, even if doing so means a slight hesitation before the latter. And following the long descending line (mm. 100–105), with a ritardando over the last two chromatic bars, the main theme sneaks in again, *piano*, back up to tempo, and with a smile. For all the *pianissimo* staccato notes I use a light hand and a quick finger and wrist motion, as if sweeping dust off the keys. I play the final chords without ritardando, all *pianissimo*, but shaped so that the very last is in fact the softest.

The slowest movement of this sonata is not an adagio but rather the Menuetto, which is moderato. The minuet is a lyrical duet between the top line and bass, and I sometimes play the first phrase of this movement softer the first time through, with more presence in the repeat. The longer singing lines contrast with the openings of both previous movements, and although the tempo is not slow, it can seem spacious and luxuriant. Playful registral offbeat jumps in the Trio (mm. 16–18) recall similar qualities of the Scherzo but in a much slower tempo. These jumps take on an improvisatory quality as well in mm. 26–29, for all feeling of meter dissolves (as in areas of the first movement) as the two-beat pattern is repeated within the 3/4 meter. A thread of connection between the Menuetto and the following Presto is set up by the chain of alternating E-flat–D–E-flat pitches of the coda; these become an integral part of the left-hand accompaniment as soon as the Presto begins. Although this reinterpretation of the pitches is not something I would necessarily bring out in any dramatic way in performance, I do believe that as a compositional link between the movements, it creates a smooth connection between them. The E-flat–D alternation is so overt in the Menuetto that I would simply play it *pianissimo*, in a calando context, reaffirming E-flat major after the slight questioning by the introduction of F-flat. I might make a slight emphasis on the first D–E-flat that one hears in the Presto (second half of m. 1) but would certainly not do anything drastic.

The Presto con fuoco starts quietly, but there is no harmonic ambiguity here; E-flat major is definitively established from the start. Although fast, the pulse should still remain a quick six beats per bar rather than two dotted quarter-notes; this gives more tensile strength to the line and allows for a greater sense of forward drive. Within the framework of *piano*, the lines can certainly be shaped with dynamic shadings according to their contour. In the middle of the development section (beginning in m. 128) the hands switch from one to the other in leading the counterpoint; first the left hand is *forte* with the main thematic motive, and then the right, with this alternation continuing until the *for-*

tissimo chords that need to be counted their full value. Although there are two initial cadences in the home key in the coda, neither is definite enough. The music continues playfully back in tempo after the ritardando of the second cadence, straying slightly from E-flat major with a brief chromatic excursion within a linear crescendo (mm. 323–328) before the final *fortissimo* cadence.

Op. 54 is one of the least frequently performed Beethoven sonatas, and I'm not sure why. It is a novel and adventurous work. The first of its two movements is surprisingly not in sonata form but is instead a highly stylized minuet. The second, which lacks a contrasting theme, extends our concept of what constitutes a sonata with so thorough a development of the main theme and its motivic fragments that a feeling of return is evinced when the main theme recurs in the home key, even though we have never really parted from it motivically. Op. 54 even concludes with a brilliant virtuosic ending. Sandwiched between Sonatas Op. 53 ("Waldstein") and Op. 57 ("Appassionata"), it is, however, considerably shorter and far less overtly dramatic than they are.

But there are similarities among the three—they comprise the third of five groups of sonatas—and particularly between Op. 54 and Op. 57. "For the life of me I should never have thought that I could be so lazy as I am here. If an outbreak of really hard work is going to follow, then indeed something fine may be the result," Beethoven wrote from his lodgings at Döbling where he spent the summer of 1804. His eventual "outbreak of really hard work" resulted in Sonatas Op. 54 and Op. 57, both of which we may humbly judge to be "fine" (Anderson 1961, 114).

They were sketched in the "Leonore" sketchbook, and since Beethoven was planning them simultaneously over a period of time, it is not surprising that there should be areas of general similarity between the two. The gentle dotted upbeat figure of Op. 54, first movement, becomes more intense in Op. 57, first movement:

Op. 54   Op. 57

Whereas the radical harmonic explorations in the finale of Op. 54 balance the harmonically conservative first movement, the last movement of Op. 57 balances its more harmonically daring first movement by being more harmonically confined. However, both finales are of almost constant sixteenth-note motion, both are in 2/4 meter, and both have repeated development-recapitulation sections followed by a faster coda.

Two immediately obvious differences between Sonatas Op. 54 and Op. 57 are the mode (F major vs. F minor) and the shape of the similarly constructed opening motive (up vs. down). The feeling at the beginning of the first movement (In tempo d'un menuetto) of Sonata Op. 54 is relaxed, as opposed to immediately high levels of drama in Op. 57. The tempo of this first movement of Op. 54 is similar to that of the last movement of Sonata Op. 49 no. 2 (also Tempo di menuetto). In fact, the general three-part form also resembles that of the minuet movement of Op. 49 no. 2, for neither movement includes a development in the classical sense nor therefore a recapitulation. Each of the two times the main theme recurs in Op. 54, it is increasingly more embellished and therefore a bit more intense.

Sonata Op. 54 is not without harmonic daring. The first theme firmly establishes the tonic key of F major. The second theme contrasts rhythmically (all triplets) and in texture (canonic, starting out all octaves), is *sempre forte*, and is centered in the key of C major (the dominant). However, without any preparation, this thematic idea moves to the unexpected key of E-flat, also *forte*. I like to shape the dynamics within the contour of the octaves here, but the beginning of the recurrence (m. 38, last beat) is a dramatic harmonic surprise.

There is no smooth transition from the first to the second theme; rather the *forte* octaves of the second theme interrupt the tranquility of the minuet. The two ideas could not be more disjunct, and they should be played that way. However, following the somewhat improvisatory flourish prolonging the dominant (m. 136), elements of both themes—the melodic line of the first theme and the triplet rhythm of the second—are superimposed in the coda, causing us to consider that a reconciliation of these ideas is possible after all.

Although the entire Sonata Op. 54 is considerably more concise than its immediate neighbors, viewed from within and therefore considering the restraints that Beethoven placed upon himself regarding the basic musical material of Op. 54—the tiny musical cells from which it evolves—the work is one of unexpectedly thorough and subtle development. The second movement is monothematic, with contrasts in mood and feeling evoked by an enormously rich harmonic palette rather than by contrasting themes. I elongate the trill at the end of the exposition ever so slightly (second ending, m. 20) to help subtly distinguish the surprise and daring move to A major that follows. With each new harmony in m. 37 on (Example 56), as the bass descends chromatically, I make sure to grow in intensity as the right hand ascends. I do not play the octaves in the bass beyond the low F (m. 40) that are indicated in parentheses in some editions, for Beethoven's piano at the time did not go below this note. However, I voice the top of the previous octaves to the top note so that the line gives the impression of continuing downward with the following E (m. 41), even though the lower octave note drops out. The main thematic ideas are frequently interchanged between the hands, and are voiced accordingly. The left hand is more prominent than the right in mm. 45–46 even though the only dynamic marking is *forte*, but the opposite is true in the following two measures, where the initial indication is *piano*. Generally, whichever hand has the moving line is the more prominent.

Example 56: Sonata Op. 54, second movement, mm. 37–44. I do not play the lower bass notes in parentheses beginning in m. 41, for they were lacking on Beethoven's piano at the time. However, voicing the octaves in mm. 37–40 to the top creates a continuous descending line.

The recurrence of the main theme in m. 114 in the home key of F major is subtle. There is no grand setting up of the dominant to usher it in, but the stable bass tremolandos and the soft dynamic for the theme evoke feelings of arriving back onto familiar turf after a journey through the rapidly changing harmonies of the development. Although this movement does not have a true second theme, it is of sonata form, and the recapitulation begins here. I take the repeat of the entire second section, which allows us to revel once again in the extraordinary density of harmonic changes in this moto perpetuo movement.

The coda, like that of Sonatas Op. 53 and Op. 57, is faster than the body of the movement. Here it is made up entirely of thematic material (as in Op. 53 but not Op. 57). The syncopated sforzandos are important, for they infuse the final cadential harmonies with a sense of unsettled urgency which is never fully resolved even in the final measure; hence the fermata over the last eighth-rest.

WHEN I WAS a student, a group of us would occasionally get together after long days of practicing at Juilliard, and if a piano were present someone might gravitate toward it to begin playing the "One Note Game." The idea was to play the first note or chord of any piece, including piano concertos, exactly the way one would play it if performing the entire work—with the same dynamics, touch, rhythm, character of approach—and others would try to guess the piece. For example, if the C two octaves below middle was played softly but seemingly as the start of a legato phrase, the piece in mind could reasonably be the Chopin's first Prelude, Op. 28, but if the same note were played softly but staccato, one would guess the "Waldstein" Sonata. Grace notes did not count as first notes, so the beginning of Scriabin's Sonata No. 6 would be the grace note plus the first main chord. Some pieces were instantly recognizable: a *piano* G major chord, voiced slightly to the top and held a little while would be a good bet for Beethoven's G major piano concerto; two long Cs, *forte*, an octave apart were most likely the Chopin G minor Ballade; two Cs, also held a while, two octaves apart, *pianissimo*, filled with tension, were inevitably the start of Beethoven's Sonata Op. 57 ("Appassionata"). So characteristic is this opening that this piece rapidly became too easy for the game.

The spare texture—the hands are not one but *two* empty octaves apart—lends a particular sense of tension to the opening, which is relieved only briefly by the harmonies in m. 3 and m. 7. Although the dynamic is *pianissimo* I keep the fingers firm and pedal very lightly, maintaining a taut and sparing texture throughout the opening figures, not allowing any harmonies to accrue until the very last note of each (A-flat–F in m. 2; G-flat–B-flat in m. 6). Sketches indicate that Beethoven originally conceived of this movement in 4/4 time. As his conception evolved, he changed the meter to 12/8. Therefore, the pulse within each measure is twelve rather than four. This results in considerably more inner tension and drive—driving force here being steady, forward propulsion, not necessarily sheer speed. The wholly unexpected move to the D-flat in m. 4 and the ensuing arpeggiation leave one with the feeling that anything can happen, that this music is harmonically unstable. The *fortissimo* outbursts in mm. 17 and 19 add to this drama, as do the frequent areas of repeated notes around which thematic fragments pirouette. The chromaticism within the descending line that leads to the second theme also adds to the feeling of harmonic instability, and the second theme itself starts out in A-flat minor (mediant of F minor), the same key relationship between first and second themes initially encountered in the first movement of Sonata Op. 53 ("Waldstein").

The pulse of twelve eighth-notes per measure should not be allowed to lapse in the cascading arpeggio figure in mm. 14–15 (which can also be shaped with dynamic shading according to the general contour of the line) and in the syncopated chords of mm. 17 and 19. In fact, a twelve-pulse heightens the effect of syncopation here, which in turn adds to the overall excitement. The repeated left-hand notes beginning in m. 24 also keep up the tension; they are derived from the repeated notes first heard in m. 10, a motive that is used later in this work and also in the Fifth Symphony. If the piano I am using is well-regulated,

I use the same finger (3) for each note and allow the key to come up just barely past the point of aftertouch before playing the next note. This type of playing allows the notes to be repeated almost as a reverberation, rather than having them interfere in the main line. In m. 35, as a point of arrival has been gradually prepared over at least four measures, I take a little time between the first and second eighth-notes in the left hand, for finally we are in a stable harmonic setting. The *dolce* indication implies that the touch is not too thick despite the low register of the instrument. The right-hand octaves—a major-key transformation of the opening theme—are played without voicing to the top but rather keeping both registers equal, enriching the contrast with the two-octave span of the opening measures. I keep the entire descending line that starts in m. 47 *pianissimo*—no shading whatsoever—so that the *forte* eruption in m. 51—the entrance of the second theme—is truly shattering. Here again, maintaining a pulse of twelve quick beats to the measure brings the music's clarity and rhythmic strength to the fore.

This is the first sonata in which the exposition is not repeated. Instead, E-flat (of the A-flat minor harmony of the second theme) is reinterpreted as D-sharp in m. 66, which in turn leads chromatically into E major, as if shifting frequencies of light in a kaleidoscope, to begin the development. I take a little extra time on the B in m. 66 to help accentuate the change in harmonic vista. When the theme is taken up in E minor slightly later (m. 79 on), care should be taken not to rush the groups of five sixteenths beginning in m. 81, for the illusion of slowing the pace here by actually keeping them in tempo adds greatly to the tension of this area. This applies as the main theme is heard in different keys, and the groups of five sixteenths switch from hand to hand throughout the entire registral range of the keyboard.

It is always a challenge to control the soft dynamic of the low repeated C (m. 134 on) which grows out of the D-flat–D-flat–D-flat–C motive and over which the main theme reenters in the home key of F minor. The low Cs immediately become softer, leading to the *pianissimo* indication in m. 135; I use as light a touch as possible to make them very soft so that they do not interfere with or obscure the top line in any way. The slur from C back to D-flat in m. 139 is a momentary increase in sonority, as the tension builds with this small chromatic ascent and reversal of the previous motive. Dramatic excitement builds even more with the introduction in m. 143 of the B–F tritone.

The large proportions of all elements—registral range of themes, extremes of dynamics, brilliant use of the keyboard—presuppose a substantial coda for balance. The coda, which begins in m. 204, is in fact fully fifty-eight measures long, and includes such improvisatory elements as cadential flourishes (mm. 227–233) a ritardando to adagio (mm. 235–237) built upon the D-flat–D-flat–D-flat–C motive, and an increase in tempo to più allegro (m. 238–262). Following a single-line restatement of the main theme throughout the full registral range of Beethoven's piano (and virtually all of ours as well) the movement concludes in a shimmer, quieter than it began (*ppp*). A ritardando here would be superfluous, for the pace of the music slows down naturally in the bass as the note values increase over the last three measures. It would be silly to slow down the trembling right-hand accompaniment, and in any case, the last chord —as a kind of final reverberation of the F minor tonality—is held under a long fermata.

For all the drama and visceral excitement of the outer movements of Sonata Op. 57 (the sobriquet "Appassionata" was a Hamburg publisher's—Cranz— not Beethoven's), the second movement is actually the most forward-looking of the three. Simply marked Andante con moto, it is a theme with three variations. The low register of both hands, the *piano e dolce* marking, and the relative still-ness of the line and conservative harmonic motion convey a sense of comfort and tranquility, feelings in complete contrast to those of the first movement. For the theme and the first variation, I voice the right-hand chords slightly to the top and play the bass as a voice equal to this line. As the variations progress with increasing density of notes (classical diminution, moving from quarter-notes to eighth-notes to sixteenth-notes to thirty-second-notes), they ascend registrally and increase in dynamic range. However, it is what Beethoven does following the third variation that is revolutionary: the theme is repeated, or rather begins to be repeated, unadorned. The first instance of a thematic restatement (Sonata Op. 26 variations conclude with a coda but without explicit thematic restate-ment), this compositional idea points forward to its eventual reuse and refine-ment in Sonatas Op. 109 and Op. 111.

However, in Op. 57 the theme is fragmented registrally, for the first two measures of each four-bar subphrase restate the theme in its original register, whereas the remainder of each subphrase is higher (Example 57). The lower register restatements of thematic fragments act as anchor points here, and except for the last, each is generally *piano* regardless of the yearning engendered by the measures that interrupt. The last of the thematic fragments (m. 93) begins a crescendo that links it with the measure that follows, forming the beginning of the last four-bar phrase of the movement. The *pianissimo* diminished seventh chord under a fermata (m. 96) leaves us hanging until the next chord, *fortis-simo*, rolled only halfway, higher by an octave, interrupts the softness, prolongs the phrase, and acts as a bridge to the last movement. In fact, the harmony remains the same at the beginning of the last movement.

Our feelings of suspense at the end of the second movement are analogous to those induced by the dominant fermata of the Introduzione of Sonata Op. 53 ("Waldstein"). However, the Rondo of Op. 53 begins immediately in the tonic key, whereas the Allegro ma non troppo of Op. 57 sustains the harmonic tension for a full nineteen measures longer, until reaching its tonic (F minor) in m. 20. Both the meter (2/4) and the incessant sixteenth-notes are features of the last

Example 57: Sonata Op. 57, second movement, mm. 81–89. The beginning of each phrase of the theme recurs in its original register but is interrupted by the remainder of each phrase in a higher register.

movements of the two earlier sonatas of this compositional group. In addition, the left hand crossing over the right to complete the theme on either side of the sixteenth-notes is a feature of the last movement of both Op. 53 and Op. 57.

As in the last movements of both Sonatas Op. 53 and Op. 54, the tempo of the last movement of Sonata Op. 57 is not fast. While the nature of the sixteenth-notes of the main theme directs us forward, the bass also engenders a strong sense of resignation, even when the rests of mm. 21–25 are replaced by chords starting in mm. 28–29. In m. 96 I like to show the thematic entrances in each hand with a slight accentuation, which is then taken up by the sforzandos and the beginning of each group of chords. This type of canonic entrance is made more intense in the continuous passage (mm. 158–167) in the development area.

As the diminished harmony that opened the movement recurs at the end of the development to lead into the return of the main theme, Beethoven specified *sempre pp* and a long pedal mark beginning in m. 192. The pedal ties together the arpeggiated diminished harmony, but careful release of the pedal as specified at the end of m. 204 leaves just the low G resonating. This is important, for this G can now act as a local dominant for the ensuing C harmony, which in turn prepares us for the return of F minor in m. 212.

This return compresses elements of the main theme and introduces a new treble line in mm. 220–221, increasing the smoldering passion of this area. The repeat of the entire development and recapitulation (but not the exposition!) of this movement creates a yearning for a satisfactory harmonic resolution in the home key. This resolution is not forthcoming, however, even as the coda starts. Similar to the codas of both Sonatas Op. 53 and Op. 54, the coda of Sonata Op. 57 is at a faster tempo, Presto (as opposed to prestissimo and più allegro, respectively), but rather than emphasizing stable tonic-dominant relationships at the outset, the two groups of massive *fortissimo* chords in the first part of the Op. 57 coda are tension-provoking tonic-mediant chords. I make sure to play the A-flat chords in mm. 316–317 with as much weight as possible, emphasizing the surprise of their presence and the lack of harmonic stability they contribute.

By contrast, when a solid F minor is attained in m. 325, the dynamic is only *forte*. I would be careful to grade these dynamics, especially since they are all on the loud side of the spectrum, to reflect harmonic and dramatic positions. *Fortissimo* is reached again in m. 341, signaling the end, for finally nothing but F minor is heard from this point until the last measure (m. 361). The main theme of this movement is a whirlwind here, and the final two chords are pedaled separately to punctuate the ending. And an ending this is, for after this work, when Beethoven returned to the genre four years later (1809), his ethos was completely different; no subsequent piano sonata is endowed with this sort of heroic passion.

Sonata in A-flat major, Op. 26 (1800–01)

Sonata in C major, Op. 2 no. 3 (1795)

Sonata in E major, Op. 109 (1820)

Of the three sonatas on this program, only the middle one, Op. 2 no. 3, does not include a theme-and-variation movement. Instead, its four movements follow the general formal scheme of the other Op. 2 sonatas (and also of Op. 7): a lively allegro movement followed by an intensely expressive adagio, a brisk scherzo, and a vivacious rondo. The two Sonatas Opp. 26 and 109 are both adventuresome in form: Op. 26 is the only Beethoven sonata to begin with a variation movement (Mozart's Sonata in A major K. 331 of 1778 also begins with one, but this is not the norm), and Op. 109 is the first sonata to end with one.

The external circumstances surrounding the composition of Opp. 26 and 109 bear similarities. In each case the sonata immediately preceding is a four-movement work (in B-flat major) of large, if not epic, proportions: Sonata Op. 26 is preceded by Op. 22, Op. 109 by Op. 106 ("Hammerklavier"). This is not coincidence. With Op. 22 Beethoven felt he had succeeded in creating a work that stands on its own—even when compared, as he must have done, with the canon of Haydn and Mozart sonatas. Perhaps he then felt freer to embark upon new paths of formal expression beginning with the next sonata—Op. 26, the first of the second group of sonatas (which also includes the Sonatas Op. 27, Op. 28, and Op. 31). Sonata Op. 26 was begun in 1800 and completed during the following year. Although variations had appeared in a Beethoven piano sonata once previously (second movement of Op. 14 no. 2), never before had Beethoven written a theme-and-variations first movement.

A challenge in playing Sonata Op. 26 is deciding how to highlight the new and different moods of each of the five variations. While all retain the same melodic and harmonic outline of the theme (AA'–B–A'), each reflects a different aspect of pianism and distributes salient melodic features in increasingly abstract ways. A facet of the theme that is subsequently exploited in different ways in the ensuing variations is the specific use of register for a melody or melodic fragment. At the beginning of the theme, each hand is voiced to the top since the main line is in unison between them. But in the B area (mm. 16/17–26) the hands alternate in importance. The sforzandos in the left hand and its single line imply that the left-hand line comes more to the fore, with the right hand coming out more for the second part of this phrase. The first variation follows the same general scheme, with more playful and extensive use of register, particularly for the A phrases. Therefore the first variation is played with more dynamic shadings than the theme.

In the second variation the melodic line is abstracted in the bass only, with equal weighting for each note of the octave, just as the octave melody at the beginning of the theme—albeit distributed between the two hands—was weighted equally. But with the different disposition of the B phrase, the roles of the hands are reversed. When the right-hand octaves move chromatically for the first four measures of this phrase (mm. 16–19) I bring out the top line more than the bass. Gone are the sforzandos of the theme and first variation (although the rinforzando of m. 18 applies to the bass B-flat–A-flat–G). In the second section of this phrase, the left hand plays out more, for it has the main line. This weighting of the hands is the opposite from the theme and the first variation. The central variation is a somber modulation into the tonic minor (A-flat minor), a harmonic practice that was not unusual in sets of variations composed in the classical era. The change of mode from major to minor increases tension, as do the incessant syncopations. Although the right hand has the main melodic line, the left-hand sforzandos provide strong metrical and harmonic anchor points, and I take a little time for the first of these (m. 10), especially within the dynamic of *piano*. In this variation the B phrase is expanded with particularly expressive triple counterpoint—sforzandos on both the upbeat and downbeat of the right hand (mm. 16–17) and the left hand entering one beat later. (For detailed consideration of the changes Beethoven made in the autograph at this point, see Lockwood 1992, 4–5.) Only on the final cadence of the third variation are the hands together, syncopation having been left behind for dissolution of tension.

A different kind of metrical stress motivates the next variation, which is back in the tonic key. With the primary stress of the melodic line on the third beat of a measure (rather than on the downbeat), a simple *pianissimo* texture acts as a conduit between the most foreign variation (the third) and the next one, the final one, while incorporating aspects of the wider ranging registers of the second variation. I play all the right-hand two-note phrases of the fourth variation as legato as possible, contrasting with the sharp staccato chords in the left hand.

With the last variation I use more pedal as a thicker texture is established. Careful voicing to the inside, while keeping the top measured "trill" as light as possible beginning in m. 9, means that the thumb and second finger of the right hand are weighted more heavily than is the rest of the hand. The idea of diminution—increasing the surface speed, leading here to measured trills—was also a feature of classical variations, one that Beethoven took to even greater expressive roles in the variation movements of Sonatas Op. 109 and 111. Sonata Op. 26 has a coda with multiple cadences before which diminution ceases; each ending of the three different sonata variation movements leaves one hanging. Here his markings of *senza sordino* and crescendo to a *piano subito* final chord serve to keep the sound of the last four measures suspended, suggesting that perhaps the ending is not quite so definite as it could be.

But the biting sforzando on the first downbeat of the next movement (Scherzo: Allegro molto) is played with vigor, even within a *piano* context. This brief move to the related minor key (F minor) was initially broached by the upbeat to the B phrase (m. 16) of the first movement, the phrase subjected to the most expressive changes within the variations. In the second part of the Scherzo, I bring out the theme, first in the left hand (m. 44) and then in the right (m. 52), the first time through. Upon the repeat I bring out the corresponding counterpoint a bit more but still keep the theme as primary. In contrast with the sharp staccatos of the Scherzo, the Trio is virtually completely legato. Careful voicing in mm. 84–87 of the top line helps continue the metrical pattern 3 | 1 2 heard so far throughout both movements.

If the first movement of Op. 26 was a surprise to Beethoven's public, the third movement must have been even more unexpected. It is a funeral march on the death of a hero: *sulla morte d'un eroe*. There is no specific hero Beethoven meant to honor. Rather, the march is a stylization of the genre, written after Beethoven heard Ferdinando Paër's opera *Achille*, which was popular at the time. As he had done with his own arrangement for string quartet of his Sonata Op. 14 no. 1 for piano, Beethoven wanted to demonstrate his compositional prowess by composing within a style that was then in vogue.

The dotted rhythms of the Marcia funebre are characteristic of the genre. What is extraordinary, however, are the enharmonic changes by which Beethoven opens new expressive vistas. In m. 8, when G-flat is reinterpreted as F-sharp, I try to hear the enharmonic change on the bare F-sharp octaves so that when the new harmony—B minor—is actually heard in the next bar, I am prepared for it. But to the listener, the B minor harmony is a surprise, and so I drop slightly in dynamic level and take a little time at the first beat of m. 9 to underscore the subtle shift of context. Tremolandos in the middle section of this movement are stylized drum roles, and as sonority builds by virtue of crescendos and keeping the pedal down, it is important for the tempo to remain very steady.

Sonata Op. 26 seems to draw upon and indeed draw together external circumstances. Chopin supposedly played the first movement of this work (Lenz

1922, 179). The Marcia funebre, while not initially intended for this use, was arranged for brass band and played at Beethoven's own funeral (Thayer 1973, 1054). The rondo finale is motivated by figuration that purposely serves as a reminder of (and successfully attempts to better) the moto perpetuo figuration in Cramer's Sonata Op. 22 no. 3 in A minor (dedicated to Haydn) with which he caused quite a sensation in Vienna in 1800 (Examples 58a and b). Beethoven could not stand by idly while his turf was being invaded.

Beethoven's Allegro is basically a gentle piece. In contrast to what happens in many of his earlier works, here the only dynamic marking for the first twenty-four measures is *piano*, with a crescendo to *forte* coming only at the first definite cadence. Of course shaping the dynamics with the contour of the lines makes for an undulating texture, particularly if the primary line is tossed back and forth

Example 58a: Cramer Sonata Op. 22 no. 3, first movement, mm. 1–7.

Example 58b: Beethoven Sonata Op. 26, fourth movement, mm. 1–9.

between the hands as indicated by Beethoven's slurring. The only area of dramatic tension follows the second statement of the theme and recalls the tremolandos of the funeral march as it delves into minor harmonies. Although sixteenth-note patterns continue, the touch is different here; to produce a more focused sound, one that is more direct and less relaxed, the fingers are a bit more curved, and I play more on the tips, with a bit more weight. The very end of the movement creates a texture similar to the end of the first, for the indication *senza sordino* in *pianissimo* allows the final A-flat major harmony to resonate as long as the strings vibrate.

IN THE quiet moments of concentration just before I begin to perform Sonata Op. 2 no. 3, I hear it internally and feel youthful, exuberant, enthusiastic, and energetic. From the start this is a virtuosic work. Even the careful articulation of the registrally restrained first measure—making sure the staccato chords of the fourth beat are indeed light and separated from the previous legato sixteenth-notes, all within *piano*—is enervating as the music seems to effervesce beneath its sparkling surface. As the main motive is tossed back and forth between the registers and hands, I maintain the general level of the *piano* so that the *fortissimo* in m. 13 is a complete and utter surprise. In the virtuosic sixteenth-note passages that follow, the touch is strong indeed, but also transparent, with pedal used only lightly. Remember that this sonata, along with the others of Op. 2, was composed in 1795; brilliant textures here are lighter than in later works, such as the first movements of Sonatas Op. 53 or Op. 111.

The first cadence of the dominant (G) leaves us hanging in a *fortissimo* setting with three beats of rest (m. 26). We would be fully justified in expecting a second theme in G major to follow, so vivacious is the mood, but in fact the theme that follows is in G minor. This unexpected change of mode requires a more legato, singing touch. The phrase seems to never end, spurred on by the syncopations in mm. 31 and 32. When G major is finally attained in m. 47, the hands initially alternate in melodic importance, and the *dolce* indication implies not only a sweeter sound but a slightly thinner one as well. I use less pedal here than in the G minor area, and keep the fingers well rounded for good articulation. I start all the grace notes to the trills at the end of the exposition before the beat; this makes for a contrast to the surrounding sixteenth-note figures, all of which begin on the beat.

Beethoven was careful about the dynamics at the beginning of the development. The left-hand chords are only *forte*, but the right-hand sixteenth-notes start *fortissimo* (m. 97). Of course the dynamics of the right-hand figures need to be shaped and graded with the general contour, which gradually becomes more confined as the music leads to a playful, *pianissimo* false recapitulation of the opening theme in the foreign key of D major. Immediately, the syncopated element of the second theme is seized upon in minor key harmonies and combined with the most salient elements of the first theme. The sforzandos in both are important, for these offbeat accents increase dramatic tension.

So expansive is this Allegro con brio that a large-scale coda is needed to balance the development area. In fact, as harmonies accrue in the coda (beginning in m. 218) analogous to the way they did in the first part of the development, they also lead to a false restatement of the theme, but now as a quasi-improvisatory cadenza. Although one might expect a cadenza in a piano concerto, it is most unusual in a piano sonata, but such was the scale of Beethoven's conception of this movement. Therefore, I take quite a bit of time with the fermata at the beginning of m. 232 and begin the ensuing right-hand figure somewhat under tempo. Even though there are no indications for articulation in this cadenza, I maintain the well-established groupings of four legato sixteenth-notes followed by two staccato eighth-notes since the cadenza is built entirely from this motive, and gradually increase the tempo to the fermata on the trill. The tremolando flourish that concludes the movement harks back also to the first theme, and although it begins *fortissimo*, I drop in dynamics immediately only to become louder again as the line rises and softer as it falls. The final two chords end most emphatically.

The slow movements of both other sonatas of Op. 2 are in the keys of the relative major and the subdominant respectively. The Adagio of Sonata Op. 2 no. 3 is in the rather surprising key of the mediant, E major. Although melodic motion is much calmer, the opening theme bears a close resemblance to the sixteenth-notes of the main motive of the first movement. When a more rhetorical E minor theme begins in m. 11, I remain basically within the *piano* dynamic range even though there are no explicit indications. Here phrase structure is unexpected with asymmetric units becoming the norm. For example, instead of the more usual 4 + 4 grouping, mm. 11–18 are 3 + 3 + 2, and mm. 59–66 are 3 + 4 + 1. This asymmetry imbues the music with qualities of melodic unsettledness and harmonic instability. In this area the right hand can be smooth but quiet, with the two voices of the left hand interacting in musical dialogue. The tempo can be slow, stately, and steady throughout, without rushing even when the harmonic motion slows (mm. 41–42), so that the reentry of the first theme (m. 43) is seamless. When this theme returns yet again (m. 67) following the only *fortissimo* outburst of the movement (which reacquaints us with C major—the tonic key of the other movements—in stentorian fashion) the touch is thinner and more concentrated for it is in a higher register and begins the long process of saying good-bye as did the ends of the slow movements of the other sonatas of Op. 2. This series of leave-takings is particularly poignant and dramatic, for the ending is not entirely soft. Sforzandos in mm. 79–80 give unexpected weight to the texture, as does the fermata in m. 80. The *forte* registral leap in mm. 80–81 links together the two registers of the previous dialogue begun in m. 11, and I change the pedal very quickly on the sforzando *pp* B, to dampen the vibrations, allowing the B to resonate as quietly as possible, leading to the last cadence.

Contributing to the playful character of the Scherzo is the delightful way the themes enter and accrue, all in a light staccato touch. This fugal opening, which becomes simply canonic, necessitates clarity of voicing and careful attention to the dynamics, specifically the *forte subito* markings in m. 13, m. 27, and m. 54. The opening notes of the Adagio are reinterpreted compositionally in different rhythmic and harmonic settings to form the opening of the Scherzo (Examples 59a and b).

Example 59a: Sonata Op. 2 no. 3, second movement, mm. 1–2.

Example 59b: Sonata Op. 2 no. 3, third movement, mm. 1–2.

Although there is no dynamic marking at the beginning of the Trio, I start it *forte*, for the A minor tonality, along with the virtuosic waves of triplets over the left-hand octaves implies a strong, dramatic character. Clarity here is also important, and therefore I pedal only lightly, sometimes touching the pedal for only the first beat of each measure, not allowing too much sound to accrue. The Trio ends *fortissimo* so that the return of the *piano* Scherzo is a stark contrast.

A consideration when playing the last movement—Allegro assai—of Sonata Op. 2 no. 3 is maintaining a unified tempo throughout, regardless of contrasting character of the themes. This is consistent with classical style; it would be a gross distortion of Beethoven's ideals if one were to play the second theme, for example, so significantly slower than the first that the tempo would be markedly different. When Beethoven referred to the tempo of a piece, he implied one idea of tempo, perhaps with some flexibility, but nonetheless singular. There are subtle ways of indicating a slight slowing or speeding up of tempo within a movement or section—such as *espressivo* (implying slightly slower) in the first movement of Sonata Op. 2 no. 2 and in the second movement of Sonata Op. 109. In the last movement of Sonata Op. 2 no. 3, I also believe that clarity of texture helps shape the style of the era and the character of the work as a whole.

Consideration of these two points together—unified basic tempo and clarity of texture—determines the speed of the beginning of the last movement, as well as the articulation of the second theme. It is certainly possible to play the opening chords very fast—particularly with a relaxed wrist—but that would lead to too rapid a tempo for clarity of the sixteenth-note accompaniment in m. 29. At this area and in mm. 8–9 I do not keep the pedal down for each half of the measure as might be expected, for this results in a texture denser and less sparkling than I would like. The tempo of the movement is therefore planned by the maximum speed allowing clarity of the second theme; although the first theme can be played faster, I believe that unity of pacing is more important.

Even taken from the second theme, the tempo—with a pulse of six per bar—is quick, and melodic sixteenth-notes need well-rounded fingers, firm but not stiff. Soaring lines are shaped with dynamics to match their registral contour, and as the two hands come together in contrary motion, *pianissimo*, in mm. 67–68, the suspense of awaiting a cadence to the tonic can be heightened by hovering just slightly with the tempo. The general level remains soft and fluid until the beginning of the development. There the arrival of D minor—a key very far away from the home key of C major—is *fortissimo*, the loudest point so far. The thirds in both hands that follow (beginning in m. 87) continue the pulse of six. If the basic tempo has been rushed, at this point it would need to be slower; better to keep everything even.

Unlike the minor-major-minor sectional scheme of the last movement of Sonata Op. 2 no. 1 and the mirroring scheme (major-minor-major) of Sonata Op. 2 no. 2, the scheme of this last movement is major-major-major. The contrast with the middle section is in choice of primary harmony (F major, the subdominant) and length of melodic line; the unit of motion is generally the dotted quarter-note, as opposed to eighth- and sixteenth-notes of the outer two sections. The general chordal texture (thirds and sixths) remains consistent. It is somewhat unusual that there are no dynamic indications for twenty-one measures (mm. 143–164). The different harmonies give a slightly more exploratory feeling to this area, but I keep everything here shaped within a general level of *piano*.

The coda is the most extroverted and improvisatory of those of the Op. 2 sonatas. In the body of this movement, the main theme is always stated by the right hand in the middle and upper registers, *piano*. The coda, however, starts with a *fortissimo* declaration of this theme by the left hand in the tenor register, under a right-hand trill on high C. It is now the left wrist's turn to stay relaxed. Beethoven suggested fingering for the virtuoso chordal passage beginning in m. 269, which I use and find helpful. (There is something intangibly wonderful about using the same fingers on specific keys as did the master himself!) The coda is densely packed with playful surprises: double and even triple trills lead to a fermata over a rest (m. 297) as the player ponders the inevitable next move to A major, definitely the "wrong" key at a point that feels close to the end of the piece. So more trials are needed, more thematic scales leading to fermatas, to arrive finally at the "right" harmony—G major, the dominant—for the final exultant cadence. Subtleties of touch, as well as the differences between calando (again, dying away, both in volume and in speed) and rallentando (becoming slower), and the differences of mode (A major vs. A minor) in mm. 298–305 all contribute to preparing the expectancy of this cadence. Throughout this area, even though a performer knows very well what is coming next, he or she mustn't reveal too much, to keep the harmonic surprises fresh and questioning, to tell the story as if it is being told for the first time.

I RELISH Beethoven's late works. They are so thoroughly composed that every expressive subtlety suggests local and global nuances, no compositional gesture is superfluous, everything matters. How does one prepare for this? As a performer returning to these works repeatedly, I find that each time there is more to understand, more to express. For a listener the experience can be similar: the more one hears, the greater one's cognitive musical memory, the more there is to hear—an endlessly rewarding cycle.

Consider Beethoven's perspective. His Sonata Op. 106 ("Hammerklavier") is a work of heretofore unimagined breadth within traditional elements of the sonata: an enthusiastic Allegro first movement, an insistent Scherzo, a dramatic slow movement of unwavering intensity which itself is almost as long as Op. 101 in its entirety, and an enormous fugal last movement. (Of the classical forms, only a theme-and-variation movement is not included.) Op. 106 therefore represents Beethoven's final summing-up of the sonata; it was proof to himself, during a time when he perceived himself to be considered old-fashioned by the Viennese public, that at least he could write bigger and more expressive sonatas than any of his more favored contemporaries (such as Hummel).

The next sonata, Op. 109, is then free to forge ahead in new ways, with new formal flexibility. The first movement is highly concentrated and compressed, the second—rather than being a slow movement—is extremely fast, and a theme-and-variation movement concludes the work.

From the start Beethoven considered the three Sonatas Op. 109, Op. 110, and Op. 111 as a single project. On 30 April 1820 Beethoven wrote to Adolf Schlesinger, the Berlin publisher, "I will gladly let you have new sonatas—but not at a lower price than 40 ducats each. Hence a work consisting of three sonatas would cost 120 ducats" (Anderson 1961, 893). Negotiations proceeded, and on 31 May Beethoven agreed to compose the three proposed sonatas within three months for a fee of 90 ducats. Several weeks after the three-month dead-

line, Beethoven wrote (20 September), "Everything will go more quickly in the
case of the three sonatas—The first is quite ready save for correcting the copy,
and I am working uninterruptedly at the other two" (902). While Op. 109 was
indeed composed in 1820, Beethoven exaggerated the implied progress of the
other two. Op. 110 was completed in 1821, and Op. 111 bears the date 13 January 1822.

Another letter to Schlesinger dated 7 March 1821 refers to Op. 109:

> But as to the sonata which you must have received a long time ago, I
> request you to add the following title together with the dedication, namely,
>
>
>
> Sonata for the
> Hammerklavier
> composed and
> dedicated to
> Fräulein Maximiliana Brentano
> by Ludwig van Beethoven
> Opus 109
>
>
>
> Would you agree to add the year as well? I have often wanted this, but no
> publisher would do it (Anderson 1961, 916).

Schlesinger did not carry out Beethoven's wish to add the year, nor did he add
"for the Hammerklavier." Opus 106 remains the only sonata known as the
"Hammerklavier."

There were additional omissions and inaccuracies as well. Beethoven's letter
of 13 November 1821 to Schlesinger points out mistakes in the engraved plates
for the printing of this sonata, and a list of twenty-eight corrections follows in a
letter dated the next day. Many of these corrections address missing ties in the
Prestissimo and missing accidentals in the variation movement. However, the
first correction points out that a phrasing slur was missing in m. 11 of the first
movement (Anderson 1961, 929–931). This missing slur does not affect accuracy of pitches or rhythm, but rather addresses the quality of sound; the slur
adds an expressive weight to these five notes, which are now a definite group
(Example 60).

The gentle opening of Sonata Op. 109 arises from silence; like Op. 14 no. 2,
there are no chords at the beginning, but harmonies accrue as the first note of
each group is held through the beat. I make the sound of the first of the two
notes in each right-hand group slightly heavier than the second, as implied by
the quarter-note voicing, but both are sustained throughout the beat. The left-
hand groups of two equally voiced sixteenth-notes have an implied diminuendo within each group; the second of the two notes is slightly lighter than the
first. Whereas we are traditionally taught to use the pedal so that changes coincide with the left hand, in the opening measures of Op. 109 and wherever this

Example 60: Sonata Op. 109, first movement, mm. 10–12. The slur over m. 11, beats 1 and 2, was initially missing; this grouping is the longest to this point.

texture recurs, the pedal should be changed with each new right-hand group, for that is where the new harmonies start. While it is easy to see a descending octave line starting from the first right-hand G-sharp, there is no reason to bring this out; it is a compositional seam of the piece, and had Beethoven considered it to be of surface thematic importance, he would have voiced the right hand differently.

A great challenge in playing this piece is the very beginning. Rather than starting slightly under tempo and then reaching stride after the first measure or so, I prefer to begin softly and sweetly (*piano, dolce*), but in tempo. The character of this music is tender but not amorphous. I hear the first several measures of the piece internally before beginning, and play only when I feel comfortable with the tempo that I have already established in my ear. This tempo continues unabated through the crescendo in mm. 5–8 as the music intensifies.

Unlike every one of his previous sonatas, Beethoven specifies a slower tempo for the second theme—it is Adagio, with the additional indication *espressivo*. The character is completely different from the first theme: the diminished harmonies are full of tension, greater changes in dynamics occur in more compressed intervals of time, the copious articulation indications assure a breathless quality to mm. 9–10, the meter is triple as opposed to duple. An enormous amount of restrained energy is concentrated in these two measures. Hence, the slurring indication in m. 11 that Beethoven specified in his letter of 13 November to Schlesinger assumes considerable significance, as it calms the sighs and gasps of the previous measures by forming the longest melodic line so far.

I make sure that I hold the pedal until the last sixteenth-note in mm. 12–13 as the music of the beginning of the second theme is abstracted into a greater registral span, one that encompasses the full keyboard of Beethoven's instrument. In particular, the legato slur for the middle notes of the left-hand chords in m. 13 (A-sharp to B) lets us feel a wonderful chromatic shift even as the pedal is being changed. With the *espressivo* marking at the beginning of m. 14—an intensification and elongation of the "missing" slur of m. 11—I expand in time as the music climbs ever higher, resuming the normal tempo for this area as the triplets begin to cascade downward.

Concerning the "incorrect" length of m. 15 (there are too many beats), the autograph score is perhaps somewhat clearer than printed editions. Beethoven put a bar line in the autograph score at the "right" place—between the treble G-sharp and A-sharp; m. 15 is three beats. The following two groups of sixteenth-notes (one beat each) plus the one beat of tempo primo add up to an additional measure consisting of three beats. However, Beethoven did specify 2/4 for the group of tempo primo, so it looks like the last group beat of a 3/4 measure is not only in the faster tempo but also has the feeling of an upbeat in 2/4 meter. The feeling engendered by the music is what's important here, not the exact notation, although the latter was pioneering in any case. However, an implication of Beethoven's bar line in the autograph concerns the tempo of the two groups of right-hand solo sixteenth-notes (from A-sharp to A-sharp). Some believe that Beethoven inadvertently left off an additional barring, intending for these notes to be thirty-second notes rather than sixteenths. This is not the case, for not only are they clearly sixteenths in the autograph, but his attempt at metrical correctness with the bar line before them implies that each group of four notes is one beat, and therefore sixteenth-notes, not thirty-second notes. (Perhaps Beethoven did not intend this bar line to be included in the published editions, for in his numbering of the measures in the autograph, he does not count this measure. The tally coincides with printed versions.) Therefore, I continue the ritardando begun at the lowest right-hand A-sharp through these notes, even though they are markedly slower than the groups of six thirty-second notes which precede them. Within these groups, tension in the second theme area first dissolves and then rebuilds as they lead us into the development area beginning on the dominant (B major).

As the music spirals higher, changing the pedal with the first of each right-hand group (rather than with the left hand) remains crucially important for harmonic and melodic understanding. A crescendo beginning in m. 42 leads to the registrally expansive recapitulation; the beguilingly simple character of the opening theme is now declamatory. When the second theme is repeated (including a *fortissimo* surprise move to C major), ending in the home key of E major, there is another long bar, m. 65. It is evident in the autograph that Beethoven tried to make this one also metrically and notationally correct. After writing out the music in ink, Beethoven frequently made another pass through, using pencil to mark changes. Here he added a light bar line in pencil just before the new time signature of 2/4, but he seems to have crossed it out immediately. The crossing-out and the light line are of the same quality of pencil stroke, and one can conjecture that he decided simply to leave the measure overly long. His numbering of the measures (also in light pencil) in the autograph score reflects this (although it is off by one; he did not count m. 64).

I make sure the rests in mm. 75–77 in the coda are given full value. They are the only silences so far in this movement, and while the harmonies they offset are three pivotal harmonies in the movement, they also create feelings of suspense. These are relieved by the choralelike phrase—fully eight measures, the longest in the movement—that leads to yet another abstraction of the opening theme. The alternating C-natural–C-sharp figures in the right hand prefigure a move from E major to E minor (the second movement), and I weight the C-naturals slightly more than the C-sharps. The crescendo in m. 92 begins on the first C-sharp, which is still a light *pianissimo*. I take a little bit of time on the sforzando C-sharp in m. 97, but then it's back in strict tempo to set up the rest in the penultimate measure. The final E major harmony reverberates, initially with the feeling of a syncopation, but then gradually just in its own aura. It is held with the pedal until the start of the second movement. There is, in fact, no heavy double bar to indicate a definite break between movements, only a light double line. The Prestissimo breaks in, *fortissimo*, without a break of silence, before the final chord of the first movement has completely died away.

E minor as opposed to E major, left-hand octaves that are not only *fortissimo* but are specifically indicated as *ben marcato*, well-defined top line and accompaniment as opposed to a melding of counterpoint, and a very fast tempo: everything about the beginning of the Prestissimo contrasts with the Vivace. The pulse should be six per bar to avoid playing in two, but the tempo is very fast. In fact, Beethoven changed the original Presto to Prestissimo in pencil in the autograph, implying a clear difference in his mind between the two (Example 61).

To achieve this sort of speed, clarity is necessary. I use well-rounded fingers and only light pedaling. The touch, except when indicated legato by a slur, is lightly detached. Each time that the second theme is stated in a single, soprano line (beginning in m. 29 and m. 120), Beethoven wrote *un poco espressivo*. Following the subtle crescendo and decrescendo in the last bar of each of these phrases, the indication is *a tempo*. The implication, therefore, is that the marking *un poco espressivo* affects not only quality of sound (a fuller, more singing sonority) but the speed of the music (a little slower) as well.

I play both trills at the top of the ascending runs before the development and coda (m. 64 and m. 164) without afterbeats; Beethoven did not indicate any, the line is stronger and more direct without them, and in any case, there is no time for them at a Prestissimo tempo. Ironically, the development area of this movement is quiet, although tension simmers beneath the surface. The main

Example 61: Sonata Op. 109, second movement. Beethoven changed Presto to Prestissimo in pencil when he went back over the autograph score.

line here (m. 70 on) is formed from the bass at the opening of the movement. While the right-hand lines form a canon, intensity is maintained by articulating each note of the left-hand tremolandos. Use light pedal only, and keep a strict pulse of six.

The crescendo in mm. 55–56 is initiated by the inner right-hand line, as is the case in mm. 156–157. But the latter seems more intense because it leads to the dominant (B minor) rather than to the dominant of the dominant (F-sharp minor), and also because it is in a lower register. This crescendo is challenging, particularly since there is an inclination to rush, but if the pulse is maintained, feelings of surging forward will be more suitably expressed. In the short coda beginning in m. 170 it is also important not to rush, although the music seems to gather momentum as more voices enter and as the dynamics increase. I keep the bass voice clear to the end and show each new line as it enters, building tension steadily while maintaining the tempo so that the final cadence comes as a dramatic relief.

The third and longest movement of Sonata Op. 109, the expressive focus of this work, is separated from the previous two by time. Several years before composing Op. 109, Beethoven had become disillusioned about traditional tempo indications, as he wrote in his letter of 1817 to the conductor Ignaz Franz, Elder von Mosel (see Chapter 3). Although Sonata Op. 106 ("Hammerklavier") is the only sonata to which Beethoven actually ascribed metronome markings, in his determination to use more meaningful and accurate terms, he described the character of the last movement of Sonata Op. 109 in both German and Italian: Gesangvoll, mit innigsten Empfindung and Andante molto cantabile ed espressivo. In the autograph manuscript, the Italian seems to have been written first and the German added later, and each variation has its own additional tempo or character indication.

Var. I:	molto espressivo
Var. II:	leggiermente
Var. III:	allegro vivace
Var. IV:	etwas langsamer als das Thema
(Var. V:)	Allegro ma non troppo
(Var. VI:)	tempo primo del tema

These variations are not restricted as closely to the overall scope of the theme as are those of Op. 26. Rather, each variation explores a particular aspect of the theme in a unique way. Each contrasts with the others, and since Beethoven abandoned the exact phrase structure of the theme (two eight-bar phrases, each repeated) in the penultimate, fugato variation, he also abandoned the designation of this one and the following as variations. They remain unnumbered as variations, each headed only by its character indication. The structural musical link among them all—in fact, among all movements of this work—is the interval of the third. This interval motivates both the first and second movements, as well as the theme and all variations of the last movement.

As implied by *mezza voce* at the beginning of the theme and again in m. 15, I use the left pedal until the crescendo in m. 13. Each eight-bar phrase of the theme is repeated, and each time I make sure the left hand is legato in the first three two-part units. The direction suggested by the left-hand lines influences the breathing of the subphrases; I do not take any time between m. 2 and m. 3, for example. The manner in which Beethoven wrote the small notes in mm. 5, 6, 13, and 14 in the autograph (and all the small notes in the first variation) indicates clearly that he meant them to be played before the beat rather than on it. In all cases these notes are written well before the actual beat they precede, not just before the right hand but before the left as well.

The first variation is perhaps slightly freer in pulse than the theme, as implied by the *molto espressivo* indication and the small crescendos and decrescendos that abound in the second part of the variation. These imply slight broadening of the tempo where they are placed. Again with the *mezza voce* in m. 15, I use the left pedal to mute the sound.

As the theme becomes more abstracted in the second variation and the surface pacing increases, clarity of texture is paramount. I use either very light pedal or none at all for the interlocking sixteenth-note areas for the first time through each thematic phrase. For the second time through each phrase, the texture contrasts, as implied by *teneramente* and the denser chords. However, the tempo remains the same. Throughout this variation, Beethoven was very specific with the placing of crescendo and diminuendo markings, and these create subtle undulations—even within the *pianissimo* passage of mm. 17–24—which add to the tenderness of this music.

So far, the first and second variation have been in the same tempo as the theme. But the third variation is marked Allegro vivace. This is the most brilliant variation of the work, as the feeling of speed is increased also by the change of meter from 3/4 to 2/4 and by the alternation of sixteenth-notes between the hands in four-measure units (rather than the expected eight-bar phrase) in the first part. I make the detached eighth-notes quite short, particularly in the fast tempo here, and take just the smallest amount of time necessary for the *piano subito* beginnings of phrases to be heard after the dramatic crescendos to *forte*.

This quick variation leads without pause into the next one, which is specified as being slightly slower than the theme. For the first part of this variation, the continuous addition of voices gives us the impression of listening to thematic motives through a kind of sonic kaleidoscope. I show the beginning of each new voice with a slight increase of weight of touch. In the second part, when the pedal is depressed slightly in m. 9 and m. 10, I make sure that the high melodic fragment is very soft indeed, so that it just floats over the harmonies. The depth of the pedal is increased somewhat with the crescendo in m. 11 but is shallow again in m. 16.

With the fifth variation Beethoven abandoned not only his numbering but the use of the term altogether. In fact, nowhere is this movement designated as a theme and variation. The reason is that strict variation form was broken here, as the second half of the theme is heard not twice but rather three times (mm. 32–39). This variation is a fugato, back in duple meter (alla breve), and is motivated most explicitly by the interval of the major third. For the second half (beginning in m. 17) this interval is inverted, forming a minor sixth, and the music is more questioning and somber. I make all the eighth-notes staccato and voice the lines as in a Bach fugue. The music is high-spirited, full of energy, so that the *piano* additional repetition of the second half is necessary to lead gradually—rather than abruptly—into the last variation.

The melodic, harmonic, and rhythmic backbone of the theme is restated in this variation, the longest one. Note values of the subsidiary voices increase in speed (diminution); in m. 5 I keep the pulse of the dotted quarter-note equal to that of the quarter-note in m. 4. In m. 12 trills—the essence of speed—are attained. The melodic line and the harmonies of the theme are abstracted around trills first in the bass (not so loud as to obscure the top line) and then in the treble. In mm. 25–32 I use the fingering 1–2 for the trill and the fifth finger for the thematic line. Using the pedal as Beethoven suggested in m. 32 creates a *pianissimo* tonic-dominant mist out of which condenses a restatement of the theme. This simple stroke—unprecedented in the sonata literature—focuses attention simultaneously on the theme itself and on the extraordinary musical transmogrifications it has heretofore experienced. (Bach also restated the Aria theme at the end of the Goldberg Variations.)

A question that inevitably arises for performances of any theme and variations concerns the seams between variations. Should time be taken? If so, how much? Should endings of final phrases be rounded off by slowing down or remain in tempo?

A subtle hint in the autograph score, one that cannot be gleaned from any printed edition, addresses these issues for Sonata Op. 109. At the end of the theme, Beethoven had initially written *ritardando*. One would assume that this indication applies to the repeated statement of the end of the theme, thus adding to the closure of the theme and separating it somewhat from the first variation. However, after completing the autograph in ink, Beethoven crossed out this ritardando in pencil. Instead he added a ritardando and a low E in the bass (also in pencil) in the equivalent place when the theme is restated after the last variation, in the very last measure of the movement (Example 62).

Since printed scores contain no marking here whatsoever, an interpreter might consider a ritardando to be in good musical taste at this point. But Beethoven's explicit crossing-out of the ritardando at the end of the theme exerts an influence far beyond its immediate locus, as does the addition of the ritardando in the final measure of the movement. The interpretive implication of the deletion is that the theme flows seamlessly into the first variation, and the first into the second, and so on. Since no ritardandos are indicated at the end of any variation, I would not take time between any two variations, nor slow the ending of any. Beethoven was very explicit about the use of this term and about manipulating the perception of time. The journey through this movement is continuous—and the overall effect of the movement is cumulative—as the music becomes evermore abstract. Therefore, there is an interpretive imperative here, for to make a ritardando at the end of the theme would be wrong. A lessening of the pace would counter Beethoven's specific expressive intentions by breaking the continuity envisioned between the theme and the first variation. The overall flow of the movement would be disrupted and the emotional impact of the musical vision lessened. The only way to be sure about all this is by consulting the autograph score. When the very end of the piece is finally attained, the singular ritardando in the last measure, the addition of the low E, and a pedal marking with no notated release for the last chord all frame the work in its own essence.

Example 62: Sonata Op. 109, third movement, theme. "Ritardando" in the last measure is crossed out in pencil.

Sonata in D minor, Op. 31 no. 2 ("Tempest") (1801–02)

Sonata in B-flat major, Op. 106 ("Hammerklavier") (1817–18)

When I first learned these works, I didn't immediately associate them with each other. But pairing Sonatas Op. 31 no. 2 ("Tempest") and the epic Op. 106 ("Hammerklavier") on this program highlights crucial aspects of expression central to Beethoven's compositional creativity. These two sonatas, although separated by some seventeen years and couched generally in traditional sonata form, are nonetheless revolutionary in similar ways. Both expand the limits of musical perception and pianistic control—consider the recitatives of the "Tempest" and the sheer exuberance and speed of the outer movements of the "Hammerklavier." Both create areas of stylized improvisation—witness the very opening of the "Tempest" and the entire Largo of the "Hammerklavier." Both also incorporate seemingly foreign stylistic elements into the sonata: the improvisatory slow music that initially seems introductory in the "Tempest" is, in fact, fundamental and motivic for the entire work, and in the fugue of the "Hammerklavier" Beethoven embraces a baroque form and pulls it into his own stylistic universe. Both works are obsessed with individual modes of expression and are dramatic to the extreme.

Unlike the other two sonatas of Op. 31, the "Tempest" is a brooding work, starting from the opening rolled chord. Although the chord can be identified as a second-inversion A major triad, there is no reason to assume harmonic stability. The Largo tempo of the first two measures, the long pedal indication, the *pianissimo*, taken together with the chord that is rolled over two octaves and then arpeggiated at a slower pace for a third—all conjure an improvisatory context in which anything can happen next. Occasionally, in my own rehearsing, I extend the slower paced C-sharp–E–A up three more octaves just to pretend that the "improvisation," which must be considered real by the performer in order to be convincing, continues this way. When I go back to what is writ-

194

ten, I hold the fermata of the last A a long time before reinterpreting this note as though part of the Allegro that follows. The two-note groupings in mm. 2–5 are linked initially into two larger metrical groups (4 | 1 2 3), each with a slight diminuendo implied by the shaping of line and by the harmonic resolutions to D minor on the third beat. With the crescendo beginning on the fourth beat of m. 4, the grouping is 4 | 1 2 3 4 | 1. I don't rush here, but I do make sure that as the line goes all the way to the sforzando downbeat of m. 6, for the first time in the piece there is a sense of forward direction. However, in this Adagio measure, even though there is a cadence to a root position A major triad, there is no real feeling of resolution. The tonality of A major is not well established, nor is there any a priori reason why it should be; we are still continuing in an improvisatory manner, as the momentary move to an implied C major in m. 7 indicates. But the first six measures—improvisatory, concentrated, and grouped as 2 + 3 + 1—are not merely introductory but rather form a strong motivic and spiritual foundation for the remainder of the movement, and in fact, the entire sonata.

Op. 31 no. 2 is the only piano sonata for which Beethoven chose the key of D minor. In trying to account for the unusual way in which the work develops and for the dramatic balance among movements—the intensity of the first movement, the songful, highly embellished Adagio, and an Allegretto built on a reinterpretation of the work's opening rolled chord—some have grasped at Schindler's revelation of Beethoven's own advice to "read Shakespeare's *Tempest*." Beethoven, accordingly to Schindler, did not explain what aspect of the play to consider (Schindler 1966, 406).

The Largo measures are slower than the Adagio of m. 6, but all the fermatas are spacious. The opening should create harmonic suspense, for the true harmonic setting of the first A major rolled chord is not yet defined. The next four bars hint strongly at D minor, but its presence is not yet stable, and the rolled C major chord (in first inversion) of m. 7 is a complete surprise. However, with the left-hand six-four chord in m. 19 and the longest line in the right hand so far, a firm harmonic grounding begins to seem likely. I make the chromatic right hand smooth and the left-hand sforzando incisive, setting up the move to D minor in m. 21. Finally, there are four measures of harmonic stability.

The long line beginning in m. 21, which establishes D minor, has its roots in the opening: although here we are in a root position chord, arpeggiation continues, and the rhythm of the *forte* arpeggiation is the same as that of m. 1 (♪ ♪ ♪ | ♩). The tender *piano* rejoinder contrasts with the intensity of the two-note groupings in mm. 2–5. But the triplet accompaniment to this rhetorical dialogue drops from its initial *forte* (m. 21, m. 25, m. 29) to *piano* after the first note of each new harmonic context, so as not to obscure the main lines. The music has evolved from the improvisatory to the definite, and so has the harmonic grounding (D minor).

Breathless qualities of the two-note groupings return in m. 41, but here we are in A minor, not an intentionally vague A major. Since both the first and second themes hark back to the very opening of the piece, it is crucial to define these measures as fully as possible, with their intended multiple layers of harmonic inference and contrasts of touch, dynamics, and tempo. Sharp staccato chords and sforzandos beginning in m. 57 contribute to the altered character of the once plaintive melody of mm. 22–23. Here the character is more gruff, with the left hand dominating in m. 63 on.

Since the development area begins with longer arpeggiated (not rolled) chords again in a largo tempo, we might wonder whether Sonata Op. 13 ("Pathétique") may have served as a general model for this work. While both sonatas do indeed alternate slower and faster tempos, the slow music of the "Tempest" is the motivic mine for the entire work; the essence of the largo measures is fully integrated into the ethos of the allegro areas. By contrast, the slow areas of the first movement of the "Pathétique" act as dramatic foils for the faster music. Each integrates slow music into a lively movement in different ways.

When we hear the largo measures after the exposition, we cannot know what follows. Three consecutive arpeggiations is a new idea; after each one, we might reasonably anticipate the music of the two-note phrases. But the arpeggiations span a greater registral range here, and since they are not rolled chords, I play them slower and with more questioning feelings than the opening largo measures. The fermatas on the last note of each are held a long time, but the rests following the first two are strictly in tempo. Only the last note of this chain—the A-sharp—is held directly into the next measure with no break in sound. I tend to hold this last fermata the longest of the three, for the surprise explosive return of the main theme in F-sharp minor is the first *fortissimo* of the movement. This key is the relative minor of A major, which was implied at the very outset. The degrees of unity in this work are multilayered and multifaceted.

As the thematic dialogue ascends from the low F-sharp (m. 99) there is once again no feeling of harmonic stability for the next twenty measures or so. The *fortissimo* in m. 121 is important, however, for it punctuates the arrival on an A harmony once again, this time interpreted retrospectively from the following measure as the dominant of D minor. Feelings of anticipation are prolonged, as sforzandos accentuate D–F chords in mm. 122–132 within an unstable six-four context, and are further heightened by the whole-note chords in mm. 133–138, all with A in the bass. D minor is virtually defined by the C-sharp–B-flat augmented second in the top line of mm. 135–136, and the grace note C-sharp–E leading to the top A in m. 137 reiterates the opening of the movement. Finally, though, instead of D minor, the A major arpeggiation of the opening recurs, and this prolongation of the expected home key is a pivotal factor in the extraordinary recitative that follows.

Beethoven's own pedal indication, the *pianissimo* dynamic, the largo tempo, and the hints of D minor within all contribute to music extraordinarily improvisatory and yet quietly dramatic. These elements further heighten the drama by seeming to extemporize on the original improvisation and by creating a sense of time suspended. Changing the pedal within this phrase, as unusual to us as the pedal marking might initially seem, destroys the line of the music.

With an enharmonic change of A-flat to G-sharp, the recapitulation starts with the most virtuosic arpeggiations in the movement, which I shape dynamically with the contour of the line. There is still no stable D minor; even the D octaves in mm. 217–218 lead to a D minor harmony, but the bass note is F (not D), and the eighth-note left-hand figuration is a final rumbling iteration of the opening first-inversion arpeggiation. I articulate the left hand as clearly as possible, but the pedal and *pianissimo* dynamic create a murmur of D minor. The last two chords are voiced slightly to the top, with the bass D as the long-sought anchor.

The Adagio begins also with a rolled chord, but this time it is a stable, root-position chord. Accordingly, I play it with more of a definite feeling, rolled straight to the top, no hesitancy or coming away from the bottom note as in the initial rolled chord of the first movement. The division of the theme into two registers—as first encountered in the main theme of the Allegro—is reversed here, with the top line answered by the lower chords. The touch here is open, singing, and relaxed, opposite to that of the entire first movement. Recurring left-hand thirty-second note triplets can help build intensity with touch and dynamics when the music suggests, such as in the crescendos beginning in m. 24 and in m. 39.

The longest sustained melodic line in the entire sonata is the second main theme of this movement, first heard in F major in mm. 31–38 and again in B-flat major (the movement's home key) in mm. 73–80. I keep the pulse even so that the thirty-second notes are clear, and use a warm, singing tone in the right hand.

When the main theme recurs in m. 50, I try to make the left-hand embellished accompaniment as light and fluid as possible. The left hand plays over the right, with flat fingers and light pedaling. A particularly dramatic moment is the solo left-hand bass B-flat making a crescendo to the low A, *piano subito*, in mm. 91–92. This bare A should not be rushed; allowed to resonate for a full measure it suggests a darker harmonic image, one that may possibly return to D minor.

In the operatic style of earlier slow movements, this movement also offers repeated takings of leave, beginning with the octave line in m. 98. But in the final measure, following the slight temporal expansion for the right-hand crescendo to a *piano subito* and the low bass B-flat, there is no fermata; the music ends quietly. If the last sound of the movement were the treble B-flat there would be a sense of full closure, but the surprising bass B-flat leaves us hanging, wondering once again what will happen next.

The Allegretto sonata-form last movement is obsessive in its use of the arpeggiated chord, but in a thoroughly composed rather than stylistically improvisatory manner (Example 63). As suggested by the careful voicing of the left hand, I give a slight extra stress to the sustained offbeat As. This helps destabilize the tonic somewhat, as has been the case in other areas of the work. The right hand is gentle, and I think it's important to maintain a pulse of three eighth-notes per bar, rather than allowing the music to lapse into a single beat per measure. This three-pulse allows for clarity and prevents the music from becoming too fast; the movement indication is Allegretto, not Allegro.

Example 63: Sonata Op. 31 no. 2, third movement, mm. 1–4. The entire first theme area of this movement is motivated by arpeggiated figures, first heard at the very outset of the sonata.

The second theme of this movement is another further-composed form of the slurred two-eighth-note figure of the first movement ♪♪ but in a different metrical and harmonic context. The entire movement is built on these two ideas (the arpeggiated chord and the eighth-note figure). There are no arching melodic lines, no areas of contrasting rhythmic or motivic patterns; although the touch is mostly gentle, an unsettling undercurrent of obsession runs throughout. I pedal lightly in the last three measures of the movement so that the arpeggio gathers in sonority only gradually, allowing the last D—finally root position—to be the most final.

ALTHOUGH Sonata Op. 106 was completed in 1818, the very term "Hammerklavier" still makes pianists quake in their boots. It is the longest of the Beethoven sonatas, infrequently played because of its extreme interpretive and pianistic challenges: it does demand Olympian concentration and tremendous emotional resources, and yet it is profoundly rewarding to performer and listener, fearful pianists notwithstanding. Both the first and last movements are endowed with immense outpourings of enormous, almost visceral enthusiasm, whereas the sublime slow movement transports the spirit into inner worlds.

Typically I learn a piece over the course of several months (while performing other works in public), play it through for some friends, work some more, repeat the intensely personal mirror of private performances, and then bring the work to the concert stage. All in all, this process of repeated rehearsal and trial performances might take up to a year, although usually less. With Sonata Op. 106 ("Hammerklavier"), it was eight years.

Beethoven himself wrote to Ries on 20 March 1819 that Sonata Op. 106 "was written in distressful circumstances, for it is hard to compose almost entirely for the sake of earning one's daily bread; and that is all I have been able to achieve" (Anderson 1961, 805). At the same time he also seems to have known that his achievement was significant, for we have seen that upon selling the sonata to Artaria, Beethoven reputedly told them that the work would still be challenging for pianists in fifty years (Marston 1991, 448).

The publisher announced the sonata in the *Wiener Zeitung* of 15 September 1819:

> Now we shall put aside the usual eulogies which would be superfluous anyway for the admirers of Beethoven's high artistic talent, thereby meeting the composer's wishes at the same time; we note only in a few lines that this work, which excels above all other creations of this master not only through its most rich and grand fantasy but also in regard to artistic perfection and sustained style, will mark a new period in Beethoven's pianoforte works (Thayer 1973, 714).

Beethoven had begun sketches for this sonata in 1817, and although he was at work simultaneously on a Ninth Symphony (and a Tenth)—both considering use of the human voice, but still without Schiller's "Ode to Joy"—the sonata was the main product of 1818. It is the longest of the piano sonatas, both in duration (about forty minutes) and in number of movements (five); it is also the only sonata for which Beethoven designated metronome markings. (Although a common description these days includes the Largo along with the Allegro risoluto as the final movement, in a letter to Ries dated 16 April 1819, Beethoven referred to the Largo as the fourth movement and the Allegro risoluto as the fifth.)

Perhaps one of Beethoven's greatest innovations in musical structure is his relating large sections of a work to one another in the same manner as the smallest details. This allows for sophisticated, multilayered experiences of listening that operate concurrently on several different temporal levels. With Sonata Op. 106 Beethoven was obsessed with the dramatic potential of chains of descending thirds, both in the small and in the large. Descending thirds can lead more abruptly than the cycle of fifths (or exact chromaticism) to more foreign keys, particularly when pitches are reinterpreted enharmonically but still remain within the classical tonal anchor, the triad. Every one of the five movements of the "Hammerklavier" is constructed with large-scale trajectories of descending thirds, as well as with themes whose principal motivating characteristic is the interval of the third.

The first movement (Allegro; ♩ = 138) is of the form that has become known as classical sonata form. It is motivated completely by descending thirds, both in the small and in the large. Furthermore, dramatic tension is engendered by a fundamental clash between the tonalities of B-flat major and B major (and B minor) which determines structure in the large, manifest by the often pivotal importance of the pitches F vs. F-sharp (or G-flat) and B-flat vs. B.

The very opening of this movement is undeniably treacherous; particularly at tempo, it is easily possible to miss one of the notes of the first chord. Milton Babbitt has told a story about Arnold Schoenberg, who used this work to illustrate several points in a course he taught at the University of Southern California: rather than risk playing the beginning of the piece himself, he made sure his left hand was ready on the first chord, with his right ready in the treble area, and asked a graduate student to play the first low B-flat.

I also make sure my right hand is ready before beginning, but not having a grad student at my disposal, I get my left hand ready on the low B-flat and then look at the area of the keyboard of the first left-hand chord. After establishing the tempo and hearing the first several bars internally, I then begin the piece, keeping my eyes focused on where the left hand needs to travel for the first chord. Wherever the eyes are, the hand is sure to follow.

The opening theme (mm. 1–8), which divides into two halves contrasting in character, dynamics, and registral disposition, is motivated by the interval of a third in both rising and descending gestures. So organic is this movement that every principal theme is closely related to this opening one. Major structural events are marked by a descent of a third. Usually the interval of a fifth is a structural determinant, but in Sonata Op. 106 adherence to the third's primacy is more pervasive than in any other sonata. Perhaps this is what was meant by the reference in the *Wiener Zeitung* to "a new period" in Beethoven's works. To help grasp the dramatic plan when I am working on the piece and then to be sure to convey the expressive interrelations of the themes in performance, I start by considering the overall compositional scheme:

B-flat major	Opening theme (m. 1); down a third to
G major	Second theme group (m. 45); down a third to
E-flat major	Opening of development (m. 124); down a third to
B major	End of development (m. 201)

This triple descent by thirds leads to a point (B major) as remote from the tonic (B-flat major) as possible within the major key tonal framework, and the ensuing tension is hardly resolved by the rather forced chromatic initiation of the recapitulation:

B-flat major	Recapitulation (m. 227); down a third to
G-flat major	Subsidiary theme in recapitulation (m. 248)

At this point the B-flat major theme has descended a third to G-flat major, which is changed enharmonically to F-sharp, the dominant of the ever-lurking B. But the cataclysm that follows is in B minor (m. 267), even more remote from the tonic than the B major of the development (Example 64).

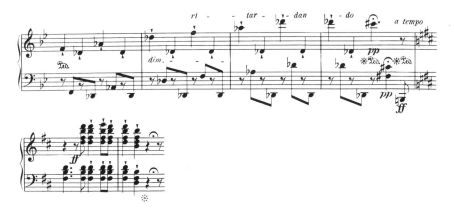

Example 64: Sonata Op. 106, first movement, mm. 263–268.

From here, another descent (by thirds, mm. 269–277) leads to F major, the dominant of B-flat, and the remainder of the movement continues firmly embedded in the tonic. The G-flat–F tension resurfaces in the coda, but the movement concludes powerfully in B-flat.

Back to playing. The fermata over the quarter-rest in m. 4 allows the reverberations of the enormous opening to dissipate and gives the performer time to prepare for the *piano* dynamic and legato touch of the melodic line that fills in the opening thirds. As the contrary motion of the hands brings them increasingly further apart, and particularly in the syncopated m. 15, I make sure that the left-hand dynamic, even within the crescendo, does not overpower the intrepid right hand as it reaches to the top of the keyboard. Beginning with m. 17, as *forte* and *piano* measures alternate, I make sure the pedal comes off quickly after the *forte* bars to ensure that the *piano* measures begin clearly.

With the introduction of an F-sharp in m. 37, the top of the right hand no longer descends but rather remains on high D for all the chords. This helps reinforce the new harmonic context, and I make sure the top D is heard plainly throughout. I also take a little time to gather momentum following the fermata in m. 38, for although the left hand remains in the thematic rhythmic pattern, the harmonic setting is completely new. The touch for the cascading lines beginning in m. 47 is much thinner and lighter than anything before, and at the right tempo, finger motions are precise, with no wasted movement.

In mm. 75–76 on, as interplay between E-flat and E natural is introduced (hinting at G minor–G major), I take a tiny bit of time for the reiteration of E-natural in the second bar of each group. I believe that the *cantabile dolce ed espressivo* indication in mm. 101–102 suggests a slight broadening of tempo, which is resumed with the trill in m. 106. As *fortissimo* and pedal is indicated in m. 112 until the third beat of the following bar, I have found it helpful to allow this sound to break off suddenly before the *piano subito* in m. 113, fourth beat. Within this G major area, the octave B-flats in m. 121*a* are a surprise, and I give them a little extra weight to drive home the fact that we are back in the home key.

Following the repeat of the exposition, the second group of E-flats in the thematic rhythm (mm. 135–136) is slightly less loud (not really softer) than the first, with the left hand playing over the right. I make sure to begin the fugue quietly and in a very steady rhythm, a strict pulse of four beats per bar. This feeling here exemplifies a sense of "working out" of the motive; the development of the opening thematic motive is thorough and consuming. The first half of the massive development section proceeds, or is motivated, exclusively by descending thirds, a level of obsession previously unheard in music. This overall concentration upon descending thirds, along with the clash of B-flat with B and F with F-sharp (or G-flat) give the music a sonority of sinuous and stern brilliance. Intensity is diminished only with the repeated Ds beginning in m. 197, but the tempo resumes as B major is established in m. 201. The touch here is once again very different. I play the beginning of the B major area with very curved, intense fingers (as opposed to the flatter fingers in the previous four measures) to produce direct but thinner qualities of sound. The sound opens up slightly with the *espressivo* in m. 205 and continues building in vigor until the reemergence of the main theme in the home key (the start of the recapitulation) in m. 229.

The autograph manuscript of Op. 106 is lost. Paradoxically, considering the extraordinary scale of the work, Beethoven seems to have abandoned his usual practice of composing in a standard-format (or desk) sketchbook. Most of the surviving sketches are from pocket sketchbooks, with a few loose leaves or bifolia (double leaves) of desk sketches. However, examination of even the earliest sketches reveals the persistence of the tonal foundation of the sonata.

An infamous textual controversy in the Allegro concerns the area of the transition to the recapitulation (mm. 225–226). Within the key signature of B major (five sharps), Beethoven did not mark a natural sign in front of each A (eight of them), and yet there is an argument that he meant to, but just forgot. An Artaria first edition in the Scheide collection has only the A (sharps), no natural signs. In the letters to Ries of 20 March and 16 April 1819—those in which Beethoven detailed more than one hundred other corrections—he made no mention of this passage. Consistent with the nature of the movement and the expressive function of this transition, the tritone of A-sharp–E generates far more tension than the bare fourth of A–E. Furthermore and perhaps most convincing, the recapitulation begins with a B-flat octave, not just a low B-flat note as in every other statement of this motive—the tenor B-flat is an enharmonic reinterpretation of the A-sharp that preceded it. The octave B-flat is also the reason that it is necessary to have a triple D in the left hand in m. 229; for the music's trajectory to continue, the third of the triad (rather than the root) is stressed. For all these reasons, I play A-sharps here.

In the recapitulation, the secondary theme is in G-flat major rather than in G major as it is in the exposition. The tonality of G-flat makes it sound lower (which it is by a half-step) and therefore slightly fuller. But it also allows for an enharmonic reinterpretation of the G-flat to F-sharp, which occurs at the end of the ritardando in m. 266. This F-sharp is the dominant of B minor, and the explosive *fortissimo* thematic outburst that follows in that key—the key farthest away from the home key of B-flat major—is the climax of the movement.

At this moment the drama is most intense, and everything that follows is denouement, bringing us back to the original tonality. The trill beginning in m. 338 is the only trill I know of in the entire literature that is surrounded by octaves in the same hand; I use the only fingering possible—2–3—except for m. 240, in which I use 1–2. Regardless of the quick tempo, it is important to allow the stark contrasts between *forte* and *piano* in the coda to be felt, as the G-flat–F-sharp tension resurfaces. Similarly, the pedal markings in the last five measures are very specific and help establish a rhythmic trajectory which, along with the progression of F–D–B-flat as the uppermost notes heard in the penultimate two bars, concludes the movement powerfully in B-flat major.

The Scherzo second movement (Assai vivace; ♩· = 80) is much smaller in formal scope than the first movement and begins so playfully as to seem a parody of the first movement. It starts in the same key: B-flat major. Repeating the top notes of each hand in the upbeat and downbeat figures is a challenge at the intended tempo. A piano adjusted for a large degree of aftertouch (see Chapter 2) can be more responsive. Even so, I play the upbeats lightly, barely depressing the keys, so that the downbeat can be played with slightly more force.

Descending thirds again motivate the progress. The contrasting long lines of areas such as mm. 19–22 sometimes require changing fingering on a particular chord to achieve a legato sound. The theme of the trio section, in B-flat minor, begins with the same rhythmic pattern (3 | 1 2) as the main theme of this movement. I begin the Presto area with a quarter-note pulse that is slightly faster than that of the previous music. Although the touch is light, the tempo cannot be too much faster if the offbeat right-hand chords beginning in m. 89 are to be clear. Although the dominant (F major) is made abundantly explicit by the series of sforzandos in mm. 106–112, I drop in dynamics for the prestissimo ascending run, which is light and gives the effect of being simply tossed off. In stark contrast is the tremolando diminished chord that follows, which I play intensely, *forte.*

Although the overall harmonic scheme of this movement is considerably more restrained than that of the first movement, there is the same insistence of B-flat–B that one hears in the first movement. Toward the end of the Scherzo, following alternating B-flat–B octaves, the opening theme is stated in Ds and F-sharps (Example 65).

Example 65: Sonata Op. 106, second movement, mm. 159–175.

I play the previous A-sharp octaves lightly, and the D–F-sharp–F-sharp–D thematic occurrence under tempo, in a somewhat improvisatory character. As in the first movement, establishment of B minor is as far away as one could be tonally from the home key of B-flat major, although here the context is *piano* going to *pianissimo,* rather than *fortissimo.* As the octave Bs become more insistent, however, and played with increasingly greater intensity, B-flat octaves break in, and the movement ends quietly and delicately. Whereas the music builds in dynamics slightly from upbeat to downbeat in mm. 172–174, I take a fraction of a second to drop from *piano* to *pianissimo* for the last measure, but make no ritard. The music just stops; the high, soft ending seems to break off, leaving us hanging.

Try playing the beginning of the Adagio sostenuto (♪ = 92) by leaving out the first measure and starting with the second. Certainly this makes harmonic and melodic sense. But now try playing the beginning of this movement again, starting with the first measure. The greater emotional impact is immediate. Interestingly, Beethoven added the true first measure only after the manuscript was already in the hands of both his London publisher (Ferdinand Ries) and his Vienna publisher (Artaria). The letter to Ries dated 16 April 1819 in which Beethoven specified a metronome marking for each movement also included (Anderson 1961, 806):

I must point out that the first bar has still to be inserted, that is to say:

Bar 1

And to Artaria he sent a leaf of music paper (currently in the Fitzwilliam Museum, Cambridge, SV 313; Mu. MS 288) containing the first two measures of the Adagio over which he wrote the instruction: "NB: the first bar must be inserted here, the second remains as before."

The Adagio sostenuto is among the longest and most dramatic slow movements that Beethoven composed in any genre. Its tonic key—F-sharp minor— is down a third from the B-flat major of the opening two movements. F-sharp minor is the dominant of B minor, the key of the climax of the first movement. It bears the additional extraordinary character indication Appassionato e con molto sentimento. Not only can fast movements be impassioned, so can an Adagio! But the opening is *una corda* and mezza voce.

The quiet intensity generated by the octave sonorities of the first measure opens into full harmonies in m. 2. I voice the chords slightly to the top and keep an inner pulse of six beats per bar to avoid playing in a slow duple pulse. The F-sharp minor harmony at the beginning of m. 13—replete with somber feelings associated with the opening of the movement—gradually moves chromatically, blossoming into a quiet, tender, optimistic floating line in G major in the next bar. Such polarity in expression is engendered by the chromatic F-sharp minor–G major relationship here, parallel to that of B-flat major–B minor established in both preceding movements, brought down by a third. But in the Adagio the chromatic relationship is between the first and second themes of the movement, whereas in the previous movements the chromatic relationship helps define larger-scale structural points.

A sketchleaf (a single page of music paper) for Op. 106 contains this move from F-sharp minor to G major, an extremely expressive element fundamental to Beethoven's initial ideas for this movement. (The present location of the sketchleaf is unknown, but it had been in the Nationalbibliothek in Vienna, and photographs of it are preserved at the Hoboken Photogramm-Archiv, also in Vienna.) Whenever these two themes recur throughout the course of the movement, contrasts of touch, concomitant with the harmonic differences, help define their character. Initially, both the first and second themes are *sotto voce*; the left pedal is held down from the beginning of the movement.

Evident on another sketchleaf is a different element of this movement that evolved through further composition: the left-hand accompaniment for the embellishment of the theme. When the main theme begins to recur in m. 27, the left pedal is lifted as indicated by *tutte le corde* (all strings: as for *tre corde*, the soft pedal is no longer depressed). Initially the left-hand figure was plain eighth-notes (Example 66a); it later evolved to the more transparent sixteenth-notes alternating with sixteenth-rests (Example 66b), allowing the top line to sing through more poignantly. I change the pedal with every sixteenth-note to avoid pedaling through the left-hand rests and negating their expressive qualities.

Example 66a: Sketch for Sonata Op. 106, part of third movement (Marston 1991, 416).

Example 66b: Sonata Op. 106, third movement, mm. 27–28.

In m. 53 a layered texture allows the sustained soprano and bass notes to be heard over the shifting harmonies of the inside voices. As the surface motion slows considerably in m. 57, I make sure to maintain an even pulse to guard against rushing, allowing the harmonies their full due. The development section of this slow movement is again a chain of descending thirds within which a duality of expression is made manifest by the alternation of *forte*, *tutte le corde*, sforzando octave phrases, and *una corda* single line phrases. We are led back to the most poignant abstraction of the main theme, where the right hand shapes dynamics to the contour of the top line. The touch burns in intensity throughout the F-sharp minor area. As a chromatic move to the companion G major theme is prepared in m. 99, the touch relaxes to allow for more open, conciliatory qualities of sound.

In certain places in this movement Beethoven's use of expressive terms implies considerable flexibility of tempo. In the area following the greatest emotional intensity, beginning in m. 107 for approximately twenty-two measures, there are two ritardando and two a tempo markings, and indicating even greater subtleties of pulse are the terms con gran espressione (m. 118), molto espressivo (m. 121), and espressivo (m. 124). Each term implies spaciousness of expression; large registral spans in m. 118 and m. 121 also broaden the music physically (for the player) and aurally as well. Following a measure or two of "grand expression," the music reverts to a more normal pacing to allow for further contrast in the area of molto espressivo.

In no other Beethoven piano work are there more una corda and tre corde markings. These directives for the use of the left pedal relate not only to quantity of sound (soft vs. loud) but perhaps more importantly to quality of sound. A pianissimo sound can be more present if the strings are struck normally (tre corde) by the hammers, or it can seem more distant if the left pedal is depressed (una corda). Hence, the placement of una corda in m. 61 (and m. 145)—one beat after the pianissimo indication—has more to do with subtle timbral differences that come into play when the left pedal is depressed than with quantity of sound, since the dynamic is already very soft. Both cases concern enharmonic reinterpretation of pitches; to maximize the expressive impact, I would be sure to place the left pedal precisely.

The connection between the decreasing dynamics of the last two chords and Beethoven's tre corde indication is also concerned with timbre. Tre corde in a pianississimo context forces one to roll the last chord a bit more slowly to make sure it is indeed soft enough, but also allows the sound to be less constrained, more open, more present. Such sensitivity to sound is particularly important since the last iteration of the theme is una corda (m. 181). It is played with the quiet intensity of touch reserved for a final statement and is the only time in the movement that the theme leads from its key of F-sharp minor to F-sharp major. Registers palpably open up, spans within each hand are as large as can be (tenths), and the tre corde breath of the final chord—although soft—is an optimistic offering. I brush each key of this chord as lightly as possible, so that as it gently reverberates in pedal over the course of the measure, the intensity of the movement is gradually relaxed, and we rise to the surface after a profound inner journey.

I do not wait any longer than the silence of the last eighth-rest of the Adagio before beginning the fourth movement (Largo; ♪ = 76). The chromatic descent from the bass F-sharp of the last chord of the Adagio to the Fs of the Largo helps establish the feeling of spontaneity of this movement. So does the continuation of the idea of rolling a chord—the thirty-second-note triplets are not much slower than the rolled chord that precedes them. This fourth movement is an improvisatory link between the Adagio and the Allegro risoluto. The improvisation is built, of course, on descending thirds. Three different themes, each contrapuntal in character, are tried and rejected. Beethoven is reaching out to the ultimate baroque musical form—the fugue—and trying to bring it into his own milieu—the sonata.

In this movement I try to bring out the feeling of searching for just the right musical direction, just the right theme. Each theme is in a different character and tempo, and each requires a slightly different touch. I begin each new theme somewhat tentatively, as if seeking the right path, but with the arrival of the third theme (G-sharp minor, m. 3) and its establishment of a more definite meter, we can feel as though we have finally found our way. Ultimately, though, this theme is also rejected, and the longest, most improvisatory train of descending thirds ensues. I start the first trill in m. 10 even slightly slower than the thirty-second notes that precede it in the brief reminiscence of the opening of the movement, before gathering momentum for each of the following trills.

As the left hand descends in thirds, the right hand ascends in register and the tempo increases. So does the intensity of touch. Just when it seems that the true destination has been reached—the bass descends a fourth from D to A, fortissimo and prestissimo, the pace slows again, and the intensity of dynamics diminishes. I make sure of a clean pedal change when the bass descends for the last time to F as the dynamics drop to pianissimo. Not only is this the same F with which the movement began—the cycle of improvisation is complete—but as the dominant of B-flat, this low F is also the pivot out of this movement into the next. It should be heard clearly.

Although the chain of trills that begins the last movement (Allegro risoluto; ♩ = 144) seems improvisatory, it is not and should not be played that way. The trills lead, with a direct and strong bass underpinning, to the theme which this time is not rejected but instead forms the basis for the entire last movement. The theme actually begins after the cadence on B-flat major, where Beethoven wrote Fuga a tre voci con alcune licenze. This directive explains the overall fugal context within the dramatic rondo-variation form of this movement, throughout which the fugue theme undergoes significant transformation. Each change, each new form of the theme, is a dramatic event set into relief both by the dynamics and by significant tonal modulations, always by a descent of a third.

Whether we are rehearsing, performing, or listening, conscious awareness of these variations helps us to understand their individual and cumulative roles in the totality of the work. The main areas of the movement are:

B-flat major (mm. 1–74)	exposition; repetition of exposition (in D-flat major) with metrical shift.
G-flat major (mm. 75–83)	variation of theme; interval of a tenth filled in with arpeggio.
E-flat minor (mm. 84–142)	theme in augmentation; return (m. 120) of variation of theme.
B minor (mm. 143–197)	theme in retrograde; new melodic counterpoint to theme.
G major (mm. 198–219)	theme in inversion.
E-flat major (mm. 220–239)	development of theme, concluding with the characteristic leap of a tenth in diminution and stretto.

These measure numbers assume that the Allegro risoluto is a fifth movement. For editions that print this movement as a continuation of the Largo, add ten to each measure number.

Up to this point, a descent of a third has marked each new section. However, the following area is a descent of a minor second from its predecessor, completely unanticipated within the total dramatic framework of this movement.

D major (mm. 240–268)	second variation of theme, a choralelike, lyrical episode formed from the main theme.
B-flat major (mm. 269–324)	reestablishment of tonic key, as the melodic line of the theme's second variation is in counterpoint with the descending element of the main theme.
B-flat major (mm. 325–390)	theme in original form and inverted form simultaneously, followed by intense stretto and coda.

The first entrance of the theme is played by the left hand. Beethoven's many sforzando indications delineate subsequent thematic entrances and motivic fragments derived from the theme. The relatively few legato markings refer to the first legato grouping in the countersubject (m. 21), and even though later recurrences of this grouping include sixths and octaves, I think they should be as smooth as possible. Although the entire movement has only one ritardando indication, I do allow the music to breathe, taking time to resolve cadences especially between the sections listed here. For example, I slow down in the last part of m. 74 at the conclusion of the first large section before moving ahead, back in tempo, in G-flat major (a new key for this movement) with a variation of the theme.

In the beginning of the third section (mm. 84–142), particularly when the theme is played twice as slowly as initially, keeping a strict pulse is important. Thus risoluto after Allegro: in a fugue so structurally complex and expressively rich, there needs to be one basic tempo, occasional ritardandos notwithstanding.

When the theme is played backward along with a new counter-melody beginning in m. 143, the feelings generated are completely different from those of unbridled enthusiasm engendered by the first occurrence of the theme. The retrograde is in B minor—the key farthest from the home key of B-flat major—continuing the dramatic B-flat major–B minor frisson begun in the first movement. Both lines are now legato, and the term cantabile is used for the first time in the movement for the character of the new top melody. As the theme is heard inverted beginning in m. 198, the texture becomes cleaner and less turgid than that immediately preceding. Just before the first high C of this inversion, I take a little time to make sure it will be fortissimo and to mark it as the beginning of a new expressive area.

There is not much time for long trills in the intense stretto of mm. 233–236. In fact, just a short trill of three or five notes is sufficient; the main idea is a concentration on the leaps of a tenth, and the trill is simply a thematic reminder. The choralelike variation that follows is surely wholly unexpected and is played with a solemn and steady grace. The only ritard of the movement is over the last three measures of this chorale and prepares for the return of the home key of B-flat major, with the theme in the middle line, pianissimo. Once again, an indication to not use the left pedal, even in a soft area—tutte le corde—is concerned with quality rather than quantity of sound. At this crucial moment of return of the two most fundamental characteristics of the movement—key and theme—the sound and feelings are open and ringing (although soft) rather than muted.

Right before m. 335, I take a bit of time to make sure the left hand is well placed over the low F, for here begins an intense section in which the theme is played simultaneously both in original form (left hand) and inverted form (right hand). The start, the low F, needs to be well defined. A cadence on the third beat of m. 356 is not conclusive enough for a movement of this magnitude and serves mainly to set up the coda. Following the poco adagio, which serves notice that the end is near, pianissimo thematic fragments, played clearly and back in tempo, lead to the opening motive back in octaves in both hands. Beethoven was careful about indicating afterbeats for the trills on these octaves. Although some editions have additional afterbeats in parentheses, I would refrain from adding them. For a motivic reason only two are indicated: they are for the thematic octaves (m. 382 and m. 386) that have the same metrical placement (upbeat and downbeat) as the motive—also an ascending third—at the very beginning of the sonata some forty minutes earlier. (The third is the essential interval here; tenths and seventeenths, for example, are octave multiples of thirds.) So interwoven is the emphasis on thirds that even the coda avoids a V–I cadence until the very end. Of course I play these chords fortissimo, but I elongate the eighth-rest before the penultimate chord by just a fraction of a second, giving the final cadence a little more drama and weight.

It is no secret that Beethoven became convinced of the necessity of metronome markings during the last decade of his life. That such markings should remain largely unrespected today is puzzling. We've seen that in December 1826 Beethoven wrote to B. Schott's Sons, asking them to withhold from publication his Missa solemnis until he had sent them his metronome markings. Some seven years earlier when Beethoven sent his many corrections for the "Hammerklavier" to his London publisher, Ries, he lamented that he could not "yet send the tempi because my metronome is broken; and I shall not have it back for a few days" (Anderson 1961, 804). Indeed these markings were duly sent on 16 April 1819 (806). Although pianists to this day have considered these markings unplayable—too fast—except those for the Largo, I disagree.

Was Beethoven's metronome faulty? Not likely. When it went wrong, he had it repaired. In a study of metronomes of Beethoven's time, Peter Standlen found that they are quite precise, but if anything, tend to beat a bit fast, which would make for readings today that are too slow. Standlen also tried slowing metronomes with the most unsuitable lubricant Beethoven could have found (according to the experts of the Clock Room of the British Museum)—green olive oil contaminated with dust, and allowed to oxidize—all to no effect (Porter 1983). Even parallax—looking up from a keyboard to a metronome scale, or down from a desk—failed to exert a significant effect. And as we have seen in Chapter 3, Beethoven considered movement character indications as the "spirit" of a composition and the metronome markings as its "body" (Anderson 1961, 727). Therefore, it must be assumed that his metronome markings accurately reflect his hearing of the piece in his inner ear.

Since Beethoven worked on Op. 106 for almost two full years and was fully immersed in its musical universe, for him the tempos were not unduly fast. True, they stretch the limits of pianism, but the work stretches the limits of musical perceptions on many levels. This piece reveals its riches with repeated hearings. Can we profess value in Beethoven's notes, phrasing, pedal markings, dynamic indications, yet ignore his specified tempos? I think not, for that would be misrepresenting his musical ideals.

   Having lived with the "Hammerklavier" for more than a decade now, learning and relearning, experimenting, playing it in many concerts, recording it, I have come to relish its challenges, and realize that to play it well, the concentration of total immersion is required. This is no ordinary state of being. The piece is in a class with the most consuming works, but the more one brings to this monumental it, the closer one is to artistic spirituality.

Sonata in B-flat major, Op. 22 (1800)

Sonata in G major, Op. 79 (1809)

Sonata in A-flat major, Op. 110 (1821)

*T*he three sonatas on this program are from three different compositional periods—the earliest, the fourth, and the fifth—and they contrast with one another greatly in form, style, and mode of expression. After playing Sonata Op. 106 ("Hammerklavier") on the previous program, I thought it would be interesting to begin this one with the only other B-flat major sonata that Beethoven wrote—Op. 22. Although Sonata Op. 106 has more in common, both spiritually and interpretively, with Sonata Op. 31 no. 2 with which it shares Program 7, the two B-flat major sonatas do share several traits in addition to, or perhaps because of, their shared key. Both are large works, Op. 22 particularly so. Considering the scale of other sonatas written around the same time, such as the "Hammerklavier," Sonata Op. 22 is also motivated to a large extent by the interval of the third, mainly in the first movement. Playing the two B-flat sonatas contiguously, on successive programs, works well.

Sonata Op. 22, a wonderful piece, is played less frequently than many, perhaps because the gentle last movement does not excite audiences to a fevered pitch. But the piece is full of rewarding musical challenges, even though not on the same epic level as those of the "Hammerklavier." (But realistically, no other piece is.) It is helpful to try to consider Sonata Op. 22 on its own terms—even, if possible, from Beethoven's perspective when it was written. By 1800, eight years after moving from his native Bonn to Vienna, Beethoven had established a secure reputation with a rather large body of compositions. He had composed twelve piano sonatas (including the sonatas that were later published as Op. 49), the first three piano concertos, the Op. 18 string quartets, the Op. 1 piano trios, the Op. 5 cello sonatas, the Op. 12 violin sonatas, and the Op. 9 string trios. An important landmark also was his First Symphony, Op. 21. The only piano sonata of the year, Op. 22, is a culmination of Beethoven's first period

213

piano sonatas; it demonstrates his mastery of high classical form, while the sonatas that follow are more experimental in nature.

Beethoven was justifiably proud of Op. 22. "This sonata is really terrific!" (*hat sich gewaschen*), he wrote when offering it to the publisher Hofmeister (Kalischer 1909, 59). He referred to it as a "Grand Solo Sonata," for in contrast to its immediate predecessors in this genre (the Op. 14 sonatas), Op. 22 is a large-scale four-movement work—Allegro con brio, Adagio con molta espressione, Menuetto, Rondo: Allegretto.

The first movement is full of life, with a high level of enthusiasm that seems to bubble just barely beneath the surface. I prefer a quick, spirited tempo, and make the opening measures very light, with the right-hand sixteenth-notes well articulated. This approach propels a listener forward to the main line beginning in m. 4, which is the only true melody of the entire exposition. To allow the high B-flat in m. 4 to sound all the way to the fourth beat, I drop the dynamic level of the left hand substantially. When the left hand has the theme in mm. 11–12, curved fingers and clear articulation will help counteract any impulse to rush. Similar articulation in the right hand beginning in m. 16 can help ensure a light texture that maintains the excitement of the music. If the top notes are held longer here, as is often the case in Schumann's piano music, the implied line would become more explicit, but the single voice of the right hand would become two voices and the texture would be denser. The lean texture would be forfeited. I consider the sforzandos in mm. 16, 18, and 20 to be sharp impulses within a general context of *piano*, with a further drop to *pianissimo* for the start of the second theme (m. 22).

The thirds at the beginning of the second theme are basically ascending, and therefore I shape each two-bar unit with a slight increase in dynamics. However, I make a slight decrescendo within each rising group of the descending thirds beginning in m. 29. Although the dominant is reached as early as m. 38, which could mark the end of the exposition, further embellishments and repeated arrivals on the dominant continue for another thirty measures. Leading up to each of these dominant arrivals, or expected dominant arrivals (such as m. 44, which actually turns away unexpectedly to A major), I like to give the impression by preparing the cadence that the section is coming to an end, but then play through the surprising continuations maintaining a trajectory all the way to m. 68. Regardless of the suspense engendered by the sense of withholding musical closure, the intervals of thirds imbue the Allegro with tonal solidity.

In the development I drop from repeated levels of *fortissimo* to levels of *piano* when elements of the first theme return in different keys (mm. 83, 87, and 91). Gradually there is a shift away from the melodic dominance of the right hand, and in m. 105, the left hand takes over as the primary melodic voice. In ever lower registers it plays the line that closed the exposition (heard initially in octaves in mm. 62–63) until reaching the lowest note on Beethoven's piano (low F, m. 116). I hold the fermata in m. 127 long enough to preserve the inherent tension of the *pianissimo* dominant chord, but not so long that the sound dies away completely. The recapitulation that follows is a slightly embellished rehearing of the exposition, but despite the breadth of the themes, there is no coda (as there is for thematic balance in the large first movements of Sonatas Op. 7 and Op. 10 no. 3). In Sonata Op. 22 repeated anticipated cadences on B-flat over the last twenty-five bars or so of the recapitulation, analogous to the repeated efforts to establish the dominant (F major) in the exposition, render any additional coda superfluous.

From the outset, the Adagio is full of operatic lyricism. I play the opening left-hand chords with a pure accompaniment touch—flat fingers gently sweeping off the keys. There is no ambiguity of role; these chords establish the tonal, melodic, and rhythmic context for the melodic line that enters later in the measure. This line is shaped parallel to its rising and falling contour, and the four bars that elongate the phrase from eight to twelve measures gradually diminish in intensity. The mood is quietly dignified, but the florid cadenzalike flourish of mm. 25 and 26, which I play with a somewhat flexible pulse, hints at further drama to come.

The abrupt and surprising move to G major (mediant of E-flat major, tonic key of this movement) in m. 31 is fraught with additional harmonic tension in the ensuing measures, as Beethoven's choice of harmonies is daring indeed. In the canon that follows, I like to establish terraces of voices, keeping each one independent in dynamics from the others. This separation is particularly important in mm. 39–42, as the top voice has subtle crescendos and decrescendos, but the middle and bottom voices remain essentially stable. To create the illusion of a crescendo on the sustained top and bottom B-flats in both mm. 43 and 44, I make a slight swell with the inner voices but then allow them to drop again as the last two eighth-notes of the top and bottom voices continue the crescendo. When the main theme returns in m. 47, I allow the embellished areas to be relaxed in pacing, in the nature of a true singing, breathing line. Just as in the first movement, there is no coda, there are no extra leave-takings as there are in many previous sonata slow movements. To me, this implies that the crescendo in m. 76 is particularly spacious. Whereas m. 30—the analogous cadential measure—is *piano*, the last measure of the movement is *pianissimo* and the registral span is greater. This gives an increased sense of finality, and therefore I wait enough time before the penultimate chord to make sure that the last two chords will indeed be very soft.

In the beginning of the Menuetto, I make a distinct difference between the singing top line and the accompaniment. But this difference blurs in mm. 9 and 13 where I make the hands more equal, possibly even favoring the left hand the second time through. I also play the initial eight-bar phrase differently in its first and second appearances: the first time arises out of silence and is softer.

Only in mm. 21 and 22, when the left hand is not under a legato slur and is more articulated within a crescendo, do I allow the left-hand dynamic level to come up to that of the right, and perhaps even momentarily to exceed it. The Minore trio is overtly dramatic. Here the left hand is prominent from the start, and the figuration hints at that of the very opening of the first movement. Keeping a steady tempo will allow the offbeat sforzando right-hand chords to sound more menacing than a pacing that rushes. A steady tempo is particularly important in the second half of the trio, when the two hands imitate each other. I wait slightly until the resonance of the final G minor harmony of the trio has cleared before beginning the minuet for the final time, starting it with more of a presence than the first time through, but perhaps slightly less than the second.

I have found that the most successful performances of the last movement (Rondo: Allegretto) are those that do not try to make this movement into something it isn't, such as a fast, impassioned conclusion, but rather accept the music for what it is—gentle and graceful—and revel in it. The tempo is not fast; it is leisurely. Even when octaves enter in the right hand in m. 9, they are not virtuosic but rather simply a fuller, more open, singing line. Throughout, harmonies are firmly grounded, and as the melodic lines evaporate (m. 22) the left hand assumes an increasingly important role in providing both a melodic and harmonic anchor.

As the top line begins to reassert prominence in m. 46, I keep the pulse strict particularly since the surface pace gradually increases with triplets and thirty-second notes. But I do take a little bit of time before the *sfp* G in m. 49, marking the reemergence of the main theme of the rondo. I also make sure that the B-flat minor harmony in m. 67 is a complete surprise—*forte*, different tone color, in a lower register than the analogous chord (B-flat major) in m. 18. In the most dramatic section of this movement, the interval of a third returns, creating a texture that recalls elements of both the Minore section of the previous movement and aspects of the first movement. Both hands are of equal importance here; the left-hand staccatos are sharp, whereas the right-hand line is smoother.

Pianistic touch becomes less intense and the pacing slightly more relaxed at the beginning of m. 111, as the alternating G-flat–F becomes G-natural–F, indicating a move away from B-flat minor to B-flat major, paving the way for a recurrence of the rondo theme, which starts here in the left hand. Here the theme is embellished considerably but retains salient rhythmic features. But when the theme recurs for the final time, beginning with mm. 164–165, right-hand triplets give a lilting feeling to the music, which becomes even more playful with the light, offbeat octaves in mm. 173 and 175.

This movement is the only one with a coda. I make sure to keep an eighth-note pulse with the seemingly long quarter-notes with which it starts (mm. 182–183) in order not to rush. The left-hand fingers are firm and articulate the thirty-second notes smoothly. The piece could end with the *fortissimo* cadence in mm. 193–194, and therefore I play it as though it does—by expanding slightly in time in m. 193 and with a clear, focused touch. But that is not the real end; the *piano subito* that follows is a surprise, and I wait a small fraction of a second before it. As this thematic fragment leads to the true final cadence, we can be led to believe that the piece will end softly—as it began—so now the tables are turned, and the last *fortissimo* dominant-tonic chords are a surprise.

Sonata Op. 22 concludes a chapter in Beethoven's creative development. With the immediate sonatas that follow—Op. 26 and the Sonatas *quasi una fantasia* Op. 27—Beethoven embarks upon new and previously unexplored musical pathways.

So CRISP and vibrant is the beginning of Sonata Op. 79 that a good performance will lift the spirits of everyone in the audience, carrying them along on soaring lines that—although they may sometimes seem to double back on themselves—always move listeners forward with unflagging energy. Before actually starting the piece, I hear the first eight measures in my mind, setting the lively musical character and the quick tempo, imagining the sharp but playful *forte* staccato touch for the opening chords. The tonality is immediately defined—no feelings of ambiguity here.

This sonata is one of the three (including also Op. 78 and Op. 81a) that comprise the fourth of the five periods of Beethoven's piano sonatas. Although this sonata is energetic, its overall formal scope is smaller than many. Each of its three short movements is in G—the lively first and last are in G major, the songful middle one in G minor. This is the only Beethoven sonata in which folk elements play a role. The first movement is Presto alla tedesca; the term *tedesca* alludes to a German folk dance in rapid triple meter, popular in the first decades of the nineteenth century. (The Alla danza tedesca of the String Quartet in B-flat major, Op. 130, is built upon an inversion of the first theme of the Presto alla tedesca of Sonata Op. 79.)

Not surprisingly, Beethoven's treatment of *tedesca* elements is highly sophisticated. The *forte* indication at the beginning of m. 8 is both unexpected and important to the drama, for it pushes forward the momentum of the phrase at a point where one would ordinarily expect the tonic cadence to conclude the phrase. The extension of the first phrase leads to a cadence on D—the dominant—that leaves us suspended. Metrical stability also dissolves as the arpeggios that follow negate feelings of three beats per bar. I play these arpeggios in the natural groupings implied (generally groups of four notes), avoiding any accents on downbeats of intermediate measures, such as mm. 13, 14, and 15 of the first group. Reestablishment of metrical stability in m. 24 provides a sense of relief, along with the cadence on A major (dominant of the dominant) as the left hand has the main line. At the end of this second theme area, there is another surprise *forte* at a cadence; we are once again propelled past the point that would ordinarily be the end of the phrase (m. 46).

I make sure not to rush the rests on the first beats of mm. 48–49, for not only do they set up the return to the beginning of the exposition, but they also establish a sense of the metrical importance of the second beat of the measure, a feature worked out more fully in the development area with left-hand registral leaps beginning in m. 59. Throughout the development the dynamics are terraced; that is, they are either *forte* or *piano* with only two crescendos marked, one leading to the restatement of the opening theme to mark the beginning of the recapitulation. But sensitivity to key is important, and I take a little time in the transition to the *dolce* E-flat major (m. 91). The pedal markings—indicated only in *dolce* and *piano* contexts in the development section—also help set new harmonic areas into relief. For each marking I depress the pedal only slightly, which helps create a delicate veil of sonority.

Although there are no long pedal markings in any *forte* areas of the development, the *forte* to mark the beginning of the recapitulation (mm. 123–124) is indeed in pedal, and the foot is depressed to the floor. There is nothing delicate about these measures; they are high-spirited and buoyant. So is the first ending of the recapitulation; mm. 170*a*–171*a* lead a listener to expect a G cadence, so the *forte* and the G-sharp in m. 172*a* are both unexpected. Therefore, I wait a little longer on the quarter-rest at the beginning of m. 172*a* just to set up the surprises.

The main theme is in the left hand for the first time in the coda (m. 176), so when it reappears in the right hand four bars later, it seems to be a rejoinder in a dialogue. But the conversation turns increasingly jovial as *forte* appoggiaturas are introduced in m. 184. I wait very slightly before each, giving as great a sense of lift and playfulness to each as possible. In m. 191 I voice the left-hand chords subtly to the top, as this area recalls the left-hand leaps of the development section.

The actual ending of the movement—the last three measures—is unique; there are no other Beethoven sonata endings like it. The dominant harmony is that of m. 198, but there are no repeated chords at the end, no *forte* pronouncements of the tonic. I try to play the ascending arpeggio gracefully and flowing to the top by pedaling only lightly and not allowing sonority to accumulate.

The beginning of the Andante is also unusual for Beethoven. The simple melody and the gentle bass, along with a 9/8 meter, create the feeling of a Venetian gondolier's song. Although Beethoven composed in this manner only this once, Mendelssohn was to espouse the aesthetic years later in many of his *Songs Without Words*. The Andante's eighth-notes determine the tempo. I allow the pace to expand very slightly at the apex of the crescendo and decrescendo throughout the first phrase. With the change of key into E-flat major in m. 10 and the longer treble lines and running sixteenth-note accompaniment in the bass, it is important not to rush. But with the group of five thirty-second notes in the embellishment of the line (m. 19), again I allow the tempo to expand slightly. The sforzando in the transition back to G minor (m. 21) is poignant, as is the portato touch in the penultimate bar. The eighth-rests in the last bar surround the final chords with silence and a ritard would be superfluous.

A feeling of openness is immediately reestablished by the Vivace, which is back in G major. During the first time through the first phrase, the right hand is primary, but in the repeat, I bring out the left-hand line a bit more. In m. 9, though, when the hands are in unison, they are equal in voicing. The relaxed left-hand accompaniment touch of m. 18 becomes considerably more intense in m. 21, as once again the hands are in unison and the context is a strong E minor (the relative minor of the tonic G major).

I'm greatly interested in the different expressive capacities of the theme whenever it resurfaces. In m. 34, before the first recurrence of the main rondo theme, I take a little extra time and exert a bit extra weight on the C-natural, for this helps establish the home key of G major. Here the theme is still quiet, even though the left hand is embellished with triplets which I play very evenly. But in m. 72 when the theme recurs after the longest episode, the G major tonality is established by the bass. Although the theme's right-hand notes are the same, the sixteenth-notes of the accompaniment provide an undercurrent of motion, making this the most intense occurrence of the theme.

The previous episode (mm. 51–71) is centered upon C major and F major; a focus upon subdominant keys rather than upon the more usual dominant helps impart a rustic character to music. Voicing in this area alternates between the hands; the left hand leads when both hands have scalar passages of sixteenth-notes, but the right hand takes over when the left hand plays chords.

The intensity of the thematic statement that begins in m. 72 is altered by the introduction of offbeat right-hand octave triplet eighths beginning in m. 80. Here it is important for the left hand to maintain the quarter-note pulse. I make the contrasts of following dynamics simple and stark. Over the last five measures, the crescendo begun in m. 113 continues through the first beat of m. 116, then I wait before the *piano subito*. Once again, the movement concludes in tempo—playfully but softly—with no ritard.

THE BEGINNING of Sonata Op. 110 is calm and expansive as implied by both *con amabilità* and the German *sanft* (gentle, soft) in m. 1, yet focused and concentrated, for the first four measures are the basis of the musical material for the entire first movement. For most pieces, I sit at the edge of the piano chair, with my back inclined slightly toward the keyboard. But in starting this work, I assume a posture of greater repose—my back is straighter, and I exhale silently before beginning to play. To play Sonata Op. 110 is to be involved in an enormous spectrum of emotion, conjured in the large by transformations of precise thematic details.

Certain elements of form that lead us to consider the entirety of a sonata as a single musical essay link Op. 110 spiritually to Sonatas *quasi una fantasia* Op.

27 and to Op. 101 and 109. All begin with a gentle, songful first movement (in Op. 110, A-flat major, with rather slow harmonic motion), which leads to a more rapid second movement with dramatic contrasts of texture and dynamics. However, the third movement of Op. 110 is wholly unprecedented. An Adagio recitative "improvisation" leads to one of Beethoven's most plaintive melodies (Arioso dolente, A-flat minor), out of which grows the subject for the ensuing fugue. A sustained dominant pedal point is interrupted by a restatement of the arioso, now in G minor. The fugue subject recurs inverted, in G major, and gradually, as the inverted subject is heard simultaneously in triple diminution and double augmentation, the original form of the theme is reached, *forte*, in original tempo and metrical position. This triumph of order over chaos, the emergence of an undisputed, transcendent affirmation, is a philosophical and musical thesis that recurs in many of Beethoven's late works: the last three sonatas (Opp. 109, 110, 111), the Opp. 130 and 131 string quartets, and the Ninth Symphony. In contrast to his increasingly chaotic external life, Beethoven created realms of unabashed optimism in his music.

As I begin to play Op. 110, I am careful not to treat the first four measures as an introduction. They are in the moderato tempo—a stately three beats per measure—of the movement, not slower, and I voice the first two measures only slightly to the top. The terms *cantabile* and *molto espressivo* that Beethoven also included in the movement heading come into play immediately, for the tone of the third measure sings out more, and with the *piano subito* and fermata in m. 4, the pulse is flexible. I begin the D-flat trill (m. 4) with a pace that grows out of the sixteenth-note that preceded it, increase the speed of the trill with the crescendo, and decrease it only slightly with the decrescendo for a smooth transition to the thirty-second notes that follow.

As the freer cadence in m. 4 leads to an intensely lyrical line over a gentle accompaniment (beginning in m. 5), the qualities of touch change with the right hand really singing out and the left becoming considerably quieter. Although the underpinning of the music confines itself to the same harmonies —tonic and dominant—as it does for virtually the entire exposition, the "variations" in the surface propel us forward, smoothly and seemingly endlessly. Distinctions between melody, accompaniment, and their usual registers dissolve in m. 12 as the thirty-second note arpeggiations are gentle abstractions within the harmonic framework. This area demands an even, light touch, with very slight accentuations on the right-hand notes that Beethoven marked staccato. I make sure not to rush here, and I change the pedal frequently.

I wait slightly before the *piano subito* in m. 20 and try to maintain a clear separation of voices in the measures that follow by concentrating on the top of the right hand. If the dotted eighth-notes are played with a little more weight, and the left-hand sixteenths are played somewhat softer, then the two voices can interact without obscuring one another. The same applies to the group of ap-

poggiaturas and trills in mm. 25–26; since the left-hand trills are in a more sonorous register, they need to be graded carefully so that they do not overpower
the more fragile right hand as the music opens up to *forte* for the beginning of
the second theme.

This theme (beginning in m. 28) contrasts with the gentle first theme in basic
ways: character, dynamics, and trajectory. Contrary motion, along with *forte*
offbeat groupings in the right hand, imbue the second theme with greater intensity, with feelings that the musical lines are being pushed apart, strained almost
to the breaking point as the right hand travels into ever higher registers. The
tension is relieved with the dynamic of *piano* and the closer registers of the last
part of m. 31, but it returns—as an emotional echo—with the smooth, high
right-hand passage in mm. 32–33.

By the time this work was composed, Beethoven—having suffered through
innumerable misinterpretations—had become increasingly specific about
placement of all manner of expressive indications. Thus, the crescendo-diminuendo in mm. 32–33 is precise: the crescendo starts with the high right-hand E-
flat (second sixteenth-note of the third beat), and the diminuendo begins with
the right-hand B-flat in the following measure (fifth thirty-second note of the
second beat). Similarly, the crescendo in m. 39, which builds intensity for the
reemergence of the main theme but in F minor (relative minor key of the tonic
A-flat major), begins with the last D-flat in the right hand and not before.

At this point we are still within the diminuendo begun in m. 38, the E-flats
that mark the end of the second theme. Intensity builds, and fingers play with
more firmness as the first two D-flats enter in m. 39, still becoming softer and
more enigmatic. I use only a little pedal for this area. But with the third beat, as
the crescendo begins, I play the D-flat a bit louder and also increase the degree
of pedal. This makes for a fuller sound and propels the music forward into the
next bar. It would be much easier to begin the crescendo earlier in m. 39, but
doing so would destroy much of the mystery of the descent from E-flat to D-
flat—bare octaves, no harmonies, becoming gradually softer. Beginning the
crescendo on the last D-flat creates a drama more intense and sustained.

The concise development concentrates solely on modulating the harmonic
context of the opening motive. Here, for the first time, harmonic motion is
intensified, and the opening motive assumes subtly different shadings of mood.
Beethoven's legato and dynamic markings are specific for each hand. The detached left-hand sixteenth-note at the beginning of each measure (mm. 44–55)
implies a change of pedal for the legato line that follows, and the crescendo-
decrescendo markings in the second measure of each two-bar grouping refer to
both hands, the fullest sound being on the second beat of these measures.

When the opening motive is played again in the home key of A-flat major in
m. 56—paired with the thirty-second notes from mm. 12–19—the effect is one
of returning to comfortable familiar territory. But once again, customary dis-

tinctions begin to blur, for after the opening is motive is heard in the left-hand (mm. 60–61), the right-hand accompaniment (alternating A-flat octaves) leads to the main line in m. 62. Therefore, in the third beat of m. 61, I continue the crescendo in the right hand so that it becomes primary by the beginning of the next measure. With the emergence of the theme in a new key (D-flat major) but within the same registral area as m. 5, Beethoven added simply *dolce*. I drop down in dynamic level and play with a very lyrical tone, but maintain the tempo. The place to expand the pulse slightly is at the end of m. 65, as the D-flat prepares to be transformed enharmonically to C-sharp in m. 66. All familiar turf is then reconsidered; as the local harmony is E major—the furthest away from the tonic in this movement—the A-flats become G-sharps, and the field of aural relationships assumes a slightly brighter quality. I play with fingers that are a bit more firm, and with quiet intensity.

The transition back to A-flat major is the chromatic move from m. 77 to m. 78. In published editions, the left-hand E-sharp and E-natural are phrased under a legato slur, but the E-flat at the beginning of m. 78 is separate. Interestingly, in the autograph score Beethoven continues the legato slur in the left hand across the bar line—that is, he seems to intend for E-sharp, E-natural, and E-flat to all be linked smoothly together. But there is some ambiguity regarding this slur in the autograph, for the first two notes are at the end of a system, and although the slur does indeed extend well beyond them, it does not actually extend the final E-flat at the beginning of the next system. The pianist has to consider both the published versions and the autograph score, and make a decision. The marking in the autograph suggests that Beethoven heard the three notes as one unit, and the chromaticism here, unprecedented in this work, creates a smoothness of transition analogous to the carefully placed crescendo in m. 39. I prefer to consider the E-sharp, E-natural, and E-flat as a single smooth line, as implied by the extended slur in the autograph, and play them as such.

The autograph score is clear about the right hand. The legato slur of m. 77 extends as far as the last G-natural octave, with a new slur for the repetition of this octave at the beginning of the next bar. This new slur makes perfect sense, since the right-hand chromatic line stops with the G of m. 77. But there is no reason to assume that the phrasing of the left hand should parallel that of the right, for the left hand continues its chromatic descent one note further.

The scalar second theme is in a lower register of the piano when it recurs in the recapitulation, for it establishes the tonic key of A-flat major. A somewhat unsettling metrical pattern of 2 3 | 1 is begun with the coda in m. 97, a pattern that continues in stark fashion in mm. 100–104. Don't rush the first chord of each two-chord group, but rather allow it to melt into the resolution—the second chord—as the music becomes increasingly softer. Intensity builds gradually with the return of the thirty-second note arpeggiations, and careful, transparent voicing is important with the cadential lines in mm. 111–114. I balance the *forte* chord at the downbeat of m. 115 so that the tension-filled notes (B-flat and F-flat) have enough sound throughout their different durations to resolve to A-flat and E-flat respectively. The last two chords are strictly in tempo, as are the quarter-rests at the end of m. 116, and lead without pause into the Allegro molto.

As in its immediate predecessor, the first two movements of Sonata Op. 110 are not separated by the conventional heavy double bar. In Sonata Op. 109 a pedal marking sustains the last chord of the first movement until the first chord of the second is played. With Sonata Op. 110, although the first movement concludes with rests, the pace continues uninterruptedly, with the first chord of the second movement coming where the downbeat of the next measure would ordinarily be. The Allegro molto is a terse movement with jagged contrasts in dynamics (F minor, *piano*; C major, *forte*), and in the trio, registral leaps (*forte*) followed by cascading figures (*piano*). The total musical effect is an unsettling one, particularly after the cantabile first movement.

Among the more immediate pianistic challenges is that of producing sharp staccato chords with the right hand in m. 6 while maintaining a legato line with the left-hand octaves. (Recall the dualism of touch suggested by the autograph score at mm. 77–78, first movement.) Using pedal would lessen staccato qualities in the right hand, but the left hand needs all the help it can get in trying to continue the legato feeling. For these reasons I use a somewhat unorthodox fingering for the left-hand octaves, starting with 5 on the bass note of the C octave in m. 5, then 4 changing rapidly to 5 for the E octave, then 4 and 3 for the G and C octaves in m. 6. The tempo is quick (but with a quarter-note pulse, not a half-note pulse) so that the change of fingering on the E octave has to be fast indeed. And with a flexible wrist I can reach the last C octave with 1 and 3. Throughout the scherzo the staccatos are sharp, and by contrast, legato areas such as mm. 21–24 are as smooth as possible. Contrasts of sound quality, and therefore touch, and dynamics contribute to the brusque character of this movement.

The two measures of rest (mm. 37–38) provide important drama and cannot be rushed. In the boisterous trio that follows, I use Beethoven's suggested fingering in m. 71; this is a tricky part, and I find his fingering helpful. When the music of the scherzo returns, Beethoven wrote out the repetition of the first eight measures in order to include the ritardando in mm. 104–107. I really do slow down substantially here but then resume the tempo immediately with the downbeat of m. 108. Tension, heightened in the short coda by the sforzando syncopated chords, is intentionally resolved only somewhat by the final F major arpeggiation. I maintain this F major sonority a long time as implied by the fermata, for the ensuing Adagio ma non troppo begins with the last F of the Scherzo in a new key: B-flat minor.

Although the first three measures of this next movement are of a single tempo, the music becomes highly improvisatory beginning in m. 4. Over the next four measures, there are six indicated changes of pacing: the Recitativo starts in the initial Adagio ma non troppo, then becomes più adagio, then andante, adagio, meno adagio, and finally adagio again before the pacing is back to Adagio ma non troppo for the Arioso dolente (Klagender Gesang) (doleful song; song of lament). This thoroughly composed "improvisation" is not an exploration of possible themes for future use, as is the case with the Largo of Op. 106, but rather an exploration of harmonies on the way to defining the tonic harmonic minor (A-flat minor) as the central key of the Arioso.

In the autograph, the pedal marking beginning with the Recitativo in m. 4 extends through the A-flat minor cadence; the release of the pedal is indicated with the first of the andante sonorities (F-flat minor). This placement of the pedal marking differs from that in some published editions, which have it the pedal release at the point of the A-flat minor cadence. I pedal very lightly here, just enough to create the impression of the sound subtly suspended in air. Having experimented extensively with both ways, I do in fact keep the pedal until the beginning of the andante. This gives the recitative a more improvisatory character.

The quality of sound of a B major seventh-chord in m. 5 is, of course, a complete surprise; accordingly, the tempo is reduced, and the pedal preserves the sonority as the top A is emphasized with a *Bebung* touch. Beethoven has indicated not only a slur for each two-note grouping of As, but also a change of fingering from 4 to 3. This implies that the first A is played in normal fashion, but the second is repeated only lightly, as if a rebound or echo. I accomplish the effect by fully pressing down the key for the first A, then letting it up just barely past the point of aftertouch (but again, not all the way up), then depressing it again softly for the second A. Along with the *tutte le corde* indication, the crescendo, and all dampers off the strings, this unusual touch for the A creates particularly expressive feelings, as if the pianist is improvising while pivoting on the A, simultaneously emphasizing its harmonic intensity and importance.

This intensity begins to diminish with the arrival of the B major chord in the left hand. The beginning of m. 6 (meno adagio) is a bit quicker than the previous measure, but the tempo slows on the third beat, as the direction toward A-flat minor begins to seem inevitable. With the change of meter from common time to 12/16 in m. 7, the pulse of a sixteenth-note triplet is established, increasing emotional intensity from this point forward. (Although the music here is much slower, this change of meter to reflect increased metric tension is analogous to the change that Beethoven made in his sketches for the first movement of the "Appassionata" Sonata Op. 57 from the meter of 4/4 to 12/8.)

Although the harmony remains stable from the second half of m. 7 through m. 9, I do not depress the pedal more than necessary to allow the strings to keep vibrating, for the build-up of too much sonority would destroy the crescendo-diminuendo in m. 8. The long, unending, songful melody begun in m. 9 is among the most plaintive, beautifully lyrical lines in the literature. In the spirit of Arioso dolente and Klagender Gesang, the singing right hand floats above the left, although clear articulation of the subtle changes and the left hand's metrical insistence are integral to its mournful nature. When inner voices enter with crescendo and decrescendo markings in mm. 21–22, I make the most of the phrasing between the doleful D and E-flat in each measure. The line and its intensity are brought down substantially by the cessation of sixteenth-note motion in m. 24, but the cadence and fermata on the octave A-flats leave us yearning for optimism.

As the solo A-flat becomes part of a fugue subject, the musical effect—major after minor, well-defined form after long, spun-out melodic lines—is as affirmation after despair. (This is made even more explicit—*nach und nach wieder auflebend* [gradually with new life]—when the fugue returns following the second arioso.) The subject of the fugue is imbedded in the concentrated opening measures of the sonata, but there is no reason to play mm. 1–4 of the first movement in a way that brings this out. The beginning of the sonata is just that; that the fugue is derived from it is something that might be heard retrospectively (Examples 67a and b). I begin the fugue subject in an almost improvisatory manner. Although the tempo is strict, the sound quality is soft and gentle, as if the theme is being coaxed from the piano.

Example 67a. Sonata Op. 110, last movement. The fugue subject is derived from a reconsideration of the opening measures of the work.

Example 67b. Sonata Op. 110, first movement. Note the right hand in the opening measures:

A-flat	D-flat–B-flat	E-flat	C–F–E-flat–D-flat	C
m. 1	m. 2	m. 3	m. 4	m. 5

Beethoven has specified entrances for each of the three voices, although the dynamic remains *piano* until m. 44. I maintain a pulse of six beats per bar and keep the tempo (Allegro ma non troppo) steady throughout. The bass entrance of the theme in m. 73 three beats early is a jarring surprise, particularly with the *fortissimo*, but I do drop slightly in dynamic level in order to rise again as the ascent of the interval of a fourth continues into m. 80. When the fugue subject is in the middle voice (beginning in m. 53, and again in m. 87) I try to make the other voices around it subservient by dividing the right hand into two dynamic terraces. Just as the fugue reaches a strong dominant—as if ready for a final cadence—the arioso returns (m. 114) in even more expressive fashion.

Beethoven has written *dolente* twice in m. 116—he really meant it. He also wrote *Perdendo le forze* (losing strength). Among the most moving features of the second arioso is the way that the line breaks off in midphrase—as if, quite literally, breathing (or sobbing) quietly but passionately—the musical result of the thirty-second–rests Beethoven introduced within the line (Example 68).

Example 68: Sonata Op. 110, third movement, mm. 120–121.

The *Bebung* touch returns in m. 125, which has an expressive nature similar to that of m. 5. So intense is the music here that following the cadence in m. 131, the piece cannot just end. Instead, improvisatory qualities resurface as the G minor harmony is changed softly into G major and then reiterated in pedal as if gaining strength. The ascending arpeggio in mm. 134–135 allows the sonority to dissipate somewhat, and then Beethoven returns to the fugue but in inverted form: L'inversione della Fuga (Die Umkehrung der Fuge). As we have seen, he also specifies *poi a poi di nuovo vivente* and *nach und nach wieder auflebend*. Considering the *una corda* and the indication *L'istesso tempo della fuga*, I reestablish the fugue tempo from the start but add life gradually by increasing the intensity and presence of sound as the voices reenter.

The nature of the fugue and our experiences in listening to it are affected by the moving experience of hearing the second arioso. The fugue cannot immediately return in its normal form; it therefore reemerges with its subject inverted. And in the midst of this return of the inverted fugal subject, Beethoven places a double augmentation of the subject in counterpoint against a triple diminution: beginning in m. 152 the music is simultaneously twice as slow (top of the right hand) and three times as fast (left hand and inside of right hand). The double augmentation is then heard in the bass, with the triple diminution in the alto and treble, beginning in m. 160 (Example 69).

Example 69: Sonata Op. 110, third movement, mm. 152–160.

Gradually, as more sound is amassed (*poi a poi tutte le corde* in m. 165), the theme fragments into its most fundamental musical component—the interval of a fourth—and a three-part texture is resumed as the normal (noninverted) version of the subject is suggested (mm. 166–167). In an unprecedented manipulation of time, Beethoven then halves the note values but cautions *Meno allegro* and *Etwas langsamer* (m. 168), all in order seamlessly to regain the original tempo and orientation of the theme and to infuse it with new life and drama. Accordingly, within this transition, he specifies *poi a poi più moto; nach und nach wieder geschwinder* (Example 70).

When the fugue subject returns in tempo (m. 174, fourth beat), the texture is no longer strictly contrapuntal, although the theme is stated first in the bass (A-flat), then in the alto (E-flat), and finally in the top (A-flat again). I maintain the same tempo once the theme subject returns in m. 174. The dynamic level is only *forte*; *fortissimo* is reserved for the final cadence. When the fugue subject becomes purely melodic (sforzando, m. 188) in this powerful ending of Sonata Op. 110, the affirmation—the journey of motivic, thematic, and emotional transmogrification—is complete.

Example 70: Sonata Op. 110, third movement, mm. 164–178.

Sonata in D major, Op. 28 ("Pastoral")
(1801)

Sonata in E-flat major, Op. 81a
("Das Lebewohl") (1809)

Sonata in C minor, Op. 111 (1822)

This program—the final one in this cycle of the Beethoven sonatas—comprises three works contrasting in expression and compositional purpose. Sonata Op. 28 is an amiable work, perhaps somewhat conservative in form when compared with its immediate predecessors—Sonata Op. 26, which starts with a variation movement, and the Sonatas *quasi una fantasia* Op. 27. Sonata Op. 81a is the only Beethoven sonata to describe an extramusical program: the leave-taking, absence, and return to Vienna of his friend and patron Archduke Rudolf during the Napoleonic invasion. Sonata Op. 111, the last that Beethoven composed, is a work of extraordinary musical concentration, scope, and vision.

WHEN I play Sonata Op. 28 in concert on a piano that is unfamiliar to me, I take some time to accustom myself to the subtle ways in which the low D key repeats (m. 1) and how the hammer is voiced. I check the degree of aftertouch to determine whether the key needs to be allowed to rise all the way to the top before it is played again in order to create a smooth, gently pulsating texture. I also experiment with both pedals. I use the left pedal if the D's hammer is a bit hard, to try to obtain a full but quiet quality of sound. The degree to which the right pedal is depressed also depends on the voicing of the hammer, as well as on the acoustics of the hall. Most often, I do not change the right pedal until the downbeat of m. 3. From the start, I depress it lightly, just enough to allow the strings to vibrate freely. The repeated Ds at the opening of this sonata immediately establish feelings of calm and stability—integral to this work—which are continued by the many different contexts and incarnations of repeated notes in each movement. Nowhere are the repeated notes fast, impatient, or throbbing with excitement (as in Scarbo of Ravel's *Gaspard de la nuit* composed some 107 years later), nor are they obsessively insistent (as in Le Gibet of the same work).

Rather, they create sturdy underpinnings, bass foundations above which (and sometimes out of which) melodic lines develop and sing forth.

From the start, I think it is important to establish a pulse of three beats per measure, rather than playing with only one beat to the bar. Solidity of pulse, along with the extended first phrase (ten bars, divided six plus four, rather than the more usual eight-bar phrase) and the repeated low bass D contribute to the opening's expansive feelings. Throughout the first theme area, I give a little extra weight to the stepwise movements of the bass while playing the right hand as legato as possible, particularly in the octaves. The sforzando in m. 23 imparts a rhythmic impulse where the line was previously purely melodic, and leads the way for further syncopated sforzandos (mm. 25–26 and in the next phrase) that impart an even greater feeling of rhythmic displacement.

The phrase in mm. 71–76, right before the start of the second theme area (m. 77 on), is again elongated; the line seems pulled out, gradually increasing in tension over the six measures. I allow the music to grow slightly in time here as well as in volume; as the crescendo reaches its apex in m. 76, I also make a slight ritard before the *piano subito* in m. 77. Just as the top and bottom lines of the first theme are smooth, I maintain a legato touch throughout the second theme area. The sense of motion of the inside eighth-notes, which are light and articulated, imbues this area with feelings of greater agitation, which reach their peaks in the measures of triplets and quintuplets (mm. 104–108 and mm. 125–130). The playful music that concludes the exposition is similar in texture and rhythm to the music that concluded the first theme area, but here (from mm. 135–136 on) the phrase begins one beat earlier. The ensuing syncopations thus seem more frolicsome, and I lift the pedal slightly before each one. The left-hand chords are sharp staccatos, with the touch becoming more modulated and gentler as the right hand descends to the bass register, meeting the left hand to begin both the repeat of the exposition and the continuation into the development.

The character of the development area becomes increasingly agitated as thematic phrases are broken down into smaller and smaller motivic units. The crescendo in m. 183 is the start; from this point forward, the last four measures of the initially major-key first theme are in minor keys, and the dynamics increase to *forte*. As the last two bars of each phrase are repeated in closer succession (m. 199 on), touch becomes more intense even though the dynamic initially drops to *piano*, and tension increases palpably. Finally, just the third measure of the initial four-bar pattern is repeated. The music at this point (mm. 219–226) is at its most concentrated—the harmonic framework is B minor, each hand plays sforzandos, and there is tension on each beat of the measure.

In m. 227 the harmony of F-sharp major is attained and the music drops suddenly to *piano*. I am careful to keep that level of dynamic even when the hands spread out to accommodate the increased registral span a few measures later. The same thematic unit (last four measures of the first theme) that underwent a thorough working-out in the development returns in mm. 256–257, first in B major and then in B minor, and I play each occurrence with increasing feelings of improvisation, creating as much suspense as possible before playing, *a tempo*, the return of the first theme.

The recapitulation is followed by a short coda, in which the main theme is linked to an ascending chain formed by the cadential motive of its last two bars. Unlike the similar chain in the development, the motive here remains in the home key of D major, while the sforzando upbeats of mm. 449, 451, and 453 (D, F-sharp, and A respectively) help with the feelings of finality by spelling out the home triad. I make each sforzando successively sharper before beginning the final decrescendo that leads to the quiet ending of this movement.

The term *andante*, though "walking pace" by definition, actually is ambiguous when applied to tempo. To establish the tempo of the Andante of Sonata Op. 28—the second movement, in D minor—I find it helpful to consider the speed of the thirty-second notes beginning in m. 47. This abstraction of the theme is melodic and can't be too fast; on the other hand, neither can it be so slow as to be lugubrious and funereal. I try to keep the right hand playing smoothly over the bass staccato notes, and maintain an eighth-note pulse within the 2/4 meter. The tempo here determines the tempo for the rest of the movement (Example 71).

Example 71: Sonata Op. 28, second movement, mm. 47–50. The flowing melodic line here determines the tempo for this movement.

Therefore, I hear this passage internally and obtain its pulse before beginning to play the beginning of the movement.

The sustained melodic line above a staccato bass is striking. Frequently the only way to maintain the right-hand legato is to change fingering on the top or middle notes of chords, for using too much pedal will connect the left-hand notes, which would not be good. This changes in m. 9, with the repeated left-hand As (dominant pitch), as the texture becomes smoother and more sustained. I would guard against the tendency to rush a bit beginning in m. 23, and I keep the quarter-note pulse steady throughout this more playful area. Although the only dynamic indication here is *piano*, it is natural to shape each cascading triplet down from the highest note.

Unlike many of the earlier sonata slow movements, this Andante concludes with no repeated good-byes but rather with an impassioned searching for the home key. Surface motion slows down considerably in m. 83 as the thirty-second notes of the previous phrase give way to a simple restatement of the opening theme starting in quarter-notes. Improvisatory qualities do enter the arena, however, with the fermatas in mm. 87 and 88, the second of which I hold longer than the first. I play the right-hand B-flat in m. 94 clearly enough so that it sustains all the way through to the A of m. 95, and then the ensuing two-note groupings of mm. 96–97 with enough diminuendo within each group so that, along with the rests, they sound almost like whispered sobs. The harmonic context becomes more definite in the penultimate measure, for the bass D–top C-sharp juxtaposition demands an inevitable resolution, which is postponed as long as possible by the poignant high sforzando E. I play the final D minor chord very softly, voicing it carefully so that the singing top notes resonate over the deep bass.

The playful Scherzo is motivated by the motion of repeated notes but reinterpreted in different registers and settings. Eight-bar phrases contribute to the feeling of solidity, with the staccato notes of the second half of each phrase contrasting to the smoothly descending octaves. A subtle two-part texture is maintained by voicing the top note of each descending octave slightly more than the bottom note; I make sure to separate the last slurred eighth-note (first beat of m. 5 on) from the second beat, just as written, even though it is considerably easier to connect the eighth-notes to the quarter-note on the second beat. A discrete separation not only creates consistency with a passage later in the movement (m. 33 on), but also makes the local ambiance more vibrant.

The Trio is the only part of this work that ventures—as a discrete section—into a key other than D. It is in B minor, the relative minor of D major, and consists of a four-bar line harmonized in both these keys six different times. I play each occurrence slightly differently, usually voicing the bass more the second time through each phrase, and taking time to make the crescendos and decrescendos intense and expressive. The overall tempo of this movement is determined by the speed of this section. If the Scherzo starts too fast, then the Trio will be either unplayable or artificially slower if the pianist slows down in order to play accurately. The Trio can be quick, but the harmonies still need to be clear, particularly since they change here at a faster rate. If the tempo is good for the lively character of the Trio, it will still indeed be fast enough for the Scherzo, even though its harmonic rhythm is slower. Getting this right can often be challenging, but rather than a very fast Scherzo and a slower Trio, I prefer a single tempo all the way through the movement. This consistency highlights the differences in musical character.

Once again, the bass sets the scene, this time for the last movement, Rondo: Allegro ma non troppo. The pulse is six eighth-notes to a measure, and as in the first movement, the low D serves as anchor point throughout the first theme. The left hand is soft, with a gentle rocking motion, shaped with increasing intensity as the implied tenor line (A–B–C-sharp–D) ascends. Playing the right hand as if the music is initially off in the distance contributes to the bucolic character of the music. (The autograph of Op. 28 bears Beethoven's own inscription, "Gran Sonate." The sobriquet "Sonate pastoral" was first applied by the publisher A. Cranz.) I start in strict tempo, ending the first two right-hand entrances as quietly and seemingly deftly as they began. The music opens up slightly with the crescendos and decrescendos in mm. 9–11, and with successive elaborations in the following bars, the most intense point of each of these measures is the third beat, not the ordinarily stronger fourth beat; playing as the markings indicate imparts a sense of going to the third beat and coming away from it, avoiding a more clichéd accentuation on the fourth beat.

A different sort of metrical emphasis is imparted by the flowing sixteenth-note arpeggiations beginning in m. 17. Here the stronger beats are the first and second, and fourth and fifth, of each measure. In rehearsal I have at times found myself rushing in this passage, so in performance I try to maintain a steady pulse here to guard against pushing the tempo; even when *forte* is reached in m. 26, the character is strong but gentle, not aggressive. I make the *forte* octaves in m. 49 also strong but the G-sharp octaves in the following measure more intense by playing them slightly louder and holding them a little longer.

Following the return of the main theme, the mood intensifies even though the dynamic level is the softest so far. In m. 79 I use the left pedal to make sure the sound is really as soft as possible, but I play each voice with tonal independence. Doing so becomes especially important beginning in m. 87, when the alto voice, which had previously been subservient to the soprano and bass, assumes the more important metrical position and therefore is played in a more forthright manner than are the other two voices. In m. 95, when Beethoven abandons the indication of two separate voices in the right hand at the point of the *fortissimo*, the implication of voicing is still that the two registers answer one another, and I take enough time after the last staccato note of each three-note figure to ensure the following one a clear beginning.

Before the theme's final entrance (mm. 113–114), I hold the fortissimo fermata long enough so that the sound dissipates considerably. This allows the *piano* A to evolve smoothly from the previous A octave sonority, rather than being an abrupt *piano subito*, more in keeping with the suave nature of this movement. The coda, which begins in mm. 168–169, grows in intensity until a dominant pedal point of A is established and repeated, beginning in m. 177. The final part of the coda—più allegro quasi presto—is the fastest surface motion of the entire work. Starting softly, with the left hand playing its opening thematic motive in light octaves, this passage grows in vigor until both hands unite in melodic arpeggios and powerful chords that bring the sonata to a brilliant conclusion. I use a light touch for the left hand and a relaxed wrist, keeping the hand close to the keyboard, and close, well-articulated fingers in the right hand. Rather than resorting to playing in two just because the tempo is faster, I still try to maintain the pulse of six per bar, albeit a very fast six, to inject the music with as much excitement and virtuosity as possible.

Does knowing that a sonata depicts an extramusical program influence the way we play it? Of course. By the same token, is our interpretive imagination thereby confined? No, I think not. Considering specifically Sonata Op. 81a, the only one of Beethoven's sonatas to embody an extramusical program, the events it portrays are central to its interpretation.

A bit of history: Austria declared war on France on 9 April 1809, but the French army's unanticipated successes led to its invasion of Austria at the end of April. The imperial family fled from Vienna in early May; Archduke Rudolf, Beethoven's friend and patron, left Vienna on 4 May. (The French bombardment of 11–12 May led to the surrender of Vienna, which eventually contributed to the five-fold devaluation of Austrian currency some two years later and Beethoven's subsequent financial distress.) The three movements of Sonata Op. 81a portray the leave-taking, the absence, and the return of the archduke. Beethoven's sketches indicate that he planned the work as a three-movement sonata from the outset. Even though the last movement shows joyful feelings upon the return of the archduke and his family, the piece was actually completed well before Rudolf's return to Vienna on 30 January 1810. Beethoven thus had it ready to present to him.

Beethoven had trouble with his publisher Breitkopf und Härtel regarding the title of the work. In May 1811 he gave them permission to publish it with both German and French titles ("Das Lebewohl" and "Les adieux") but "certainly not in French only" (Anderson 1961, 322). The publisher followed this instruction for the first edition (July 1811) but not for the second and third (September 1811 and November 1821), which included French headings only. On 9 October 1811 Beethoven wrote to Breitkopf und Härtel, complaining that he had

> just received the "Lebewohl" and so forth. I see that after all you have published other copies with a French title. Why, pray? For "Lebewohl" means something quite different from "Les adieux." The first is said in a warm-hearted manner to one person, the other to a whole assembly, to entire towns (Anderson 1961, 337–8).

Typically, Beethoven's appeal was ignored, and Op. 81a is most commonly known as "Les adieux." However, Beethoven cared about these meaningful linguistic subtleties, and therefore I prefer to consider this work as he did: "Das Lebewohl." Beethoven specified sobriquets for only two of his piano sonatas—this one and Op. 13, "Pathétique."

The opening Adagio introduces the motive over which Beethoven wrote *Lebe wohl* with a sense of intimacy (consistent with the connotations of the term): *piano* and *espressivo* (Example 72).

Example 72: Sonata Op. 81a, first movement, mm. 1–2.

Although the first measure has no firm harmonic grounding, the strong implication is E-flat major, so I play the surprise C minor harmony in m. 2 with a softer, more questioning touch. The C-flat minor in m. 8 is also unexpected, and playing both of them with feelings of hesitancy helps impart to this musical introduction feelings natural to any forced separation between friends. The rests beginning in m. 12 are also important, particularly those of the last measure of the Adagio (m. 16), for they set up the A-flat chords as sighing and unresolved, yearning for harmonic and melodic stability.

Although the first measure of the joyful Allegro is in a new, fast tempo, I hold the first chord of m. 18 just a little longer than the beat would ordinarily be, as implied by the tenuto indication above it. I also try to play the left-hand chromatic descent clearly, giving an added dimension of strength to the music. When eighth-notes are played beginning in m. 21, the left hand becomes lighter, but the right hand continues its crescendo up to the top B-flat octave, before which I like to wait just a tiny fraction of a second, postponing the sforzando with an imperial gesture. This Allegro, while cheerful and even playful in character, nevertheless maintains an air of resignation in the *espressivo* second theme. In both m. 50 and m. 54 I take a bit of time for the left-hand appoggiaturas and maintain careful voice-leading with the hints of B-flat minor (m. 58 and m. 60) that create feelings of instability.

The "Lebewohl" motive is the melodic basis for most of the development area, as it is played in a wide range of different harmonic settings as if the music is searching for just the right path to continue. Although the dynamic from m. 73 to m. 89 remains *piano*, I shape the levels of sound in this area to reflect the surprises and intensity of the harmonic changes. Generally, the single right-hand notes are softer and the chords (for example in mm. 75 and 79) a little fuller in sound, with the left-hand motives falling away in dynamics as well as in register. The recapitulation that follows gathers momentum similar to the way the opening of the Allegro unfolded from the Adagio.

The coda of this movement is, uncharacteristically, considerably longer than the development area. But here, finally, the "Lebewohl" motive is heard in stable form, remaining in its implied E-flat major context, beginning in m. 197. A lighter touch is implied by the marking *dolce* and by the fact that the motive is now in a higher register. For the first time, the motive is accompanied by fluent eighth-notes; we have no feelings of starting and stopping as we do in the development.

The leave-taking becomes understandably more prolonged with the motive's repetition in its barest form beginning in m. 223, but the tempo remains steady. I take a little extra time on the poignant high C appoggiaturas in m. 248 and again in m. 250, the final questioning phrases of this movement before the final crescendo beginning with the octave Cs (m. 252) ensures that the work finishes strongly, in tempo.

The second movement—"Abwesenheit" (absence)—is not a slow, songful Adagio but rather a restless Andante espressivo. It is as though Beethoven were not so much mourning the absence of the imperial family but rather restlessly awaiting their return. As we have seen, this movement marks the first instance in which Beethoven used German as well as the traditional Italian to indicate the spirit of the music as he sought greater specificity in tempo and musical char-acter. In addition to Andante espressivo, Beethoven specified In gehender Bewe-gung, doch mit Ausdruck (in forward motion but with expression).

The opening figure is closely related to the upbeat figure in the opening Ada-gio—it is an inversion in contour. (It is also identical rhythmically to the upbeat figure in the Introduzione of the "Waldstein" Sonata Op. 53, another restless movement.) An important difference here is the metrical placement; all caden-tial resolutions in the Andante espressivo occur in weak metrical positions—I play the first note of this figure with the most weight—which makes the music seem searching and not firmly grounded.

In mm. 13 and 14, as the musical line takes flight, I still maintain a pulse of four to the measure, increasing the weight of touch with the portato marking at the end of m. 14 and playing with a decidedly more singing tone as the legato line enters in m. 15. The left hand takes over as it assumes the main line in m. 19, with the right-hand chords lightly detached. Although the right hand plays octaves at the end of m. 30 and on into the legato line of the next bar (analogous to m. 15), the quality of sound is vibrant but not as full as in mm. 14–15: the tonality here (C major) is more closely aligned to E-flat major than the tonality (D major) of the first occurrence of this theme.

But an altogether different quality of sound, one more mysterious and intense, is invoked by the subtle use of the right pedal in mm. 37 and 39. As with such markings earlier, I depress the pedal not fully to the floor but just enough to raise the dampers off the strings, allowing them to vibrate freely for the duration of the pedal marking. The final dominant pedal of the movement holds sound suspended until the reiteration of the chord as the first one—*forte*—of the last movement.

I know of no greater outpouring of musical exuberance than the first ten bars of "Wiedersehen." Marked not only as the extreme Vivacissimamente but also Im lebhaftesten Zeitmaasse, these measures—a prolonged dominant preparation for the tonic, signaling the return of the Archduke Rudolf—are extremely brilliant and virtuosic. Following the first chord, I drop in dynamic only to let it rise again as the line does. The diminuendo in m. 5 continues until the *forte subito* in m. 9, and once again, I drop to a lower dynamic level to start the rising line, which I play without slowing down, with increasing intensity in touch and dynamics. The *piano* that follows for the start of what turns out to be the main theme of the movement in m. 9 is a surprise, and I allow for a short break in sound to clear the air before this theme enters. Of course it is in the home key of E-flat major.

When the left hand plays this theme beginning in m. 23, the right-hand accompaniment is far more brilliant than that of the left hand in m. 11. But balancing of voices is important, and the left hand, along with its sforzandos, is the more important of the two here. The pedaling in mm. 29–30 and mm. 33–34 is not subtle—the context is *fortissimo*, the tonality is purely E-flat major, and the pedal is used to amass sound so I push it down as far as it will go. The same ideas of pedaling pertain to m. 37 and m. 41, although the staccato sforzando lines need to be shaped in dynamics according to their contour. Even the quieter second theme, to which this area leads, is brilliant in its extroversion. Crescendos and decrescendos are shaped by the inside measured trills beginning in m. 53. When the right hand plays off the beat (m. 69 on), I make sure not to pedal too heavily, so that the left hand remains clear and the main beats are not lost in a mass of too much sound.

Harmonic daring in this movement is confined to the development. An enharmonic reinterpretation of D-flat as C-sharp (m. 87) leads to a brief B major statement of the second theme, which I play more carefully as if improvising, since the key is so foreign to the home key of E-flat major. In m. 107, at the height of an increased canonic concentration of the main theme, I take a little time before the last beat, as the right hand descends chromatically, seemingly forcing a modulation from the local C major to A-flat major. The last C of the left hand is detached in any case, and the implication is that while the right-hand chromaticism is smooth, the left hand is detached and the pedal is changed.

The coda is marked *poco andante*, which I interpret to mean that each eighth-note of the 6/8 meter is heard at a walking tempo. So the pace really is quite a bit slower, considering that the body of the movement is at a most lively tempo. I like to consider the beginning of this coda as quasi-improvisatory—as if one is free to develop the opening motive of the movement—and particularly with the *espresssivo* marking in m. 181, I allow the pulse to be quite flexible. For the first part of the coda, V–I cadences are avoided. But the final flourish, back in the original tempo, leads to a true, emphatic dominant-tonic cadence. The archduke has returned and is here to stay.

I REMEMBER that when I was in my early twenties working on Sonata Op. 111 for the first time, I would often save it for my afternoon practice session. But after lunch, when I was motivating myself to return to the piano, I would actually be frightened of the necessary level of concentration and intensity I knew I'd need to put forth to do a good job working on this piece. Most of the time I managed to summon the mental fortitude, put myself into the right frame of mind, and just go off to work on it without worrying how much I needed to concentrate. But occasionally I'd be unable to do this, and Op. 111 would languish for a while, and so would I, feeling guilty about not working on it. Finally I would just make myself start. That was always the hardest part, for I knew that total involvement is necessary for a good performance (or practice session) of this work. Don't misunderstand—it was my idea (not my teacher's) to learn this piece, and I've always found Op. 111 unusually passionate and moving. The more I immerse myself in this piece—either by playing or listening to it—the more rewarding it is, but the process of immersion itself is intense.

Musical considerations aside, the publication of Op. 111 was also intense. It was the only one of Beethoven's sonatas to be published initially in four cities—Berlin, Paris, Vienna, and London. However, every aspect of its publication was fraught with an unusual degree of turbulence, even for Beethoven. In 1820 he had agreed that Schlesinger *père et fils* (Berlin and Paris) would publish three sonatas (Opp. 109, 110, 111) in those two cities, and in a letter dated 31 May 1820 Beethoven agreed that the arrangement included the Schlesingers' right also to sell these works in England (Anderson 1961, 895). That the Schlesingers each received an autograph copy of Op. 111 is confirmed by their letters to Beethoven on 3 and 13 July 1822, expressing concern that Beethoven had cheated them since the sonata had "only" two movements. (On 3 July 1822 Schlesinger *fils* inquired from Paris whether a third movement had not been forgotten at the copyist's, and on 13 July Schlesinger *père* suspected from Berlin that he had not received as much music, measured in detached movements, as he had paid for: where was the rondo finale?) On 6 July 1822 Beethoven wrote to his former pupil Ferdinand Ries in London, suggesting that Ries act as an agent for a separate publication of Op. 111 (and Op. 110) in England: "I should be glad if you could obtain the same sum of 26 pounds sterling for these, for I can dispose of them in Germany as well without injuring either the English or the German publisher. *If you can get more, all the better*" (Anderson 1961, 954). Beethoven had either forgotten that the Schlesingers had rights to the English market, or simply chose to ignore this fact.

Again on 25 April 1823 Beethoven wrote to Ries: "Do see that the C minor sonata is engraved immediately. I promise the publisher that it will not appear anywhere else first" (Anderson 1961, 1026). Ries dutifully arranged for another publisher in London—the enterprising Clementi—to publish Op. 111, but by the time Beethoven actually sent him the manuscript, the sonata had already been published in Paris (early 1823). Beethoven had demanded to see a third set of proofs for the Paris edition, owing to the extraordinary number of mistakes even in the second set of proofs. When Schlesinger *fils* did not comply with this request and forged ahead with publication, Beethoven was understandably furious. Furthermore, a pirated edition, based on the faulty Paris edition, was subsequently brought out in Vienna by Sauer and Leidesdorf. Then Diabelli, Beethoven's friend, obtained a pirated copy and also planned a quick (pirated) reprint in order to capitalize on business in Vienna.

At this point Beethoven cast aside any ethical concerns he may have had and decided to cooperate fully with Diabelli (whom he seems to have mistrusted the least) in order to correct as many of the mistakes as possible. He realized that neither he nor Schlesinger could prevent Diabelli (or anyone else) from marketing such a reprint, and Beethoven's sense of artistic self-preservation came to the fore. He knew he had to undo the damage caused to him by Schlesinger's having initially brought out so faulty an edition. Diabelli's pirated edition became the authoritative one.

Even the dedication of Op. 111 is convoluted. Beethoven had initially considered dedicating the work to Antonia Brentano. However, on 1 July 1823, several months after the first Schlesinger printings of Op. 111, Beethoven wrote to Archduke Rudolf, suggesting that the work be dedicated to him. This was to be the case for the Berlin, Paris, and Vienna editions. But Ries must not have been informed that Beethoven had changed his mind, for the London edition appeared with Brentano as dedicatee.

The date at the top of the first page of the Op. 111 autograph—"am 13ten Jenner [13 January] 1822"—does not indicate the date of completion, but rather the date that Beethoven began writing out the manuscript of the first movement. This is the same date written on the page of the sketchbook (Artaria 201) in which first movement sketches end and sketches for the second movement begin. Thus, Beethoven seems to have started work on the autograph first movement before having sketched the second. However, more than one sketchbook was used, and additional sketches for the first movement (the opening Maestoso) appear contemporary with the autograph (Johnson, 385–386). Beethoven completed Op. 111 by late March 1822, but a letter dated 9 April (Anderson 1961, 942) to Schlesinger *père* refers to a second copy of the variation movement to replace the one that had initially been sent.

Beethoven had already composed several two-movement sonatas, each of which is confined to just one key. Both movements of Sonata Op. 54 are in F major; both of Op. 78 are in F-sharp major; and both of Op. 90 are in E, but the first is in E minor and the second in E major. (Even though they are much earlier works, the two Sonatas Op. 49 are each also of two movements—the two movements of the first sonata are in G minor and G major, and both movements of the second sonata are in G major.) The minor-major scheme of Op. 90 points forward to that of Sonata Op. 111, for the two movements of the last sonata contrast most intensely on all levels: C minor vs. C major; Sturm und Drang vs. profound serenity; anguished diminished harmonies vs. tonic, dominant, and relative minor harmonies; a 4-meter vs. triple meter. The relationship of these movements aesthetically resembles the relationship of the two primary areas (Arioso dolente and Fuga) of the finale of Op. 110—the triumph of order over chaos, of optimism over anguish. With Op. 111 Beethoven expanded this thesis into a complete sonata; any further musical gestures would have been superfluous.

There was no expressive need for Beethoven to compose additional sonatas. Op. 111 brings to an end the processes of formal experimentation begun with Op. 90. Beethoven began with an intimate two-movement minor-major scheme, continued with Op. 101 as a *quasi fantasia* that incorporates the element of fugue, followed this with the epic "Hammerklavier" with all its movements (including the fugue) on an almost superhuman level, and concluded with Opp. 109, 110, and 111 as the completion of the expressive quest for expanding sonata form in a fusion with both fugue and variation. Op. 111 is the apotheosis; with its conclusion, Beethoven had done everything that could be done with the sonata as a genre.

His only subsequent works for piano were the Diabelli Variations Op. 120 (1819–23) and the Six Bagatelles Op. 126 (Cyclus von Kleinigkeiten) (1823–24). (Of the eventual grouping Bagatelles Op. 119, Nos. 7–11 had been published in 1821 as *Five Bagatelles for Pianoforte* and Nos. 28–32 in *Wiener Piano-Forte-Schule* by Ferdinand Starke, Kapellmeister. The autograph manuscript of Nos. 1–6 bears the date November 1822, although there is sketchbook evidence that Nos. 2–5 were conceived some twenty years earlier.) After this—no more. Beethoven declared in 1826 that he was too dissatisfied with the pianofortes of his time: "It is and remains an inadequate instrument" (Thayer 1973, 984). Regardless, Op. 111 is an enormous expressive challenge to pianists, to pianos, and to listeners, for no matter how many times we have played or heard this work, there are new aural connections to be made, deeper realms of emotional involvement, new perceptions to be felt.

The drama is riveting from the start. I sit up straight, and when I have heard the tempo of the opening measures internally and established the maestoso (majestic) feeling of the opening, I place my left hand on the first E-flat octave, keeping my right hand on my right knee. I then look at the second octave that the left hand plays—the F-sharp octave—hearing once again the tension inherent in this diminished seventh interval, and only then do I play the first two chords, using the thumb as a guide to make sure that there are no extraneous notes. While the F-sharp octave is reverberating, I place my right hand on its first chord and complete the first two-measure phrase, insuring that the trill receives special dynamic emphasis and that the chords in m. 2 are voiced subtly to the top, establishing a line beginning with B–C–D. The pedal on the third beat of m. 2 insures that the arpeggiated G sonority lasts through the entire beat, but the notation as an eighth-note (rather than a quarter-note) implies that the sound—although *forte*—is more transparent and that the hand comes off sharply after playing the chord, rather than playing it heavily and holding the keys down for the full beat.

As the second and third diminished chords (mm. 3–4 and m. 5) continue in higher registers, the sound becomes even more intense, as does the top line of the right hand that continues with E–F–G (m. 4). Although each of the three groups of diminished chords resolves temporarily, no firm tonality is established. In addition to the top line that continues in m. 6, I bring out slightly the bass chromatic ascent, which heightens tension still further. When the left-hand Ds dip into the lower bass (m. 8), the quality of sound is deep but still *pianissimo*. The crescendo is saved for m. 10, which concludes with the sharpest staccato chords yet. Although the local harmony is back in G, the underlying feeling is of considerable restlessness.

Finally there is a legato line—albeit a short one—in mm. 11–12, for the detached ascending eighth-notes following the resolution of the first two diminished chords (m. 2: B–C–D and m. 4: E–F–G) continue with the fully voiced G–A–B–C. I make the most of the dissonant F-sharp–G in the bass (m. 12 and m. 14) as the line resolves temporarily. The right hand is finally calm in m. 16, but I play the chord with a more pointed touch so that even though the dynamic is *pianissimo*, the sound will last for the entire measure. The left hand is calm too, but only for the first note, G. The A-flat that follows—and the bass rumble for the entire m. 16—is unsettling. But I keep the tempo steady, giving no indication of the passion that follows.

Even Beethoven's musical handwriting in his autograph score becomes more intense with the Allegro con brio ed appassionato. Whereas the distances between notes and chords in the Maestoso were quite pronounced, implying that as he was writing out the autograph he heard the spaciousness of the music, the notes and the measures of the Allegro are considerably closer together, written more intensely, conveying an obvious sense of urgency. So in mm. 17–18 I increase the tempo and the level of intensity, playing the right-hand chords so that the top D and G are voiced subtly, as well as making a dramatic crescendo in both hands. I also make sure that the line (G–A–B–C) at the end of m. 18

into m. 19 is clear. This motive is repeated more explicitly beginning in the up-beat at mm. 19/20 before forming the first part of the true first theme in mm. 20–22.

The opening Maestoso provides the initial impetus for this theme, although the beginnings of the line are subtle indeed. It also establishes a dramatic con-text for the main theme by creating a prologue in which salient harmonic and linear dimensions are set forth. I've experimented in my own rehearsing by starting to play Op. 111 at the point of the Allegro; it just doesn't work. There is no point of reference. Although the music of the Maestoso does not explicitly return, it is integral—thematically, referentially, emotionally—to the entire work.

Following the brusque first statement of the main theme—fully in C minor —the mood changes and becomes somewhat more reflective, if only for part of m. 23, as the second half of the theme is reconsidered, slower and softer. As the theme here is then elaborated and climbs registrally and in intensity, I find that Beethoven's suggested fingering (put down long after he withdrew from playing publicly) is very helpful in this tricky passage. In mm. 30–31 and particularly with the *espressivo* in mm. 34–35, I allow the cadences to open up, to expand temporally, for the pace to relax. But vigor returns as the theme receives a terse counterpoint beginning in m. 35. Once again, as in the Maestoso, the only three possible diminished chords—the maximum in intervallic intensity—are played out as the theme is heard first in the alto, then in the bass, and finally at the top registers of the keyboard in mm. 35–47. In each thematic occurrence I make sure that the theme is primary and the counterpoint secondary.

When I am playing so intently, it is difficult to make a sudden pronounced change in pace—particularly harmonic pace. But in m. 48 the harmonic rhythm slows considerably (now only one harmony per bar) as the right hand effec-tively unites the registers of the first theme. This confluence of register prepares for the second theme, which is an astounding contrast with the first. Suddenly, for the first time in the piece, we enter the major mode (A-flat major) with no hints of diminished chords, the register is higher, the dynamic is *piano* rather than *forte*, and the theme is basically a descending single line with left-hand accompaniment. Its character is gentle and optimistic whereas the first theme is extremely intense. Its pace is also flexible, as the immediately following elabo-ration is marked *meno allegro* and then *ri-tar-dan-do* and then finally adagio. I play this music with as sweet and gentle a touch as possible. But tension is still inherent in this theme, for with E-flat in the bass, the A-flat harmony is spelled as the unstable second inversion chord.

Although the slow, seemingly uncomplicated pace of the second theme lasts only six measures as tempo primo is resumed in mm. 55–56, the influence of this theme remains, as the mode continues in major for the rest of the exposi-tion. I play the elements of the first theme that return in m. 58 in a triumphant manner; finally the bass plays A-flat, and the harmony is stable. The sforzandos in the ascending line that leads to both the first and second endings prevent it from being played in a headlong manner, and by emphasizing the A-flat triad (A-flat–C–E-flat) plus F, they add enormous vitality.

Suspense is heightened by the contrasting dynamics (*fortissimo, piano,* crescendo, sforzando, *piano*) at the start of the development area (mm. 69*b*–72), as well as by long silences (rests) between the dramatic chords. I play the full-octave statement of the theme beginning in m. 72 with a very light touch, and pedal carefully to avoid accumulation of harmonies, for this area is more exploratory, improvisatory, and even mysterious, as opposed to the more declamatory statements of this theme earlier in the piece. The theme is undergoing a transformation and beginning in m. 76 is set against itself in a quasi-fugal texture, as the right hand initially plays the first notes of the theme in double augmentation (twice as slowly as originally), while the left hand plays the theme metrically displaced, starting on the third beat of the measure rather than the first. Tension builds as the bass leads chromatically to syncopations in m. 85, which I bring out strongly. The characteristic beginning of the main theme returns to its original shape and metrical position in m. 86, but that is only the start of a five-bar trajectory in which it grows higher and higher and the harmonies, although they all start on the dominant G, become increasingly dramatic. Finally, in m. 90 the original key (C minor) of the theme is attained and both hands join to complete its second half. I give a slight emphasis to the last three sixteenth-notes of m. 91—the G–A–B—for they form the upbeat figure to the next *fortissimo* double octave thematic declamation.

As the key of D-flat is temporarily established in mm. 98–99 (it also led into the second theme in mm. 48) the impact of C minor is temporarily lessened, and I allow the pace to slow a bit with the *espressivo* and *poco ritenente* of m. 99, before resuming with the tumultuous first theme in m. 100. The recapitulation takes the theme to extreme registers of the piano. The musical effect is one of barely controlled drama; so tightly organized is the music, so compelling its attraction, that when the upper register limitations of Beethoven's piano demanded that he bring the theme down slightly lower (Example 73), one is almost thankful for the momentary lessening of the tension. At the end of m. 110, the right-hand line is brought down an octave, for Beethoven's piano could not accommodate notes higher than the high C. The effect—then and now—is initially startling, but tension is momentarily lessened as the span between the hands is reduced.

The second theme returns, this time in C major. Further elaborations lead to the left hand's playing it, but in F minor, the only time this theme is in a minor mode. I use a singing, deeper tone than in the major key right-hand instances; the effect here is more plaintive. But this has to be the case, for again, through flexibility of tempo, we are led back to the first part of the main theme (m. 135)

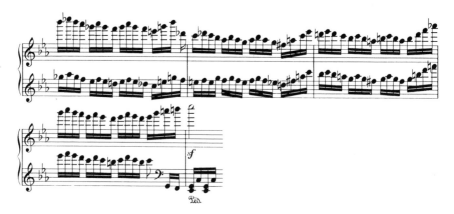

Example 73: Sonata Op. 111, first movement, mm. 110–113.

in an exultant setting, but since we are nearing the end of the movement, the mode is minor (rather than major as in m. 58 on).

I play the diminished chords in mm. 146–147 as strongly and emphatically as possible, changing touch with the first one in m. 148. Since the chords are all off the main beats, the rests—held for their full duration, not rushed—are crucial for maintaining the metrical frame of reference here, and thus the backbone of the music. Rather than the more usual dominant harmony (in this case, G minor) motivating the coda, F minor—the subdominant—in combination with C major, is primary. This gives the music a sense of unsettledness, a degree of harmonic instability, of not being quite finished. I use only a little pedal here, keeping the contour of the restless left-hand figuration clear but allowing the right-hand phrases to sing and to be legato. The intensity of each phrase increases as the central note rises higher and higher, until the B, the longest one, the one fraught with the most tension as it resonates over an undisguised F minor arpeggiated bass harmony, leads inexorably to the top C. Even though the pedal is held for the last two measures, the final chord sounds hollow, for only the upper and lower registers are played. There is nothing in the middle. We are left suspended.

The middle is filled in with the start of the Arietta, the theme of which is, in the words of Thomas Mann, "destined to vicissitudes for which in its idyllic innocence it would seem not to be born" (p. 54). This movement is motivated also by three basic harmonies, but instead of the three possible diminished seventh chords and their inherent tension, these harmonies are basic and serene: C major (the home key), G major (its dominant), and A minor (its relative minor).

From the start, this movement evokes feelings of spaciousness with the wide disposition of the chords, the simple phrasing, and the meter of 9/16. I maintain a pulse of nine sixteenth-notes for each measure. At the beginning, I play the left hand very quietly but make sure that the general sonority is full and round. The right hand is also quiet, although it is voiced to the top to bring out the arietta line. The point at which the line opens up the most is the apex of the crescendo in m. 6, after which the intensity diminishes. However, I do play the top note (G) of m. 8 (both times) with enough sound so that even though the bass and the inside have a slight crescendo-decrescendo, the G continues to sound clearly throughout. I change the quality of the sound markedly for the second part of the arietta, which begins in A minor. The mood is more contemplative, more questioning, for four measures, and I drop slightly in sonority. But with the crescendo that begins on the first G harmony of m. 13, everything grows to the highest level of intensity (sforzando in m. 16) in the arietta.

In this movement Beethoven integrated variation and sonata-allegro form. The surface pace increases from the theme through the third variation, while the basic unit of metrical pulse (the sixteenth-note) remains constant (Example 74).

Example 74: Sonata Op. 111, second movement, theme.

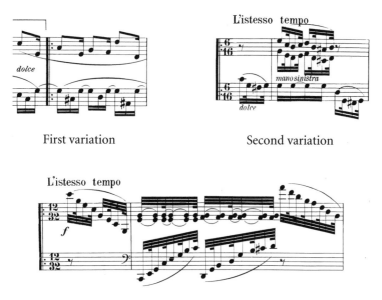

First variation   Second variation

Third variation

The first and second "variations" (Beethoven himself did not use the term) follow the same dynamic outline as the "theme." But the density of the notes is greater, and the increased surface speed allows us to feel that the music is growing in intensity. As we saw in Chapter 3, although the duration of each measure remains the same, the smallest rhythmic unit (the thirty-second-note triplet) is simply twice as fast as the smallest rhythmic unit (the sixteenth-note triplet) in the previous variation. In the second variation, Beethoven begins to make the registers more abstract, for the start of the first phrase of the theme is played by the left hand, with the remainder of the phrase being completed by the right (mm. 33–34). Whereas the A minor area of the first variation had subtle shadings and was more open than that of the theme, I play the A minor area of the second variation, although a four-part texture, somewhat held back in dynamics. The top and bass are slightly more prominent than the inside, but the two inside voices provide expressive coloring.

The third variation is dramatically different. Beginning *forte*, the surface motion is twice as fast again as that of its predecessor, and the opening interval is immediately extended from a simple fourth to a complete two-and-a-half-octave arpeggio. I drop in dynamics in the right hand as the left-hand arpeggios sweep up the keyboard. This variation compresses the rhythm at the beginning of the theme:

p

to the ultimate:

and creates the syncopations throughout. Beethoven was not the first jazz musician; rather the music here is the natural outgrowth, as extreme as it may be, of the music that preceded it.

Following the third variation, the musical line becomes far more abstract, but the basic harmonic and metrical backbone is unchanged. I use the left pedal throughout the *pianissimo* area and change the right pedal with every right-hand rest. The first occurrence of each half of the theme is played over a softly undulating left-hand accompaniment, and the giddy heights to which the line ascends, *pianissimo*, in the transformed echo of each half of the theme, often over a simple repeated note for harmony and pulse, leave one suspended as if over a yawning abyss. These sections I play very quietly, with only the most subtle shading particularly in mm. 94–95, as tension increases palpably with the ascent up to B-flat in the left hand, and then to B-natural before the sought-after cadence to C major in m. 96. Music cannot be more abstract or beautiful.

At this point, classical variation form is broken, for the texture of this variation continues longer than it seems as though it should, and another one does not begin right away. Instead, Beethoven brings back the idea of the theme with a simple (but not simplistic) reaffirmation of the three basic harmonies (mm. 100–105). I play these measures as two groups of three, with a substantial crescendo in each. That of the second group goes all the way to the end of the phrase. We are then faced with the issue of how to continue.

The fundamental approach of classical variation diminution has brought the music to this point but can take it no further. So after restating the three fundamental harmonies, Beethoven brought in the ultimate in diminution (or speed)—the trill. The C–G–G motive is heard, now *forte*, in the bass only, under the D–E trill:

The trill also allows the music to dissolve, and the motive recurs in new, foreign harmonies as the trill changes to D–E-flat. At this point the music is no longer a further variation but is rather a nascent development of the generalized C–G–G motive in new harmonic contexts. The trills grow with the crescendo starting in m. 114, and the bass B-flat in m. 116 can be played truly sforzando, for the right-hand trill continues above it. Careful consideration of the registers is needed, however, in mm. 118–119, for I try to keep the right-hand high B-flat sounding over the resonant bass G-flat—F as the crescendo continues to the right-hand A-flat.

Development of the main thematic motive continues more explicitly in the measures that follow (mm. 120–130). As the music descends in register and is heard in more harmonic contexts, it diminishes in intensity. From m. 125 on, I keep the top line of the right hand as the main thread, while the left hand plays the light, subtle rhythmic outlines of the abstracted theme as begun in m. 120.

The C major harmony is once again attained in m. 130, and the theme recurs. But I try to make this melting into C major very subtle. I do not play the reemergence of the theme with greater emphasis than anything around it. Rather, the crescendo that began in the previous measure continues through the beginning of the theme and keeps going. The left-hand accompaniment changes too, and in fact the last part of m. 130 has ten notes instead of nine. But I just elongate the last dotted eighth-note of m. 130 by that one extra note, the only concession to the start of the recapitulation. I prefer for the listening experience to be some-what retrospective here—we realize that we are back on home turf only after being there a little while.

The three-part texture here makes for a fuller sound; after its extraordinary transformations, the theme returns as an affirmation. I keep the same tempo with which the movement began. The restatement of the theme ends in m. 146, with the cadence on the second beat. Therefore, the sforzando on the third beat is of particular importance; rather than another variation beginning at this point (which would be unthinkable considering everything else that the music has gone through), the main motive (♪♪ ♩) continues on its own, abstracted, exploring new harmonies. Intensity reaches a peak in mm. 159–160, as all that is left is a trill on high G.

As a near-final transformation, the theme (G–C–C) is played with the trill in counterpoint, first above, then below—recalling the giddy registers of the fourth variation. The left hand is a mere shimmer, the trills very soft, and the melodic notes not so much played as caressed. In this context, the motive becomes even more poignant with the addition of a C and C-sharp before the D. The C–C-sharp–D–G–G, as Kretschmar describes in *Doktor Faustus*, "is the most moving, consolatory, pathetically reconciling thing in the world. It is like having one's hair or cheek stroked, lovingly, understandingly, like a deep and silent farewell look. It blesses the object, the frightfully harried formulation, with overpower-ing humanity" (Mann 1948, 55).

Finally, the motive C–G–G is itself inverted; it becomes G–C–C to end the sonata. This is a moment of transcendence; after nearly thirty minutes of music, time seems to stand still, even to reverse itself. Such a phenomenon cannot be explained, but it can be experienced by total involvement—either by playing or listening. Nothing can be added. The musical journey, the transformation, is complete; this sonata, the sonata cycle, the sonata as Beethoven's form, comes to an end.

Glossary

afterbeat   *Nachschlag*; small, unaccented, decorative note (may be several) to be played after the note or trill to which it is appended; trill suffix

aftertouch   the distance a key travels downward after the initial point of resistance at which the hammer-jack is tripped

alla breve   literally "to the *breve*" or "short"; a direction to count in two beats, a half-note to the beat, in a measure of four quarter-notes

appoggiatura   literally "leaning note"; a grace note or small decorative note that is played before the note to which it is appended

autograph   complete score written in the composer's hand; often, but not always, the copy that is sent to the publisher for engraving

Bebung   a wavering tone; on the piano, an echo or rebound in which a second note is rearticulated

calando   dying away, both in volume and in speed

cantabile   singing

con sordino   with dampers (also *sordini*)

fair copy   a copy of a work made by a copyist (not the composer) but corrected by the composer and then sent to a publisher for engraving

fermata   long pause

Heiligenstadt Testament   a profoundly moving document written by Beethoven in the summer of 1802 in which he admitted for the first time the onset of deafness

l'istesso tempo   same tempo

legato   smooth

mezza voce   half voice

mit einer Saite   with one string

Nachschlag; Nachschläge (plural)   *See* afterbeat

249

octave register   Various systems are in use for designating pitch levels. In this book, the following scheme applies (thus c–c¹ designates an octave):

$$CCC \quad CC \quad C \quad c \quad c^1 \text{ (middle C)} \quad c^2 \quad c^3 \quad c^4$$

ossia   or; rather; an alternative, often easier, version of a passage

portato   semidetached; detached but weightier than staccato

rallentando   slowing down gradually

ritardando   slowing down gradually; also ritard

ritenente   held back; played immediately slower; same as ritenuto but less frequently used

ritenuto   held back, played immediately slower. *See* ritenente

senza sordino   without dampers; with the right pedal depressed (also *sordini*)

sotto voce   in a low voice

staccato   detached

stretto   literally narrow; imitation of musical motives at progressively shorter time intervals

tre corde   three strings sound, implying that the soft pedal is not depressed

tremolando   with tremolo, the rapid repetition of a single pitch

tutte le corde   all strings: as for *tre corde*, the soft pedal is not depressed

una corda   one string sounds, implying that the soft pedal is depressed

Urtext   a term often misused to imply "original text" but in reality an edition that has at least some degree of critical editing

Bibliography

Anderson, Emily, ed. and trans. 1961. *The Letters of Beethoven*. 3 vols. New York: St. Martin's Press; London: Macmillan.

Bach, Carl Philipp Emanuel. 1949. *Essay on the True Art of Playing Keyboard Instruments*. New York: W. W. Norton. Translated and edited by William J. Mitchell. Originally published as *Versuch über die wahre Art das Clavier zu spielen*. Leipzig: Schwickert, 1787 (Part 1) and 1797 (Part 2).

Beethoven, Ludwig van. 1932. *Complete Pianoforte Sonatas*. Edited by Harold Craxton; annotated by Donald Francis Tovey. London: Associated Board of the Royal Schools of Music.

Beethoven, Ludwig van. 1935. *32 Sonatas for the Pianoforte*. Edited by Artur Schnabel. New York: Simon & Schuster.

Beethoven, Ludwig van. 1947. *Klaviersonaten*. Edited by Heinrich Schenker. Revised by Erwin Ratz. Vienna: Universal Edition.

Beethoven, Ludwig van. 1949. *Klaviersonaten*. Edited by Max Pauer. Frankfurt: C. F. Peters.

Beethoven, Ludwig van. 1952. *Klaviersonaten*. Edited by Bertha A. Wallner. Munich: G. Henle.

Beethoven, Ludwig van. 1979. *Sonate Op. 13*. Edited by Johannes Fischer. Leipzig: Edition Peters.

Blackham, E. Donnell. 1965. "The Physics of the Piano." *Scientific American* (December) : 96.

Blom, Eric. 1938. *Beethoven's Piano Sonatas Discussed*. New York: Dutton.

Burnham, Scott, and Michael Steinberg, eds. 2000. *Beethoven and His World*. Princeton, New Jersey: Princeton University Press.

Drake, Kenneth. 2000. *The Beethoven Sonatas and the Creative Experience*. Bloomington, Indiana: Indiana University Press.

Flamm, Christoph. 1970. Ein Verlegerbriefwechsel zur Beethovenzeit. In *Beethoven-Studien: Festgabe der österreichischen Akademie der Wissenschaftern zum 200. Geburtstag von Ludwig van Beethoven*. Vienna: Akademie der Wissenschaftern in Wien.

Grier, James. 1996. *The Critical Editing of Music: History, Method, and Practice.* Cambridge: Cambridge University Press.

Harding, Rosamond E. M. 1978. The *Piano-forte: Its History Traced to the Great Exhibition of 1851.* Cambridge: Cambridge University Press. Original edition 1933.

Hoyle, Fred. 1962. *The Black Cloud.* New York: Harper and Brothers.

Hughes, Rosemary. 1970. *Beethoven: A Biography with a Survey of Books, Editions and Recordings.* Hamden, Connecticut: The Shoe String Press; London: Bingley.

Johnson, Douglas P., Alan Tyson, and Robert Winter. 1985. *The Beethoven Sketchbooks: History, Reconstruction, Inventory.* Berkeley: University of California Press.

Kalischer, Ulrich, ed. 1909. *Beethovens Sämtliche Briefe.* Berlin and Leipzig: Schuster & Löffler.

Kolisch, Rudolf. 1993. Tempo and Character in Beethoven's Music. *The Musical Quarterly* 77 (1): 90–131; 77 (2): 268–342.

Lenz, Wilhelm von. 1922. *Beethoven.* Berlin: Schuster & Loeffler.

Lockwood, Lewis. 1992. *Beethoven: Studies in the Creative Process.* Cambridge, Massachusetts: Harvard University Press.

Mann, Thomas. 1948. *Doctor Faustus.* Trans. H. T. Lowe-Porter. New York: Knopf.

Marston, Nicholas. 1991. Approaching the Sketches for Beethoven's "Hammerklavier" Sonata. *Journal of the American Musicological Society* 44 (3): 404–450.

Newman, William S. 1988. *Beethoven on Beethoven: Playing his Piano Music His Way.* New York: Norton.

Porter, Andrew. 1983. Ta Ta Ta Ta Ta . . . Dear Maelzel. *The New Yorker* (24 October) : 151–157.

Reichardt, Johann Friedrich. 1915. *Vertraute Briefe geschrieben auf einer Reise nach Wien und den österreichischen Staaten 1808–09.* 2 vols. Edited from original edition of 1810 by Gustav Gugitz. Munich: Georg Müller.

Rosen, Charles. 1997. *The Classical Style.* New York: Norton.

Rowland, David. 1993. *A History of Pianoforte Pedaling.* Cambridge: Cambridge University Press.

Schenker, Heinrich. 1970. *Beethoven: Sonata Op. 101 in Die Letzten Sonaten—Kritische Einführung und Erläuterung.* Vienna: Universal Edition.

Schindler, Anton F. 1966. *Beethoven As I Knew Him.* Edited by Donald W. MacArdle and translated from the German edition of 1860 by Constance S. Jolly. London: Faber.

Schnabel, Artur. 1961. *My Life and Music.* New York: St. Martin's Press.

Solomon, Maynard P. 1998. *Beethoven.* 2d edition. New York: Schirmer Books. Original edition 1977.

Stanley, Glenn. 1998. Genre Aesthetics and Function: Beethoven's Piano Sonatas in Their Cultural Context. *Beethoven Forum,* vol. 6. Lincoln, Nebraska: University of Nebraska Press.

Thayer, Alexander Wheelock. 1973. Reprint. *Thayer's Life of Beethoven.* Revised and edited by Elliot Forbes. Revised edition, Princeton, New Jersey: Princeton University Press, 1967.

Tovey, Donald Francis, Sir. 1931. *A Companion to Beethoven's Pianoforte Sonatas: Complete Analyses.* London: Associated Board of the R.A.M. and the R.C.M. Reprinted New York: AMS Press, 1976; Reprint Services Corporation, 1993.

Tovey, Donald Francis, Sir. 1945. *Beethoven.* London, New York: Oxford University Press. Reprinted 1965.

Index of Beethoven Piano Sonatas

Semicolons between movement designations indicate that sections follow without pause.

Sonata in F minor, Op. 2 no. 1 (1795), 18, 28, 36, 47, 59, 74–76, 86, 90, 98, 129, 147, 176, 180, 181, 183; Program 1: 99–104
  Allegro
  Adagio
  Menuetto: Allegretto; Trio
  Prestissimo

Sonata in A major, Op. 2 no. 2 (1795), 15, 18, 24, 26–27, 28, 53, 56, 86, 90, 98, 103, 121, 129, 137, 147, 153, 176, 180, 181, 183; Program 2: 117–120
  Allegro vivace
  Largo appassionato
  Scherzo: Allegretto; Trio
  Rondo: Grazioso

Sonata in C major, Op. 2 no. 3 (1795), 18, 29, 61, 63, 73, 75–76, 77, 86, 90, 98, 129, 131, 147, 176; Program 6: 180–184
  Allegro con brio
  Adagio
  Scherzo: Allegro
  Allegro assai

Sonata in E-flat major, Op. 7 (1797), 18, 45–46, 47, 53, 55, 86, 129, 131, 152, 176, 215; Program 4: 143–148
  Allegro molto e con brio
  Largo, con gran espressione
  Allegro
  Rondo: Poco allegretto e grazioso

Sonata in C minor, Op. 10 no. 1 (1796–98), 9, 18, 75, 76, 86, 98, 147, 156; Program 3: 129–132
  Allegro molto e con brio
  Adagio molto
  Finale: Prestissimo

Sonata in F major, Op. 10 no. 2 (1796–98), 18, 47, 76, 86, 98, 129, 130, 131; Program 3: 132–134
  Allegro
  Allegretto
  Presto

Sonata in D major, Op. 10 no. 3 (1796–98), 18, 47, 53, 54, 86, 91, 98, 129, 131, 215; Program 3: 134–136
  Presto
  Largo e mesto
  Menuetto: Allegro; Trio
  Rondo: Allegro

255

Sonata in C minor, Op. 13 ("Pathétique") (1798–99), 16, 18, 47, 86, 98, 143, 196; Program 4: 156–161
Grave; Allegro molto e con brio
Adagio cantabile
Rondo: Allegro

Sonata in E major, Op. 14 no. 1 (1798–99), 18, 47, 86, 92, 98, 117, 178, 214; Program 2: 120–123
Allegro
Allegretto
Rondo: Allegro comodo

Sonata in G major, Op. 14 no. 2 (1798–99), 18, 47, 56, 86, 98, 117, 120, 176, 185, 214; Program 2: 123–124
Allegro
Andante
Scherzo: Allegro assai

Sonata in B-flat major, Op. 22 (1800), 18, 38, 47, 55, 75, 77, 86, 98, 104, 176; Program 8: 213–217
Allegro con brio
Adagio con molta espressione
Menuetto
Rondo: Allegretto

Sonata in A-flat major, Op. 26 (1800–01), 17, 18, 19, 38, 56, 86, 98, 104, 173, 190, 217, 229; Program 6: 176–180
Andante con variazioni
Scherzo: Allegro molto; Trio
Marcia funebre sulla morte d'un eroe
Allegro

Sonata quasi una fantasia in E-flat major, Op. 27 no. 1 (1800–01), 17, 18, 46, 48, 56, 60–61, 69, 73, 86, 98, 99, 125, 127, 137, 138, 176, 217, 220, 229; Program 1: 104–107
Andante–Allegro–Tempo I;
Allegro molto vivace;
Adagio con espressione;
Allegro vivace–Adagio–Presto

Sonata quasi una fantasia in C-sharp minor, Op. 27 no. 2 ("Moonlight") (1801), 16, 17, 18, 19, 41, 48, 53, 84, 86, 98, 117, 137, 176, 217, 220, 229; Program 2: 124–128
Adagio sostenuto
Allegretto; Trio
Presto agitato

Sonata in D major, Op. 28 ("Pastoral") (1801), 18, 56, 86, 176; Program 9: 229–234
Allegro
Andante
Scherzo: Allegro vivace
Rondo: Allegro ma non troppo

Sonata in G major, Op. 31 no. 1 (1802), 18, 25, 38, 69–71, 74, 75, 86, 98, 113, 120, 143, 165, 176, 194; Program 4: 148–152
Allegro vivace
Adagio grazioso
Rondo: Allegretto

Sonata in D minor, Op. 31 no. 2 ("Tempest") (1801–02), 15, 18, 24, 25, 37–39, 53, 55, 59–60, 62–63, 86, 98, 125, 148, 165, 176, 213; Program 7: 194–198
Largo; Allegro
Adagio
Allegretto

Sonata in E-flat major, Op. 31 no. 3 (1801–02), 18, 47, 59, 71–72, 77, 86, 98, 148, 162, 176, 194; Program 5: 165–168
Allegro
Scherzo: Allegretto vivace
Menuetto: Moderato e grazioso; Trio
Presto con fuoco

Sonata in G minor, Op. 49 no. 1 (1798), 18, 86, 240; Program 5: 162–163
Andante
Rondo: Allegro

Sonata in G major, Op. 49 no. 2 (1796), 18, 47, 86, 162, 169, 240; Program 5: 163–165
  Allegro, ma non troppo
  Tempo di menuetto

Sonata in C major, Op. 53 ("Waldstein") (1803–04), 9, 10, 15, 16, 18, 19, 27–28, 33, 41–42, 45–46, 55, 59, 60, 66–67, 84–85, 86, 90, 98, 99, 117, 125, 149, 168, 170, 171, 173, 174, 180, 236; Program 1: 110–116
  Allegro con brio
  Introduzione: Adagio molto;
  Rondo: Allegretto moderato

Sonata in F major, Op. 54 (1804), 18, 47–48, 55, 87, 98, 107, 110, 162, 164, 174, 240; Program 5: 168–170
  In tempo d'un menuetto
  Allegretto; Più allegro

Sonata in F minor, Op. 57 ("Appassionata") (1804–05), 18, 19, 20, 26, 46, 56, 60, 71, 74, 87, 88, 90, 98, 107, 110, 114, 162, 168–169, 170, 224; Program 5: 171–175
  Allegro assai
  Andante con moto;
  Allegro ma non troppo; Presto

Sonata in F-sharp major, Op. 78 (1809), 18, 19, 77–78, 87, 98, 99, 117, 217, 240; Program 1: 107–110
  Adagio cantabile; Allegro ma non troppo
  Allegro vivace

Sonata in G major, Op. 79 (1809), 18, 56, 87, 108; Program 8: 217–219
  Presto alla tedesca
  Andante
  Vivace

Sonata in E-flat major, Op. 81a ("Das Lebewohl") (1809), 18, 44, 48, 56, 69, 78, 87, 98, 108, 138, 152, 217, 229; Program 9: 234–238
  "Das Lebewohl": Adagio; Allegro
  "Abwesenheit": Andante espressivo (In gehender Bewegung, doch mit Ausdruck)
  "Wiedersehen": Vivacissimamente (In lebhaftesten Zeitmaasse)

Sonata in E minor, Op. 90 (1814), 18, 19, 44, 45, 48, 87, 98, 107, 108, 138, 143, 240; Program 4: 152–155
  Mit Lebhaftigkeit und durchaus mit Empfindung und Ausdruck
  Nicht zu geschwind und sehr singbar vorzutragen

Sonata in A major, Op. 101 (1816), 18, 20, 31, 44, 48–49, 53, 55, 60–61, 64, 72, 74, 83, 87, 90, 98, 129, 184, 220, 240; Program 3: 136–142
  Etwas lebhaft und mit der innigsten Empfindung: Allegretto ma non troppo
  Lebhaft. Marschmässig: Vivace alla marcia
  Langsam und sehnsuchtsvoll: Adagio, ma non troppo, con affetto;
  Geschwind, doch nicht zu sehr, und mit Entschlossenheit: Allegro

Sonata in B-flat major, Op. 106 ("Hammerklavier") (1817–18), 9, 11, 15, 16, 18, 19, 23, 28, 29–30, 31–33, 36–37, 44, 49, 50, 51–54, 60, 64, 72–73, 78, 82, 83, 87, 89, 91, 94, 98, 134, 138, 140, 176, 184, 185, 190, 194, 213, 224, 240; Program 7: 198–212
  Allegro
  Scherzo: Assai vivace
  Adagio sostenuto
  Largo; Allegro; tempo I;
  Allegro risoluto

Sonata in E major, Op. 109 (1820), 9,
18, 19, 20, 42, 44, 46, 50, 54–55, 56, 66,
67–68, 83, 87, 88, 98, 109, 123, 137, 138,
140, 173, 176, 178, 183, 220, 223, 240;
Program 6: 184–193
  Vivace
  Prestissimo
  Gesangvoll, mit innigster
    Empfindung

Sonata in A-flat major, Op. 110 (1821),
9, 18, 19, 28, 44, 50, 55, 56, 63–64, 65,
78, 83, 87, 98, 138, 140, 184, 185, 238,
240; Program 8: 219–228
  Moderato cantabile molto espressivo
  Allegro molto
  Adagio ma non troppo; Arioso
    dolente; Fuga: Allegro ma non
    troppo;
  L'istesso tempo di arioso; L'istesso
    tempo della fuga

Sonata in C minor, Op. 111 (1822), 9,
18, 19, 21, 22, 26, 29–30, 36, 42, 43, 44,
50, 56–57, 66, 67, 68–69, 79, 83, 87, 98,
107, 140, 153, 156, 173, 178, 180, 184,
185, 220, 229; Program 9: 238–248
  Maestoso; Allegro con brio ed
    appassionato
  Arietta: Adagio molto semplice e
    cantabile